Inside The&World's

Export Credit Agencies

William A. Delphos

THOMSON
™

Australia · Canada · Mexico · Singapore · Spain · United Kingdom · United States

THOMSON
™
SOUTH-WESTERN

Inside The World's Export Credit Agencies
William A. Delphos

VP/Editorial Director:
Jack W. Calhoun

Production Editor:
Darrell E. Frye

Senior Designer:
Mike Stratton

VP/Editor-in-Chief:
Dave Shaut

Production Manager:
Patricia Matthews Boies

Production House:
Argosy

Acquisitions Editor:
Steve Momper

Manufacturing Coordinator:
Charlene Taylor

Printer:
Phoenix Book Technology
Hagerstown, MD

TABLE of Contents

Acknowledgements

The publication of this book would not have been possible without the dedication and cooperation of a significant number of people within Delphos International. It is impossible to mention everyone who has contributed to the book. However, I would like to thank in particular my colleagues at Delphos International, namely Linda Habgood, Slav Gatchev, Todd Morath, Juan Fronjosa, Tsewang Namgyal, Suzi Sidek, Briana Fichtner, Melissa Faubert, Elena Batallia, Robert White, William Casey, Jeremy Arditi, Adam Holt, Tara Dempsey, Dave Whittingham, and Nicolas Nannetti.

Our diligent and dedicated research team spent many hours working to provide the most up-to-date, comprehensive information possible. Once the information was obtained, it was synthesized and rewritten for a business audience, based on a practical use of the programs.

I would like to also extend a special thank-you to our good friend, Delio E. Gianturco, president of First Washington Associates and author of *Export Credit Agencies, The Unsung Giant of International Trade and Finance,* for his comments and suggestions.

Alan J. Beard
November 2002
Washington, D.C.

Preface

Over the past decade, the world has seen exponential increases in international trade. In 1999, total trade by the United States alone reached a record USD 2.18 trillion. One can almost see the day when the term "international trade" will become an anachronism. With the globalization of the world's economy, it is just as likely that your business partner is in Asia or Europe as in California or New York. Today we no longer talk in terms of "interstate trade." In the future we may no longer feel the need to differentiate between transactions across international borders, just as we no longer differentiate those transactions between different states.

Notwithstanding the interconnectedness of world commerce, the Asian contagion of 1997, the Russian financial crisis of 1998, and the current problems in Latin America remind us that there are still substantial risks involved in conducting business overseas, particularly in emerging markets. While doing business in Western Europe or certain Asian countries entails a little more risk than doing business within the United States—with the exception that businesses must adapt to a new set of rules, regulations, and customs—doing business in emerging markets does expose businesses to additional risks. However, the developing world presents some of the greatest business opportunities. In the last 30 years, merchandise trade in these countries grew at an annual rate of 12 percent as compared to 10 percent of the world as a whole.

Finance is the lubricant of commerce. Without financing, in all of its varieties (i.e., short-term trade credit, letters of credit, medium- and long-term capital equipment loans, and project finance), most international opportunities would be difficult to capitalize upon. Imagine the business that foolishly sells products and services with only a cash up-front policy. Equally as silly is the business that offers any buyer anywhere consignment terms. Financing forms the bridge between reality and the dreams of businesses.

An important source of trade finance, particularly for transactions in emerging markets, is the world's export credit agencies (ECAs). These are typically government agencies that provide risk mitigation tools to financial institutions extending credit on behalf of their country's exporters and/or funding support directly to importers to promote their national exports. By using ECAs, exporters can sell on more liberal terms than the cash in advance policy previously referenced, and still have a high degree of certainty that they will get paid. Or alternatively, the financial institution that is uncomfortable exposing itself to the risk of another country can extend the necessary credit to allow an importer with insufficient funds today to purchase the products and services it needs. ECAs are one of the largest sources of trade finance and cover some USD 1 trillion of exports each year. The size of support by ECAs vary from country to country. According to the General Accounting Office analysis in 1997, Canadian and U.S. ECAs support only 2 percent of their exports in contrast to Germany's 9 percent, France's 18 percent, and Japan's 32 percent.

As an economic tool of national governments, ECAs take additional risk to promote exports as a government subsidy. Therefore, their primary goal is promoting national exports, or what is known in the industry as "content." This should not be confused with the ownership of the exporter, rather it is where the production takes place. Ultimately ECAs are about creating jobs in their host market. Hence, a company may be a well-known national symbol in a country but unless it actually manufactures, processes, or in some way adds value from that market, its products may not qualify for the ECA subsidy. On the other hand, a company may be known as not having local ownership, but because it is producing in the host market its goods and services may qualify for ECA support. An example of this is the Israeli geothermal power generation company Ormat. Because Ormat frequently sources much of its production from the United States, it has qualified for U.S. Export-Import (Ex-Im) Bank support on many different occasions, including one of the first ECA project financings ever done. Ex-Im Bank's support opened a market for Ormat that it had been unable to penetrate, while at the same time providing high-paying manufacturing jobs in the United States.

Given the degree of globalization that has occurred, it is frequently difficult to source the goods and services for a transaction in a single country. Consequently, ECAs have had to adapt and permit more nonhost country content. There is also the recognition that ECA's may be required to co-finance transactions with other ECAs in order to support their respective country's content. Through this book business executives learn that when sourcing products from many countries, ECA support is available, which may allow them to then offer not only cheaper prices to their buyers but also attractive financing. During the past few years there has been a significant increase in the number of ECAs among developing countries, which provides a certain amount of flexibility in sourcing product that didn't previously exist.

The British ECA was one of the first to be established early in the twentieth century. Most of the major powers of Europe and the United States followed suit and created their own ECAs before World War II. Each government supported their exporters using similar financial tools, but the structure, terms, and pricing varied greatly. With the intensification of global competition between major industrial powers and the rise of newly industrialized countries such as Korea and Taiwan, ECAs were frequently confronted with providing ever more aggressive financing terms in order to win business for their countries. In the high-interest environment of the 1970s and the financial crises in Mexico and Brazil, ECAs began generating huge losses for their respective governments. The U.S. Ex-Im Bank was particularly hit hard with delinquent loans in Latin America and negative interest rate spreads on some of the credit it was extending. Under political pressure to reduce the losses and curtail the subsidy, the United States and the major European powers began a series of discussions that evolved into a formal agreement. In 1978, the Arrangement on Guidelines for Officially Supported Export Credits (the Arrangement) was signed under the auspices of the Organization for Economic Cooperation and Development (OECD) to limit highly subsidized competition. This "gentlemen's agreement" was based on the understanding that acceptable competition should be based primarily on the quality and the price of goods and services exported. The initial participants of the arrangement were Australia, Canada, Austria, Belgium, Denmark, Finland, France, Germany, Greece, Ireland, Italy, Luxembourg, the Netherlands, Portugal, Spain, Sweden, the United Kingdom, Japan, Korea, New Zealand, Switzerland, and the United States. Many non-OECD countries have also undertaken to comply with the guidelines of the Arrangement. Subsequent to the initial agreement, additional reforms have been taken to further codify support and rein in ECA support for transactions in the developed world—the basic premise being that there are sufficient commercial alternatives with which the public sector should not compete.

Inside the World's Export Credit Agencies is a practical guide to who these organizations are, what they offer, and how they can be used in a business's overseas activity. The book deals with the basic services offered, the types of information needed to obtain ECA support, industry jargon, and information on some major pitfalls. Some of this is U.S. Ex-Im Bank–specific, but the majority of the information is generic and applicable to most of the ECAs mentioned in this book. Following a primer on ECAs are chapters covering most of the ECAs currently in existence. While we do not suggest that this publication is comprehensive, every effort has been made to include detailed descriptions of each of the major ECAs available at the time of publication. Throughout we have provided case vignettes of companies that have successfully used the products described. We also provide specific contact information so that interested executives can follow up with the agencies themselves.

We are confident that if your company is actively working overseas in emerging markets, this book will become a valuable one-stop shop for financing. ECAs are not the only financing solution, but in many cases they may be the best.

William A. Delphos
November 2002
Washington, DC

INTRODUCTION

Export credit agencies (ECAs) provide three basic functions. First, they help exporters meet officially supported foreign credit competition. (When foreign governments subsidize their companies' exports by offering buyers below-market, fixed-rate financing, exporters often find it difficult to offer financing that matches those subsidized rates.) Second, and perhaps their most important function, ECAs assume risks beyond those that can be assumed by private lenders. Third, ECAs provide financing to foreign buyers when private lenders cannot or will not finance those export sales, even with the risks removed. ECAs do not compete with private financial institutions. To the contrary, they enhance the ability of their country's lenders to compete internationally. It should also be noted that ECAs do not offer development assistance to other countries; other agencies typically fulfill this role.

The approximately 100 officially supported ECAs share common features in their application process, eligibility requirements, risk classifications, terms, and pricing. They also have essentially the same mission: to increase jobs through exports while not competing with the private sector. The similarities among the ECAs are a result of common business practice, as well as an international treaty signed by most governments and known as the OECD Arrangement. As mentioned in the preface, OECD is the organization through which regulations on official credit agencies are promulgated. In this chapter we discuss the provisions of the OECD Arrangement, unique requirements and basic financing programs offered by ECAs, trends, and pitfalls to provide the reader with a holistic approach to using this valuable resource.

Generally ECAs are accessed through a country's banking institutions, where the international divisions of larger financial institutions typically have a person or staff that specializes in their use. Essentially banks extend this type of export credit based on the support being extended to them by their governments. Increasingly, ECAs work directly with the exporters, consultants, attorneys, and advisors. This is particularly the case in the United States where financial intermediation tends to be more fragmented and no longer the exclusive role of banking institutions. For example, the U.S. Ex-Im Bank permits companies to obtain preliminary financing commitments directly without any involvement of a financial institution.

ECAs address two fundamental risks involved in an export transaction. The first is political risks, which refers to those events that occur due to political actions taken by the government that impact payment by the buyer. These may include transfer risk (inability to exchange the local deposit to that of the ECA country), expropriation, war risks, cancellation of an existing import or export license, and/or political violence. The risks of countries are usually evaluated by the Organization for Economic Cooperation and Development (OECD) and classified into seven categories depending on their risk profile. Countries rated 1 have the lowest risk and those rated 7 have the highest risk. The second risk ECAs address is commercial, which refers to nonpayment as a result of bankruptcy, insolvency, protracted default, fluctuation in demand, unanticipated competition, shifts in tariffs, and/or failure to take up goods that have been shipped according to the supply contract and other factors not covered under political risks.

The solutions ECAs provide address five basic financing needs of an exporter:

- Pre-export working capital
- Short-term export terms extended to importers
- Medium- to long-term financing support to overseas importers
- Project financing
- Special export structures (e.g., leases, aircraft financing, on-lending credit facilities, etc.)

Working capital support from ECAs significantly reduces a lender's risk on the goods or services for export. This support may also assist in posting standby letters of credit needed to secure down payments, post bid bonds, or other activities required in anticipation of an export sale. An ECA's primary function is to shield the exporter from the commercial and political risks of selling overseas. This can be done as a supplier credit where the ECA guarantees the obligation of the importer on terms extended by the exporter. Or it can take the form of a buyer credit where the ECA supports the obligation of the importer directly. Finally, ECAs have recognized the need to support turnkey solutions with project financing support, as well as tailoring their support to work with the special financing needs of specific industries.

ECA support comes in three basic forms:

- Insurance
- Guarantees
- Loans/credit facilities

ECAs offer a variety of export credit insurance policies to exporters and financial institutions to reduce repayment risks on foreign receivables due to political or commercial events. Policies may cover single or repetitive sales to single or multiple buyers. As determined by the product, repayment terms are available for short-term sales (up to 180 days, exceptionally 360 days) and medium-term sales (up to five years). Loans are made directly by some ECAs to overcome financing gaps and compete against foreign subsidized competition with the lowest interest rates allowed under international guidelines. Typically this is on a limited basis since their goal is not to compete with the private sector. By reducing repayment risks, guarantees from ECAs allow lenders to offer financing to exporters and/or their foreign customers with fixed or floating competitive rates.

Lenders use these programs for several reasons. By limiting the risk inherent in international lending, ECA programs enable lenders to assist their current customers with international sales they otherwise would be unable to finance. These programs also help lenders develop new relationships with exporters and foreign buyers that may grow into long-term, profitable lending relationships.

These programs help exporters meet two critical financial needs. First, ECAs help obtain the working capital financing they need to produce or buy their goods and services for export. Creditworthy exporters sometimes have difficulty securing such financing for a number of reasons: they have reached their borrowing limit with the lending institution; the lender has no relationship with the exporter; or the lender will only provide a low percentage loan against the exporter's collateral, thereby constraining the firm's cash resources. Second, ECAs help exporters secure credit for foreign buyers. Often the exporter cannot complete the sale unless competitive financing can be provided. In some cases, the exporter could expand business with current customers if credit is extended.

ECA POLICY CONSIDERATIONS

Unlike private lending institutions, ECAs have a political agenda. While their primary role is to sustain their country's exports, in carrying out this mandate they are also required to adhere to certain policies and guidelines, some imposed by their governments, others imposed by the OECD Arrangement. These policies are unique to each ECA but generally fall into the following broad categories.

Foreign Content Policy

ECA programs support sales of goods and services produced in their country. However, as globalization has occurred, sourcing of components and services from around the world have made this policy evolve into a more loosely defined view of what is "manufactured/produced/built" in a given country. In many countries ECAs now support goods and services that provide a "substantial benefit" to their economy. Other countries take the view that if the majority of the good or service is made in their country then the entire amount of the sale can be supported. In the case of the United States, however, there are fairly rigid rules of what the U.S. Ex-Im Bank is willing to support.

When providing medium-term or long-term financing support, if the U.S. export contains foreign-made components, Ex-Im Bank will provide support only for the U.S. content, as long as the total U.S. content is at least 50 percent of the entire cost of the exported good or service. Of course, under the OECD Arrangement the total amount supported by Ex-Im Bank must not exceed 85 percent of the contract price. When supporting short-term export transactions (less than 360 days), Ex-Im Bank will support the entire gross invoice value, assuming the product is at least 50 percent U.S. content, exclusive of price markup.

Military Sales

Generally, ECAs do not support sales of military equipment or services. However, the following are some exceptions for financing the sale of defense articles and services to less-developed countries: drug interdiction purposes, dual use items and humanitarian purposes.

Environmental Considerations

ECAs such as Ex-Im Bank are committed to increasing their level of support for exports of environmentally beneficial goods and services and they have designed special program enhancements to support such exports. In general, ECAs are prohibited from supporting transactions that damage the environment. The environmental policies of ECAs vary although a uniform approach is being developed. Generally ECAs adhere to the environmental policies of the World Bank Group. Certain ECAs such as the U.S. Ex-Im Bank have voluntarily established several strict guidelines relating to environmental issues. The World Bank defines three categories (A, B, and C) of transactions for environmental purposes. Category A defines transactions that have little environmental impact and are therefore excluded from review. Category B identifies locations vulnerable to impact from a project. This includes tropical forests, wetlands, national parks, endangered species habitat, etc. For projects that do not fall into Category A or B, review is handled on a case-by-case basis and placed into Category C.

Bribery

The OECD Convention on Combating Bribery of Foreign Public Official in International Business Transactions was put in force in February 1999. Subsequently, in 2000 an Action Statement on Bribery and Officially Supported Export Credits was issued. OECD countries have taken the issue on bribery seriously while considering the differences in the judicial systems of different countries.

Sales to Certain Countries

ECAs may not support exports to or for use in certain countries. This does not include situations where the ECAs stop supporting business in a country for credit reasons, which occurs from time to time when the economic picture is so bad that a reasonable assurance of repayment can no longer be found. There are countries that are cut off from ECA credit as a matter of that country's foreign policies. For example, the United States will not permit credit to be extended to Iraq or North Korea.

Economic Impact

Some ECAs, most notably the U.S. Ex-Im Bank, are required by law to assess whether supporting an export is likely to cause substantial direct injury to the country's industry. For example, Ex-Im Bank will not extend support that would have a net adverse economic impact on U.S. production and employment. (This prohibition does not apply if benefits to industry and employment in the United States resulting from the export transaction outweigh the injury to U.S. producers.)

Additionality

The concept of additionality within the context of export finance is defined as the probability that a transaction would not go forward without the ECA's support. Ex-Im Bank is the only significant ECA that applies this policy, and there are a variety of influences and circumstances that can affect the degree of additionality associated with a given transaction.

Ex-Im Bank supports transactions when at least one of the following two conditions exists:

1. A lack of adequate financing available from other sources, such as commercial banks or the capital markets.

2. A foreign ECA is offering financing support on behalf of a foreign exporter that is competing with a U.S. exporter for the same transaction.

At the time of application, Ex-Im Bank must make a positive determination that at least one of these conditions applies. Because the factors, which influence the degree of additionality present in a given transaction, are not always quantifiable or precise, the measurement of additionality is typically a probability of additionality related to an export transaction rather than to an absolute.

Risk Premium (Exposure Fees)

ECAs charge a fee for supporting export transactions. The basic sovereign risk exposure fee (i.e., the minimum fee for a country) is determined by several variables: exposure fee level of the country, percentage of cover, the quality of product provided, the length of the draw down and repayment periods, and how the fee is to be paid. Exposure fee levels are established for all markets where it is possible for ECAs to provide cover consistent with OECD country classifications.

Percent of Cover (e.g., 90 percent, 100 percent)

The OECD norm for coverage is 95 percent. However, the U.S. Ex-Im Bank's normal coverage is 100 percent for medium-term insurance, guarantees, and loans. A premium is applied for this additional coverage. Ex-Im Bank is in the process of evaluating the merits of offering a long-term insurance product that may provide less than 100 percent cover.

ECA Products Offered (from least to most expensive)

There are three quality levels of financing product:

1. Below Standard (conditional insurance product that does not cover post-default interest). The U.S. Ex-Im Bank does not currently offer a below standard product.
2. Standard (conditional insurance product that covers post-default interest).
3. Above Standard/Superior (unconditional coverage). Guarantees and direct loans are priced as "above standard."

ORGANIZATION FOR ECONOMIC COOPERATION AND DEVELOPMENT (OECD)

This section delineates ECAs financing terms and conditions, which are governed by agreements, reached among official export credit agencies under the auspices of the Organization for Economic Cooperation and Development (OECD) and guided by conventions established by the Berne Union.

Several basic export credit definitions are required:

Export contracts are transactions that involve the cross-border sale (or sometimes the lease) of equipment or services. The OECD Arrangement defines export contract value to include the entire value of imported goods and services contracted between the buyer and supplier.

Export credits are financial obligations that arise from particular export contracts and are directly and explicitly "tied" to such contracts. Financings that simply make funds available to buyers for general foreign purchases are "untied."

Officially supported export credits are those that benefit from the financial support of ECAs, which are nationally based institutions that provide financial support for national exports. ECAs benefit from varying degrees of explicit or implicit support from national governments. Some ECAs are divisions of government trade ministries. Others act as autonomous or even private institutions that operate an official export credit scheme on behalf of the government. Ex-Im Bank is the official ECA of the United States.

Pure cover is an ECA offer of protection against nonrepayment by the buyer. Ex-Im Bank's guarantees and insurance are both forms of pure cover. Guarantees typically imply 100 percent cover. Insurance implies a small risk-sharing deductible, which may increase under certain conditions. Most ECAs provide insurance, with some degree of supplier or financial intermediary risk sharing. Ex-Im Bank and its British counterpart, ECGD, offer 100 percent cover under medium-term insurance policies, but not short-term insurance policies. The interest rates associated with export credits under pure cover are a matter for negotiation between suppliers (or their financial intermediaries) and the buyers.

Official fixed-rate support is an ECA offer of protection against increases in interest rates during the life of an export credit. Official fixed-rate support is delivered by different means by different ECAs. Ex-Im Bank provides official fixed-rate support by means of direct fixed rate loans, where Ex-Im Bank itself serves as the financial intermediary on behalf of the supplier. Other countries (usually not the ECA) guarantee banks a fixed margin over a floating rate cost of funds when they provide fixed rate financing at arrangement interest rates.

Tied aid credits are a special form of official export financing support involving, at least in part, grants or interest rate subsidies provided by government development assistance (aid) agencies. As with export credits, such support is tied to particular export sales. Tied aid credits are readily identified by their large grant components, very low interest rates (relative to market rates in the currency offered), or exceptionally long terms.

The OECD Arrangement on Guidelines for Officially Supported Export Credits is an evolving agreement among 22 OECD member governments (the "rich" industrial democracies) containing conventions for international cooperation and competition in officially supported export credits with a term exceeding two years (except for defense items and agricultural commodities), including guidelines for many of the export credit financing terms and conditions explained in this section. Annexes provide additional special terms for the special sectors of aircraft, nuclear power plants, and ships. The agreement also contains conventions and guidelines for the provision of tied aid credit supported by OECD countries. The agreement holds the force of law within the European Union, and is elsewhere considered a binding document, morally if not legally. Note that the OECD Arrangement is an agreement among governments, involving oversight ministries, while Berne Union arrangements are agreements among member organizations.

The Berne Union (The International Union of Export Credit and Investment Insurers) is a group of export credit and investment insurers, including official ECAs (the large majority of which provide export credit) as well as private companies. Unlike the membership of the OECD, Berne Union members are made up of institutions not only from "rich" industrial democracies but also developing countries. The Berne Union maintains guidelines for customary repayment terms (stricter than the OECD Arrangement's maximum terms). More importantly, the Berne Union serves as a forum for the exchange of information among export credit insurers on cover policies for various borrowing countries, data on arrears, claims, and recoveries.

Cash Payments

It is customary in export sales and in export credit financing, as in domestic lines of business and their financing, for suppliers and their financiers to require a significant good-faith cash payment from prospective buyers. The OECD Arrangement codifies this practice by requiring, at a minimum, a cash payment equal to 15 percent of the export contract value for all export credits.

Ex-Im Bank adheres to the minimum 15 percent guideline in its medium- and long-term programs. Ex-Im Bank requires a prior certification of cash payments before making disbursements. In projects involving progress payments, each disbursement of Ex-Im Bank–supported financing must be preceded by cash payments from the buyer equivalent to 15 percent of the portion of the transaction financed.

In practice, buyers often secure alternative financing for the 15 percent cash payment. This is permissible as long as the ECA does not officially support such financing. Private financial intermediaries often extend it on relatively shorter terms, and at relatively higher interest rates, than financing provided under pure cover guarantees or insurance. In many cases, private financial intermediaries will extend financing for 100 percent of the value of the export credit contract, on the same repayment terms applying to the 85 percent officially supported.

Export Contract Coverage

In effect, the OECD Arrangement's 15 percent cash payment requirement normally limits the volume of officially supported export credit coverage to 85 percent of the price of an export contract.

However, for transactions involving in-country construction expenditures, it is possible that coverage might effectively exceed 85 percent of the export contract value. This is because a portion of local costs, as well as interest accruing during construction (which is often considered a project expense), may be financed. (See the relevant sections below.)

For many projects in developing countries, 100 percent financing of all project costs (goods and services imported from the United States, foreign third-country costs, and local installation or construction costs) is often specified as a bidding requirement. Prospective bidders are responsible for combining various sources of financing to meet such bidding requirements. Ex-Im Bank support would cover only the portion of such project financing eligible for export credit support.

Disbursement Periods and Repayment Starting Points

The OECD Arrangement requires the first payment of principal and interest on an officially supported export credit no later than six months after the proper "starting point," a date which reflects the nature of the underlying export contract. Many exported goods and services are delivered to buyers. For these goods, the proper starting point is delivery.

Many exported capital goods are installed. Some are installed in broader projects that must be constructed. For export credits involving such capital goods, the proper starting point is the conclusion of physical installation or construction. For projects involving the installation of multiple units of imported capital goods, the arrangement requires either the use of multiple starting points or of an average starting point.

An export credit's disbursement period is the period between the export credit's first disbursement and the starting point for repayment. For delivered products, the disbursement period is usually very short; in some cases, there may be a single disbursement. For projects under construction, the disbursement period can be as long as four or five years, or perhaps even longer. In such cases, partial disbursements are made as various construction milestones are achieved.

Interest always accrues on outstanding balances during the disbursement period. In most cases, Ex-Im Bank expects accrued interest to be paid every six months, even during the certain limited-recourse projects. Ex-Im Bank is willing to permit the capitalization of accrued interest during the disbursement period. Such interest during construction, or IDC, represents an additional cost eligible for Ex-Im Bank financing.

Repayment Pattern and Frequency

For export credit loans, the OECD Arrangement requires equal repayments of loan principal, on at least a semiannual frequency, beginning six months after the starting point defined above. Quarterly frequencies are permitted, but are not as common as semiannual frequencies. Interest payments are also to be made on at least a semiannual frequency. In practice, principal and interest are paid in single payments. These are larger for the first payments due than for the last payments due.

For lease, the OECD Arrangement permits mortgage-style level total payments of principal and interest. This payment pattern has the cash flow advantage of lower payments during the first few years of a term credit. However, there are larger payments during the last few years, and export credit principal is paid down at a much slower pace.

In some cases, particularly aircraft transactions, "special purpose vehicles" (SPVs) serve as buyers and obligors in Ex-Im

Bank–supported transactions. The SPVs on-lease the purchased assets to end users, collect rental payments from end users, and pass through such payments. In such structures, Ex-Im Bank requires the end-user's payments to the SPV also to meet OECD Arrangement payment requirements. Ex-Im Bank will not permit end users to make reduced streams of payments in violation of OECD Arrangement guidelines, even though such reduced payments, if they can be designated under local laws or accounting as operating rentals, might have tax advantages to the end users.

Interest Rates

Many ECA-guaranteed export credits involve floating rates. Typically, these rates are adjusted semiannually, and are pegged at some spread over an adjustable base rate, often six-month U.S. dollar LIBOR. The extent of the spread is often related to the quality of the guarantee offered by the ECA, and is established at the time of disbursement.

For loans under an Ex-Im Bank comprehensive guarantee covering 100 percent of principal and interest with no risk deductible, the spreads usually are rather small, as there is no residual credit risk taken by the lender. The remaining spreads represent compensation for administrative expenses in making the loan and an element of lender's profit. For loans guaranteed by those ECAs that cover only 98 percent, 95 percent, 90 percent, or lesser amounts of principal and interest, the lending spreads can be substantially larger, as they seek to compensate for residual credit risk.

Some ECA-guaranteed export credits involve fixed rates. Typically, the private financial intermediary establishes these rates at the time of disbursement. They are pegged at a spread over the yield (at time of disbursement) for a U.S. Treasury bond of comparable average life. The spread over Treasury yields typically has two components: first, the same administrative/profit/credit risk spread described in connection with floating rates; and second, a LIBOR-minus-Treasury "swap spread," which is more or less the credit spread between six-month LIBOR and the rate on a six-month Treasury bill. Again, Ex-Im Bank's 100 percent guarantee of principal and interest helps to minimize the first component of the spread over yields for comparable Treasury bonds.

Also, since notes issued under Ex-Im Bank's 100 percent guarantee represent the "full faith and credit" of the U.S. government and are freely transferable, such notes can be securitized with relative ease. A financial intermediary's Ex-Im Bank guaranteed loan can be repackaged as smaller investor-held certificates, each with its own 100 percent Ex-Im Bank repayment guarantee. Securitization may involve higher legal costs than a straightforward Ex-Im Bank guaranteed loan, but the increased access to a wider pool of investors' funds often lowers the cost of such funds and permits lower spreads to borrowers.

As noted above, private financial intermediaries usually fix their rates at the time of each disbursement, which is when funds for lending are accessed. However, in a rising interest rate environment, some borrowers will want to lock in rates prior to disbursement. Some lenders, including PEFCO, will offer to lock in such a "forward rate," which will usually be somewhat higher than the current spot rate for the equivalent term (although probably less than the future spot rate that will prevail at time of disbursement).

Ex-Im Bank, like most ECAs, provides official fixed-rate financing support. For Ex-Im Bank, this support takes the form of direct fixed-rate loans offered to borrowers. The Japanese and Canadian export credit systems also operate in this manner, while the British, French, and Italian systems deliver fixed-rate loans.

The OECD Arrangement strictly regulates the minimum interest rates associated with official fixed-rate financing support, whether it is provided via a direct loan or interest rate make-up mechanism. Each OECD currency has at least one commercial interest reference rate, or CIRR, which is 100 basis points (bp) greater than the yields of government bonds of comparable average life. The CIRRs for each currency are recalculated on the fifteenth of each month.

The U.S. dollar remains the most common currency in long-term export credit finance. There are three U.S. dollar CIRRs, one for each of three repayment terms.

Term (Number of Payments)	Formulation of U.S. Dollar CIRR
Up to 10 semiannuals	3-year treasury yield plus 100 bp
Over 10 & less than 17 semiannuals	5-year treasury yield plus 100 bp
Over 17 semiannuals	7-year treasury yield plus 100 bp

The OECD Arrangement permits a firm CIRR to be established only after an export contract has been signed. Under Ex-Im Bank's system, firm CIRRs (held for the life of the financing) are permitted only in the context of final commitments (see below), which are authorized only after export contracts have been signed. In the context of export credit financing offers (letters of interest or preliminary commitments), no particular monthly

CIRR may be quoted for a period extending beyond the applicable month, except with an additional "hold" spread. (See below.)

For an export contract involving immediate or near-term delivery in an environment of stable or declining interest rates, a CIRR is often less attractive than the rate set by a private financial intermediary under an Ex-Im Bank guarantee, because the spread established on a guaranteed loan at the date of disbursement is normally lower than 100 basis points. However, for an export contract involving deferred delivery or a relatively long disbursement period in a rising interest rate environment, a CIRR established immediately after contract signing can ultimately prove significantly more attractive than a rate set at disbursement under an Ex-Im Bank guarantee.

Moreover, the OECD Arrangement permits ECAs to temporarily maintain CIRR "hold" rates in export credit financing offers for a four-month period prior to export contract signing. A CIRR hold rate consists of the monthly CIRR rate being held, plus an additional 20 bp. The Arrangement permits the choice of the hold CIRR rate or the current spot CIRR rate, whichever proves more attractive after contract signing. In effect, the use of CIRR hold rates is similar to the market's use of interest rate caps, except that the 20 bp per annum cost of the interest rate cap is paid only if the hold rate is actually used.

It may be interesting to note that for years, the OECD matrix (SDR-based) rate constituted the greatest potential source of subsidy in standard export credit financing. In the fall of 1994, OECD governments reached an agreement to stop issuing Matrix rate offers, effective September 1, 1995.

Foreign Tied Aid

"Tied aid" is concessional government-to-government foreign assistance that is explicitly tied to the purchase of exports of goods and services from suppliers in the donor's country. Tied aid financing is always more attractive to government borrowers than standard export credits, which are likewise tied but that offer, at best, maximum standard OECD Arrangement terms. However, tied aid financings are subject to their own set of OECD Arrangement rules and procedures.

One key element is that nearly all forms of tied aid financing (grants and near-grants are the exception) require prior notification of at least 30 working days before a firm offer or commitment is made by the offering government. The major purpose of prior notification is to ensure that other governments have the opportunity to provide matching tied aid financing—an opportunity that the United States has seized with Ex-Im Bank's Tied Aid Capital Projects Fund. Another key element is the use of "no aid" common lines. The OECD Secretariat will issue, on behalf of any member government and on a confidential basis, a request to OECD governments that they accept a "no aid" common line for a particular project. Any government can reject this common line request; however, if all OECD governments either accept or remain silent, the "no aid" common line is approved. Ex-Im's Bank's Tied Aid Capital Projects Fund uses the common line procedure to ensure that an attempt is made to preserve standard OECD terms. Tied aid sometimes takes the form of stand-alone grants for 100 percent of an export contract. Grants do not need to be repaid. Other times, a grant element of 35 percent or more of a contract is combined with an export credit, on standard OECD Arrangement terms, covering the remaining 65 percent or less. This structure is called a mixed credit. Tied aid can also be offered in the form of soft loans, which are exceptionally long-term (20–40 year) credits at highly concessional interest rates. Sometimes, a soft loan can be combined with a standard export credit, or a grant, to form additional mixed credit permutations. According to the OECD Arrangement, export credits cannot be combined with grants aid credits without the entire package being defined as a tied aid financing.

"Concessionality" is a measure of the financial stability of the recipient government. The concessionality of tied aid credits is typically underwritten by development assistance (aid) agency budgets rather than export credit agency budgets. A stand-alone grant offers 100 percent concessionality, a stand-alone export credit offers zero percent concessionality, and a mixed credit with a 35 percent grant portion offers 35 percent concessionality. For a soft loan, concessionality depends on the present value of such financing, discounted at a market-related rate in the currency of the financing offered. The lower the present value, the higher the concessionality. The lower the interest rate relative to market rates in the currency of the financing offered, or the longer the repayment term, the more concessional is the soft loan. Most tied aid credits involve concessionality at, or just slightly higher than, 35 percent. The minimum concessionality level specified in the OECD arrangement is 35 percent.

Government-to-government tied aid is concentrated in several markets. China and Indonesia solicit bilateral aid financing for priority capital projects, and historically have been the largest recipients of tied aid by a wide margin. Several other developing countries, mostly in Asia, welcome bilateral tied aid financing for capital projects, even if they may not actively solicit such financing for a large spectrum of projects. While tied aid is not as significant a commercial factor in key markets in Europe and the Americas, the OECD Arrangement prohibits tied aid use in a number of developing country export markets including Mexico, Brazil, Argentina, Venezuela, Russia, Poland, Hungary, the Czech Republic, the Ukraine, South Korea, Hong Kong, Singapore, and Taiwan.

Several Eastern European governments are willing to accommodate China, Indonesia, and other countries with bilateral tied aid offers. These donor governments mix two competing motives in providing tied aid: transferring financial resources to recipient countries and supporting national export and domestic employment. Once a tied aid offer is in hand, recipient governments are unwilling to take serious negotiations with other exporters who cannot likewise demonstrate that they bring along matching tied aid financing.

The OECD Arrangement has a provision that helps shift tied aid use away from those areas most likely to cause trade distortion—the OECD Arrangement's "commercial non-viability" rule, by which the only projects eligible to be supported by tied aid financing are those that are found "commercially non-viable," in the sense that their operating revenues would not be able to service the debt contracted on standard OECD arrangement terms. This rule, as well as the OECD challenge and consultations process established to clarify and enforce the rule, has led to a major shift in foreign tied aid offers away from commercial projects in manufacturing, power, and telecommunications—preserving the primacy of standard export credits in these important sectors. There are still some gray areas where some projects are found commercially viable and some are not, but generally projects that generate positive operating income are found commercially viable. However, there are many kinds of projects that offer minimal or no commercial viability and yet are sufficiently commercially attractive to attract foreign tied aid credits. These are the kinds of projects where Ex-Im Bank's Tied Aid Capital Fund can be used to counter foreign tied aid credit offers.

Ex-Im Bank's Tied Aid Capital Projects Fund

Ex-Im Bank uses the Tied Aid Capital Projects Fund to counter those trade-distorting foreign tied aid credits not prohibited under the OECD Arrangement. Ex-Im Bank's countering activities take advantage of the matching provisions contained in the OECD Arrangement. The Fund is not used to initiate U.S. tied aid credits into foreign competitive situations, where foreign tied aid is not already a factor. Its mission is to provide tied aid counteroffers to known foreign tied aid offers. Tied aid preliminary commitments, which are directly convertible to Final Commitments, are only available once a foreign tied aid offer has been prior-notified to the OECD, and have cleared the OECD challenge-consultations process.

A tied aid credit is trade distorting when the target export contract would likely have been financed on standard export credit terms, but where introduction of concessionality (nearly 35 percent) is clearly intended to sway procurement decisions, not only for the immediate contract, but also potentially for many follow-on contracts. Ex-Im Bank is unlikely to approve a tied aid credit if it is apparent that the sale is a unique opportunity, with no significant follow-on sales opportunities.

Sometimes, other OECD governments offer tied aid financing of very high concessionality (50 percent or higher). Such offers are expensive for Ex-Im Bank to match, in terms of budget, and Ex-Im Bank is unlikely to provide a matching tied aid offer. Sometimes, foreign tied aid will be provided to less creditworthy governments, which otherwise have limited access to standard export credits. Typically, even standard Ex-Im Bank export credits to these governments involve high budget costs; these costs are far higher when tied aid is involved. It is unlikely that Ex-Im Bank will match a foreign tied aid credit in riskier markets.

In countering a foreign tied aid offer, the Ex-Im Bank's intention is to frustrate a foreign government's intention to use tied aid to advantage its exporters on sales to a capital project. Ex-Im Bank's intention is either to supplant the foreign export sale in its entirety, dollar-for-dollar, or to deny foreign exporters the full volume of exports originally intended as a result of their aid financing by helping the U.S. exporter win part of the sale. Ex-Im Bank will not permit a matching tied aid offer to be diverted to a second project or to a second phase of the initial project. In determining project scope for matching purposes, Ex-Im Bank relies on information included in foreign tied aid notifications to the OECD, and also in commercial viability studies whenever these are prepared for an OECD tied aid consultation.

SPECIAL PROGRAMS

Lending Facility

Here the ECAs work with financial institutions so that they can provide financing to buyers of exports. Both the ECAs and users benefit from such facilities. The ECAs can leave the work of analysis to the local banks that have a better understanding of the local companies. ECAs reduce the repayment risks of the local company, and users of such facilities do not have to go through the ECA application process.

Exchange Risk Insurance

Exchange risk insurance protects exporters against currency depreciation, prior to the receipt of payment for goods sold, when the majority of their contract is in a foreign currency. Coverage is usually limited to one year, but may be as long as five years.

In the event that the exporter's currency depreciates against the foreign currency of the contract, it is often the policy that the exporter pays the insurer a portion of the profit.

Premiums of the insurance are calculated based on a per-case risk of the specific foreign currency and the length of coverage. In the case of the Ex-Im Bank, only a select list of hard currencies are subject to guarantees. In addition to premiums, credits are also subject to a risk-based exposure fee and a commitment fee of $\frac{1}{8}$ of 1 percent on the undisbursed amount of credit. Exchange risk guarantees are most beneficial to those industrial nations whose own currencies are appreciating against the dominant currencies of the developed world.

Project Finance

This form of financing has been growing in popularity due to the flexibility it provides the sponsors, as they have limited or no recourse. In this type of structure, the future cash flow backs the debt instead of the sponsor's balance sheet. This form of financing is particularly useful in natural resources and infrastructure-related projects. In these types of projects, long-term purchase agreements can be executed, thus insuring the project cash flow.

Leases

Certain ECAs such as the U.S. Ex-IM Bank provide financial support in the form of loans, guarantees, and insurance programs to facilitate leases, especially in the area of large products, such as aircrafts. The terms and conditions of ECA aircraft programs are governed by the OECD sector understanding on Export Credits for Civil Aviation (Annex III to the OECD Arrangement). Here the dependent factors are the type, size, and age of the aircraft. Category A aircrafts include turbojets and turboprops. The terms are usually for up to ten years. Category B is turbine-powered aircrafts and have repayment terms of seven years. Category C aircrafts include all other aircrafts and have five-year repayment terms.

Large aircrafts (i.e., those that have over 70 seats) are usually financed through asset-based finance lease structures. OECD Arrangement terms require a maximum of 12-year terms and principal to be repaid in equal periodic installments. The repayment terms for used aircraft are shorter than for new aircraft and usually do not exceed five years.

Similar to aircraft, ECA financing support for locomotives ("rolling stock" equipment), ships, and trucks are governed by the OECD Arrangement. The terms and conditions are influenced by the country category of the borrower. See terms.

PITFALLS

Through our experience in providing trade finance services, we have noticed that many firms seeking ECA support make the same mistakes or have the same misunderstandings. We will attempt to address these in this section.

The most common misunderstanding is that ECA financing is subsidized. In most cases this is not true. The staffs of ECAs use sound policies and procedures in reviewing applicants. The result of this can be seen by the profitability and relatively low default rates of most ECAs in the last decade. Applicants must be creditworthy and face the same analysis as they would with a private bank. Since the rates charged by ECAs are regulated, the financing benefits are neutralized and, therefore, firms have to ultimately compete in the quality of their products and services. In certain limited circumstances, certain ECAs such as Canada's EDC offer rates that are lower than the OECD-required rates. This is achieved when it is determined that the private sector has rates below the OECD rates.

The second most common mistake by exporters is their lack of proper understanding of ownership and content. The requirements vary among ECAs. Exporters assume that just because the product is exported from the home country it will be eligible for ECA support irrespective of the percentage of foreign content. Others assume that the products exported must contain no foreign products. Proper management and understanding of ownership and content allows more financing to leave the table. In general the content requirements are more stringent for medium- and long-term programs than for short-term programs. For example, for medium- and long-term programs, Ex-Im Bank will support either 100 percent of the U.S. content or 85 percent of the net contract price. However, for short-term programs, Ex-Im requires products at least U.S. origin exclusive of mark-up.

Applicants should also be aware that the application process tends to take longer than clients anticipate. ECAs have policy requirements such as environmental and workers rights issues that need to be met. ECAs outside of the United States tend not to work directly with exporters and importers. They are more likely to wholesale products to banks and often rely heavily on local banks. The timing of application differs among ECAs. In general, ECAs require that the applications be submitted prior to the product being shipped.

Applicants of ECA support need to be aware that certain ECAs require that the vessels used in export trade must be those of the country of product origin. For example, exporters from the United States must meet the MARAD requirements. However, waivers can be obtained for a certain percentage of products, if no U.S. vessels are available destined to the country of export, and if it is one of those countries with a country waiver.

Clients need to be aware of the down payment requirement of buyers. As mentioned earlier, the OECD Arrangement codifies this practice by requiring, at a minimum, a cash payment equal to 15 percent of the export contract value for all export credits. The down payment can be paid by an alternative source of financing such as private financial intermediaries.

In theory, ECAs are supposed to work cooperatively with each other and with other multilateral lending institutions. In reality, all of these institutions see themselves as senior lenders and thus sharing of collateral is often a problem. This lack of cooperation and consensus results in projects being delayed, and thus clients lose valuable time and money.

CONCLUSION

New ECAs continue to form and existing ECAs evolve in recognition of their importance and the changing environment. It is anticipated that the formation of more regional ECAs will be developed due to their benefits, such as flexibility in content requirements, better terms, economy of scale, and as a result of regional integration such as the European Union. Already regional ECAs such as the African Export-Import Bank (AFREXIM), Inter-Arab Investment Guarantee Corporation (IAIGC), and the Latin American Bank for Exports (BLADEX) exist to stimulate intra-regional trade.

To facilitate financing with other ECAs, "One-Stop-Shop" co-financing facilities are being set up. "One-Stop-Shop" arrangements allow products and services from two (or more) countries to benefit from a single ECA financing package. Without co-financing, the parties would have to make separate financing arrangements with two (or more) ECAs to ensure support for exports from various countries. The country with the largest share of the sourcing and/or the location of the main contractor will generally determine which ECA leads the transaction. The lead ECA will provide export credit support for the entire transaction and will arrange for support from the follower ECA behind the scenes. As a result, the lead ECA is able to provide one set of documents, one set of terms and conditions, and one set of disbursement and claims procedures for the entire transaction. The buyer will benefit from the ease of a streamlined financing package and the involvement of the follower ECA should be invisible to the buyer.

Finally, in recent years there has been a growth in privatization and development of capital market in developing and former socialist countries. As a result of the free market economy, most countries no longer provide sovereign guarantees to support export transactions. Indeed, at times countries are pressured by institutions such as the World Bank from providing such guarantees. In certain cases, there has been a shift to sub-sovereign guarantees as witnessed in Russia. Here the city of Moscow now provides such guarantees to the U.S. Ex-Im Bank, but for the most part ECAs are looking to private institutions to provide the comfort that a reasonable assurance of repayment can be made.

FOREWORD

It is with great pleasure I welcome the publication of another of Delphos International's practical guides to government resources for international business. This book, in particular, will be an important resource guide for anyone doing business with an export credit agency (ECA) such as the U.S. Export-Import Bank.

As Chairman of the U.S. Export-Import Bank, I personally witnessed the important role of ECAs in international trade. In order to illustrate this point, I use our agency as an example. From its humble birth in 1934 by a decree by President Franklin D. Roosevelt, Ex-Im Bank has grown to become an important ingredient in U.S. economic growth, particularly in the growth of exports. In 2001, exports represented about 10 percent of the nation's GDP and supported approximately 12 million jobs (Department of Commerce), including one in five manufacturing jobs. And lest there be the wrong impression that most of this was conducted by large companies such as Boeing and GE, medium- and small-sized companies represented 97 percent of U.S. exporters. Jobs in the export sector on average pay wages that are 13 to 18 percent higher than the national average of non-export jobs (Department of Commerce). In 2001, Ex-Im Bank supported exports valued at USD 12.5 billion.

I believe *Inside the World's Export-Credit Agencies* will allow more firms to tap the resources of ECAs in the rapid rush of globalization. Since straightforward information is not always easy to obtain, even with the Internet, a practical guide such as this puts valuable information at the busy executive's fingertips to refer to again and again. Ex-Im Bank is proud to be a part of this initiative in taking some of the confusion out of this very specialized world that is so critical to the U.S. export engine.

Chairman
November 2002
Washington, D.C.

Experts from around the world welcome
Inside the World's Export Credit Agencies:

"A major global credit insurance player, Coface offers its customers an unrivalled local service in 99 countries. With its country risk expertise and extensive database covering 45 million companies worldwide, Coface is today the international trade facilitator with the most comprehensive range of services. This book is important as it provides operators with the keys to understanding the inner workings of credit agencies that guarantee medium- and long-term contracts."

Francois David, Chairman and Chief Executive, Coface

"As the official export credit agency of the United States, Ex-Im Bank helps U.S. companies to sustain and create jobs by providing financing for U.S. exports that fills trade finance gaps in commercial lending and levels the playing field for U.S. exporters competing with foreign companies backed by their governments."

Eduardo Aguirre, Vice Chairman,
First Vice President and Chief Operating Officer, Ex-Im Bank

"We at FMC Technologies, Inc., use the Delphos International guide on *Inside the World's Export Credit Agencies* frequently. Given our global presence and major project focus, particularly in our FMC Energy Systems businesses, the publication is a valuable tool for our general managers and controllers."

Wolfgang H. Thoene, Director, Marketing
and Business Development, FMC
Technologies, Inc.

"Our firm has found this book and the resources described in it to be invaluable in raising financing for our projects."

Claudio Bruzual, Managerial Consultant, Grupo EDC

Official Export Credit Agencies of OECD Member Countries

AUSTRALIA
EXPORT FINANCE AND INSURANCE COMPANY (EFIC)

I. INTRODUCTION

EFIC is owned by the Australian government. While it is semi-independent, it receives direction from the Ministry for Industry, Technology and Commerce. It was established in 1956 to help promote and facilitate Australian exports by providing finance and insurance. From 2000–2001, EFIC supported more than AUD 6.8 billion (USD 3.7 billion) to over 170 countries. The majority of the loans were to small- and medium-sized enterprises. EFIC offers a wide variety of credit options, insurance plans, and guarantees.

II. PRODUCTS—SHORT, MEDIUM, AND LONG TERM

Direct Loans (Buyer Credit)
These credit facilities with overseas buyers help to fund their purchases of Australian capital goods and services. The funds of the loan are normally advanced directly to the exporter, but in certain cases a buyer can be reimbursed after his purchase.

Specifications
The loan amount is up to 85 percent of the total value of the contract, or 80 percent in the case of ships. The exporter must receive a cash payment of 15 percent of the contract value before the first advancement of the loan (not eligible for EFIC credit). Interest is payable semiannually, beginning within six months of the first draw down. The loan is repayable semiannually as well, beginning within six months of the end of the draw down period

with a maximum term of ten years. To be eligible, a contract must generally be over AUD 1 million (USD 540,000), have over a 60 percent content of Australian capital goods or services, and comply with EFIC's environmental policy. The entity receiving the loan can be the buyer, a parent or holding company, a bank representing the buyer, or the Ministry of Finance representing a government department.

Clarity International

With EFIC's assistance, Clarity, an operational support system software developer, was able to secure a multimillion dollar contract to supply software, hardware, and management expertise to the Philippine Long Distance Telephone Company (PLDT). EFIC structured a direct loan for PLDT, enabling the buyer to expand and improve its infrastructure with Clarity's products. In 2001 Clarity won the award for being the Communications World Best Software Vendor. The company has derived more than 80 percent of its revenues from the export market and describes the PLDT success as an integral moment in its history.

Export Finance Guarantee

EFIC issues this guarantee in order for Australian and international financial institutions to issue loans to the buyers of Australian capital goods and services. This guarantee helps Australian exporters by allowing them to take advantage of the vast networks of international banking institutions. Under conditions of high political and/or commercial risk, this guarantee stimulates banks to extend credit under conditions where they normally would not. The funds of the loan are normally advanced directly to the exporter, but in certain cases a buyer can be reimbursed after purchase.

Specifications

The guarantee covers up to 85 percent of the total value of the contract (80 percent for ships), but the lender of the credit can also choose to take a higher percentage of the risk. The exporter must receive a cash payment of 15 percent of the contract value before the first advancement of the loan (not eligible for EFIC credit). The repayment of the loan guaranteed by EFIC is made semiannually, beginning within six months of the first draw down. To be eligible, a contract must generally be over AUD 2.5 million (USD 1.36 million), have over a 60 percent content of Australian capital goods or services, and comply with EFIC's environmental policy. The entity receiving the guarantee should be a bank granting credit to a foreign buyer of Australian capital goods and services.

Documentary Credit Guarantee

With this guarantee, EFIC assures the payment of interest and amortization to a bank that confirms an irrevocable documentary credit issued to an exporter by another bank. This allows the bank that confirms the letter of credit to share the risk with EFIC.

Specifications

The guarantee covers up to 85 percent of the total value of the contract, but the confirming bank can also choose to take a higher percentage of the risk. The structure is similar to the previously mentioned programs. To be eligible, a contract must generally be between AUD 1–10 million (USD 540,000–5.4 million), have over a 60 percent content of Australian capital goods or services, and comply with EFIC's environmental policy.

Documentary Credit Finance

This allows exporters to receive the funds granted to them through irrevocable documentary credits by making EFIC the beneficiary. EFIC then pays the exporter the amount covered on the letter of credit.

Specifications

It is recommended that transactions are over AUD 500,000 (USD 272,000) and have a minimal number of shipments.

Bonds and Related Guarantees

EFIC can provide a bond in order for an exporter to assure the buyer for advanced payments or to support its obligations according to a contract. EFIC issues bonds directly or provides guarantees to banks issuing bonds.

Specifications

EFIC usually requires a minimum security of 5 percent of the bond value. To be eligible, the contract value generally must be over AUD 500,000 (USD 272,000), have over a 60 percent content of Australian capital goods or services, and comply with EFIC's environmental policy.

Political Risk Insurance

This insurance covers exporters from political risks including expropriation, war or armed conflict, and currency inconvertibility and exchange transfer blockage. The insurance can be for an investor or a lender. The investor equity insurance protects against repatriation of capital or investment earnings. The lender debt insurance protects those who provide nonshareholder loans for overseas entities if political events make the servicing or repayment of debt impossible.

Specifications
The political risk insurance for investors will cover 100 percent of the cost of the investment and the amount insured will be indemnified up to 90 percent. The term can be for a period of up to 10 years, but can be granted up to 15 years on a case-by case basis. To be eligible, the investment value must generally be over AUD 500,000 (USD 272,000). The political risk insurance for lenders will also cover up to 100 percent of the debt amount, and the amount insured will be indemnified up to 100 percent. The term should not exceed the term of the loan, and the repayment of the loan should not exceed 10 years. To be eligible, the loan value must generally be over AUD 2.5 million (USD 1.36 million).

Export Credit Insurance
This insurance protects Australian exporters from the political and commercial risks involved when granting credit to a buyer. There are different policies for exporters that have an annual turnover of more than AUD 10 million (USD 5.4 million), and for medium- and small-sized exporters with a turnover of less than this amount.

Specifications
EFIC covers exporters against the following risks and will indemnify accordingly:

- Political risks: 100 percent
  - Blockage on currency exchange or transfer
  - Import bans
  - War or armed conflict
  - Legislation against performance of a contract
- Commercial risks: 90 percent
  - Default on debt by the buyer
  - Buyer insolvency
  - Wrongful failure to accept goods
  - Bank that issues an irrevocable letter of credit and does not honor its obligations

The length is generally based on payment terms of 180 days. Medium-term payment insurance is also available. To be eligible, exports should have over a 60 percent content of Australian capital goods or services, and comply with EFIC's environmental policy.

III. CONTACTS

Head Office:
Export Finance and Insurance Corporation
22 Pitt Street
Sydney NSW 2000
Australia
Tel: (61-2) 9201-2111
Fax: (61-2) 9201-5222

Mail:
Export Finance and Insurance Corporation
P.O. Box R65
Royal Exchange NSW 1223
Australia
Internet: www.efic.gov.au
Email: info@efic.gov.au

Michael Clarey
Head of Structured Trade and Project Finance and Natural
    Resources
Tel: (61-2) 9201-2268
Email: MClarey@efic.gov.au

Nancy Howie
Senior Manager Infrastructure and Engineering Services
Tel: (61-2) 9201-2136
Email: NHowie@efic.gov.a

Peter Johnson
Assistant Manager Manufacturing and Services
Tel: (61-2) 9201-2206
Email: peterjohnson@efic.gov.au

Craig Scullin
Senior Manager Transportation
Tel: (61-2) 9201-2147
Email: CScullin@efic.gov.au

Peter Swan
Senior Manager Information Technology
Tel: (61-2) 9201-2173
Email: PSwan@efic.gov.au

AUSTRIA
OESTERREICHISCHE KONTROLLBANK
AKTIENGESELLSCHAFT (OEKB)

I. INTRODUCTION

OeKB is Austria's primary financial and information service provider for the export industry. OeKB operates on the government's account as agent for the Republic of Austria. Founded in 1946, the bank provides risk coverage services to companies and financial institutions. OeKB is a quasi-sovereign borrower with yearly long-term funding volume of USD 3–4 billion. OeKB holds a majority of shares in Prisma Kreditversicherungs AG, a private credit insurer, as well as a majority stake in Osterreichischer Export-funds GmbH, Austria's export refinancing specialist for small- and medium-sized companies.

II. PRODUCTS

Short, Medium, and Long Term

Export Credit Insurance
OeKB provides short-, medium-, and long-term export credit insurance to reduce the risks for Austrian domestic and foreign trade. OeKB's insurance programs promote Austrian exports by covering both political and commercial risks. OeKB provides a single-buyer turnover guarantee and a multi-buyer turnover guarantee, which support short-term export credit sales; the difference between the two is that the first provides services to only one buyer while the second supplies services to all buyers or countries. All export companies are eligible to apply.

Specifications
The main criterion for insurance eligibility is that the transaction insured create a positive effect on the Austrian current account. Austrians, as well as foreign companies, are eligible for cover as long as they follow the Berne Union's Guidelines. The risk category of the transaction determines the percentage of foreign content. If the transaction falls into categories 1 to 3, which are low-risk transactions, OeKB will accept up to 100 percent foreign content; for transactions in categories 4 and 5, which are medium-risk transactions, 50 percent foreign content is accepted; and for categories 6 and 7, which are high-risk transactions, 40 percent foreign content is accepted.

Terms: OeKB provides insurance for short-, medium-, and long-term contracts. Terms are as follows: Short-term contracts, including raw materials, semi-finished goods, and consumer goods, typically have a term of 6 months; medium-term contracts, including capital goods, have a term of between 2 and 5 years; and long-term contracts, including large projects, have a term of as much as 10 to 12 years.

Coverage: OeKB provides comprehensive coverage plans protecting Austrian exporters against both political and commercial risks. For political risks including war, revolution, transfer risks, nonpayment, and expropriation, OeKB will cover losses up to 100 percent of the transaction costs. For commercial risks, including nonpayment and insolvency, OeKB generally covers between 70 and 95 percent of the transaction costs.

Interest Rates and Fees: Rates are determined on a case-by-case basis depending on the risk category, creditworthiness of foreign importer, contract duration, the amount insured, and loss experience. However, for both commercial and political risks the premium is fixed between 0.2 and 3.2 percent. OeKB also issues a handling/administration fee of 0.1 percent of the amount covered.

Guarantee

OeKB offers bank guarantees to protect Austrian lenders against the nonrepayment of short-, medium-, and long-term credits involving high-value capital goods and services. Guarantee programs cover commercial and political risks for up to 95 percent of the contract value. Bank guarantee agreements are made between the lending institutions and OeKB. If the foreign buyer defaults on its loan repayments, then OeKB will make direct payments to the owed lending institution.

Specifications

The main criterion for an OeKB guarantee is that the transaction creates a positive effect on the Austrian current account. If the amount exceeds EUR 10 million (USD 9.78 million), OeKB will accept 30 percent foreign content in the goods or services exported; if less than EUR 10 million (USD 9.78 million), OeKB will accept 40 percent foreign content. Specifics of OeKB guarantee contracts are tailored to the creditworthiness of the parties involved and the nature of the transaction.

Terms: OeKB provides guarantees for short-, medium-, and long-term contracts.

Coverage: OeKB will assume between 90 and 100 percent of losses due to political claims, and between 75 and 95 percent for commercial claims depending upon the creditworthiness of the importer and country.

Fees: Guarantee interest rates and fees are determined on a case-by-case basis with all aspects of the transaction considered. OeKB also issues a handling/administration fee of 0.1 percent of the amount covered.

Case Study

In December 1998, OeKB guaranteed ABB Export Bank for a DEM 11.9 million (USD 6 million) loan for Slovenské Elektrárne (SE). SE is the national power generation utility in Slovakia and accounts for over 80 percent of power generation in the country. The guarantee allowed SE to obtain credit financing for the purchase of needed power generation turbines and transformers from Austrian suppliers.

Export Finance

OeKB provides financing schemes for Austria's export industry. The export financing program provided by OeKB includes support of both exports and foreign investments.

Specifications

A corporation must be domiciled in Austria or abroad exporting products wholly or partially (up to 30 percent foreign content can be accepted) manufactured in Austria. Transactions must serve, directly or indirectly, the improvement of the Austrian current account balance.

Terms: OeKB provides export financing schemas for all term limits, but medium- and long-term contracts generally range between 2 and 15 years.

Fees: Rates are decided on a case-by-case basis, but the average interest rates as of July 1, 2002 were as follows: short-term interest rates (under two years) are 4.3 percent, medium-term interest rates (two and five years) are 4.8 percent, medium- to long-term interest rates (five to under eight years) are 5.3 percent, and long-term interest rates (eight years and more) are 5.6 percent.

Medium and Long Term

Project Finance

OeKB has greatly increased its support of the project finance program in the past years assessing about 270 projects in Central and Eastern Europe. Commitments for projects have amounted to more than USD 3 billion.

Specifications

There is no limit on industry for project financing, but power, pulp, metalworking, and infrastructure are encouraged. There is a requirement that the origin of the product or service is at least 60 to 70 percent Austrian.

Terms: OeKB considers all contracts on a case-by-case basis, though term restrictions include a maximum repayment term of 14 years and a maximum grace period of 2 years.

Fees: The principle interest rate for project financing is also determined on a case-by-case basis, but where a project's repayment term exceeds 12 years an additional 20 basis points will be added to the contract's interest rate.

Government Bonds

OeKB is the most important government bond issuer in the Republic of Austria, capturing 54 percent of the total market. Austrian government bonds are typically issued on an auction system, with OeKB acting as the government and paying agent.

Specifications

The interest payment period of a bond begins on the first day of the bond's term and ends on the day before its redemption date. The interest payment is effected via the bank's holding accounts and is redeemed on the redemption date. Austrian government bonds cannot be terminated by issuer nor the bondholder, and claims for the payment of principal and interest expire after 3 years in the case of interest and after 30 years in the case of the principal.

III. CONTACTS

Head Office:
OeKB
A-1011 Wien Am Hof 4; Strauchgasse 1-3
Tel: 43 (1) 531 27-0
Fax: 43 (1) 531 27-698
Internet: www.OeKB.co.at
Email: public.relations@OeKB.co.at

Capital Market Department
Name: Erich Weiss
Tel: 43 (01) 53 127 305
Email: erich.weiss@oekb.co.at

Project Analysis Department
Name: Werner Schmied
Tel: 43 (15) 31 27 240
Email: Werner.schmied@oekb.co.at

Guarantee Department
Name: Brigitte Peraus
Tel: 43 (15) 31 27 601
Email: Brigitte.peraus@oekb.co.at

Credit Department
Name: Dieter Nell
Tel: 43 (15) 31 27 240
Email: dieter.nell@oekb.co.at

BELGIUM
OFFICE NATIONAL DU DUCROIRE/NATIONAL DELCREDERENDIENST (ONDD)

I. INTRODUCTION

Ducroire-Delcredere (ONDD), established in 1939, offers programs designed for exporters, investors, banks, traders, and credit insurers, as well as tailor-made programs for those whose needs do not fit inside specific programs. An autonomous body guaranteed by the Belgian government, Ducroire-Delcredere offers a full range of services for exporters and banks. ONDD offers its programs both with and without the state guarantee. Ducroire-Delcredere supported Belgian exports with over EUR 5.8 billion (USD 5.6 billion) in 2000.

II. PRODUCTS

Ducroire-Delcredere offers a wide range of programs to support the Belgian economy, with its primary focus on insurance. Over 600 of its 670 clients are small to medium enterprises. In addition, about 50 percent of the companies insure less than EUR 750,000 (USD 732,000).

Short Term

Ducroire-Delcredere offers short-term services on credits of less than 360 days.

Comprehensive Insurance Policies

This policy covers both consumer and capital goods and services by securing transactions from buyers, allowing an exporter to enhance its turnover. Nonpayment may arise from war, riot, foreign currency transfers, insolvency, cancellation, or the arbitrarily calling in of bank guarantees. Comprehensive insurance covers all of these events.

Specifications
Coverage includes 95 percent of political risks and 90 percent of commercial risks. Companies eligible for these policies are exporters to developing countries located in Belgium or tied to Belgium through a parent company, subsidiary, or origin of the good exported.

Small to Medium Enterprise (SME) Policies
This policy allows smaller corporations exporting consumer or capital goods and services to non-EU countries to cover their overseas risks.

Specifications
The SME policy is for Belgian businesses with an annual turnover that generally does not exceed EUR 5 million (USD 4.8 million) and overseas exports amounting to less than EUR 620,000 (USD 605,000). Coverage is available for up to 95 percent of political risks and 90 percent of commercial risks.

Medium and Long Term

Ducroire-Delcredere classifies terms over 360 days as medium to long term.

Foreign Investments
This insurance covers losses due to infringement to rights of ownership or nonpayment. These losses can be due to a number of events, including expropriation, transfer, breach of contract, and government action. Three basic packages are available. The full basic package offers coverage for war, expropriation, or government action, while the other two offer coverage for expropriation and government action, or war. The principal and profits are insured.

Specifications
All investors who are integrated into the Belgian economic community are eligible for this program. Losses are insured up to 90 percent.

Buyer Credits
These loans are issued to buyers of Belgian exports. The bank fulfills the buyer's obligations to the exporter. A variation of this

involves a bank-to-bank credit instead of a direct buyer credit. Ducroire-Delcredere thus assumes the risk on behalf of the exporter.

Specifications
Repayment to Ducroire-Delcredere varies from 2 to 12 years, depending on the value of the transaction, the nature of the products, and the buyer's country. Payments are made semiannually, with the first payment due upon delivery or upon the provisional acceptance. Under direct buyer credits, given the 15 percent advance payment made by the buyer, the credit cannot exceed 85 percent of the contract.

Project Financing
Ducroire-Delcredere offers this program to protect companies that undertake projects utilizing Belgian goods and services. Special-purpose companies set up for these projects may apply for project financing, or investment cover where Belgian investors are involved.

Specifications
Ducroire-Delcredere complies with OECD agreements and regulations regarding project finance. The bank will provide exporters and financing banks with cover for commercial and political risks. In addition, the bank will cover exchange rate risks. Terms are capped at 5.25 years in OECD countries and 7.25 years in other countries.

Cockerill Mechanical Industries used the project financing program to construct power plants in Izmir, Adapazari, and Gebze, Turkey. The construction and operation of these plants is organized in the form of a "build-own-operate" concession, after a tender by the Turkish Ministry for Energy and Natural Resources. A similar method was used to insure the political and the commercial risks linked to the implementation by Siemens-Atea of a cell phone grid in Kenya.

III. CONTACTS

Head Office:
Square de Meeus 40
B-1000 Brussels
Tel: 32 (2) 509 42 11

Fax: 32 (2) 513 50 59
Telex: ONDD B 211 47
Internet: www.ducroire.be
        www.delcredere.be
Email: ducroire@ondd.be
        delcredere@ondd.be
        bu-ondd@ondd.be

Richard Maroquin
Tel: 32 (2) 509 44 79
Email: r.maroquin@ondd.be

Didier Nicaise
Tel: 32 (2) 509 44 96
Email: d.nicaise@ondd.be

Herman Christiaens
Tel: 32 (2) 509 42 66
Email: h.christiaens@ondd.be

Lieven Dupon
Tel: 32 (2) 509 42 31
Email: l.dupon@ondd.be

CANADA
EXPORT DEVELOPMENT CANADA (EDC)

I. INTRODUCTION

EDC is a Canadian financial institution dedicated primarily to supplying trade finance services to Canadian exporters and investors in over 200 markets. Many of the markets it operates in are emerging markets, which provide a wealth of opportunity for Canadian exporters and investors, but at a greater risk. It has been been providing trade finance services since 1944. EDC operates both on a commercial account, and as an agent of the government, under the Canada Account.

In the year 2001, Canadian businesses concluded CAD 45.4 billion (USD 28.7 billion) in export and domestic sales and investments in markets using EDC trade financing services, which was up 13 percent from the previous year. EDC works primarily with small businesses—nearly 90 percent of their customers are smaller corporations. EDC provides credit insurance, bonding and guarantees, political risk insurance, and direct loans to buyers. Long-term joint venture projects and equity participation are also provided but on a limited basis. EDC can mobilize more than CAD 14.6 billion (USD 9.2 billion) in capital to support exports.

II. PRODUCTS

EDC prides itself on being flexible in the services offered. Short-term financial services focus on credit and political risk insurance. Medium- and long-term financial services include bonding and guarantees, political risk insurance, direct buyer loans, and lines of credit. More specialized financial services include highly structured, limited recourse financing arrangements (debt and equity to support individual projects)—joint ventures or projects that involve long-term leasing arrangements.

Short Term

Accounts Receivable Insurance
EDC covers up to 90 percent of losses resulting from a wide range of commercial and political risks, including war in the buyer's country, refusal of goods by the buyers, insolvency, and payment delay due to blockage.

Specifications
EDC will work for any company, regardless of its size, functioning in any sector of the economy in Canada. Because it is a federal Crown corporation, it requires that the transactions economically benefit Canada. Thus, any transaction with over 50 percent Canadian content is qualified.

Export Credit Bank of Turkey
Turkey has always been an important market for EDC in Europe and it predicts even better things to come. Over the past few years, EDC and Canadian exporters have been active in Turkey on several fronts. In 1996, EDC signed its first line of credit (LOC) with the Export Credit Bank of Turkey (Turk Eximbank). The purpose of this LOC was to help Canadian exporters take advantage of Turkish companies' strong links to the countries of the former Soviet Union and Eastern Europe, and to enable EDC to work with Turk Eximbank to support joint Canadian-Turkish projects. Under this facility, EDC supported projects for Nortel and its Turkish subsidiary Netas in Russia. This first LOC expired in 1999, and in August 1999 EDC signed a new USD 50 million LOC with Turk Eximbank.

Short-Term Credit Insurance

Short-term credit insurance policies cover sales of products or services on credit terms of up to 180 days. Global political insurance provides cover to an exporter against specified political risks inherent in export sales made on short-term credit.

Specifications

Export credit insurance also supplies cover to exporters with sales of CAD 5 million (USD 3.16 million) or less against commercial and political risks. Coverage is for 90 percent of the lesser of the outstanding amount under the operating line of credit or the eligible foreign receivables.

Medium and Long Term

Political Risk Insurance

Political risk insurance insures loss against transfer and inconvertibility of funds, expropriation, and political violence.

Specifications

In order to be eligible the investment must benefit Canada and the host country. EDC provides up to 15 years of coverage and will supply coverage for the investor's equity investment, as well as retained earnings coverage of up to 200 percent of the equity investment.

Political Risk Insurance of Loans

Political risk insurance of loans is an expanded form of the political risk insurance because it provides the following: augmented safety for loans, a bigger range of financing solutions for investors and exporters, increased accessibility of commercial bank financing, potential to increase project capital, and flexibility to organize projects.

Specifications

Loans can be from both Canadians and non-Canadians. Eligible structures are loans to Canadian-sponsored projects, project loans involving non-Canadian investors but from which Canadian benefit will result, and loans for Canadian export sales.

Direct Loans

There are three conditions that must be met when EDC finances a Canadian export transaction:

1. A person or a company must be operating in Canada.
2. The transaction can only be an export.
3. The products and services that are to be exported have an acceptable level of Canadian content.

In order to obtain approval for a loan, EDC needs information on the exporter, buyer, borrower, guarantor, and the transaction. It will then underwrite the transaction on a case-by-case basis.

Inland Technologies, Inc.

When Brunei Shell Petroleum Company started looking for an environmental company to clean up more than 100,000 tons of oily sludge in the Sungai Bera Holding Basin, Inland Technologies Inc. of Truro, Nova Scotia, was quick to respond. Having worked in Brunei since 1997, Inland was familiar with the market and the challenge. It put together a joint venture with two other Nova Scotia-based companies, plus a local partner in Brunei, each with specialties in key environmental niches. After three years of intense negotiations with Shell, local officials, Canadian banks, and EDC, the partners were awarded the three-year USD 15 million contract, even though they were far from being the lowest bidder. EDC was able to couple a performance guarantee with insurance to assist the consortium in completing the project.

III. CONTACTS

Head Office:
151 O'Connor
Ottawa, Canada
K1A 1K3
Tel: (613) 598-2500
Fax: (613) 237-2690
Telex: EXCREDCORP OTT 053 4136
Internet: www.edc.ca
Email: export@edc.ca
Small businesses (up to CAD 1 million (USD 600,000) in annual
    export sales): 1-866-283-2957
Large businesses (over CAD 1 million (USD 600,000) in annual
    export sales): 1-866-278-2300

Regional Offices:
Western Region:

Lewis Megaw
Regional Vice President
Tel: (403) 537-9800
Fax: (403) 537-9811
Email: contactwest@edc.ca

One Bentall Centre,
Suite 1030
505 Burrard Street, Box 58
Vancouver (British Columbia)
V7X 1M5
Tel: (604) 638-6950
Fax: (604) 638-6955

Home Oil Tower,
Suite 606
324-8th Avenue S.W.
Calgary (Alberta)
T2P 2Z2
Tel: (403) 537-9800
Fax: (403) 537-9811

10010-106th Street
Suite 905
Edmonton (Alberta)
T5J 3L8
Tel: (780) 702-5233
Fax: (780) 702-5235

Commodity Exchange Tower
Suite 2075
360 Main Street
Winnipeg (Manitoba)
R3C 3Z3
Tel: (204) 975-5090
Fax: (204) 975-5094

Ontario Region:

Ruth Fothergill
Regional Vice President
Tel: (416) 640-7600
Fax: (416) 640-7634
Email: contactontario@edc.ca

150 York Street
Suite 810
P.O. Box 810
Toronto (Ontario)
M5H 3S5
Tel: (416) 640-7600
Fax: (416) 862-1267

148 Fullarton Street
Suite 1512
London (Ontario)
N6A 5P3
Tel: (519) 963-5400
Fax: (519) 963-5407

151 O'Connor Street
Ottawa (Ontario)
K1A 1K3
Tel: (613) 597-8523
Fax: (613) 598-3811

Quebec Region:

Françoise Faverjon-Fortin
Regional Vice President
Tel: (514) 908-9200
Fax: (514) 878-9891
Email: contactquebec@edc.ca

800 Victoria Square
Suite 4520
P.O. Box 124, Tour de la Bourse
Montreal (Quebec)
H4Z 1C3
Tel: (514) 908-9200
Fax: (514) 878-9891

2875 Laurier Boulevard
Suite 1340
Ste-Foy (Quebec)
G1V 2M2
Tel: (418) 266-6130
Fax: (418) 266-6131

Atlantic Region:

David Surrette
Regional Vice President
Tel: (902) 442-5205
Fax: (902) 442-5204
Email: contactatlantic@edc.ca

Purdy's Wharf Tower II
1969 Upper Water Street
Suite 1410
Halifax (Nova Scotia)
B3J 3R7
Tel: (902) 442-5205
Fax: (902) 442-5204

735 Main Street
Suite 400
Moncton (New Brunswick)
E1C 1E5
Tel: (506) 851-6066
Fax: (506) 851-6406

90 O'Leary Avenue
St. John's (Newfoundland)
A1B 2C7
Tel: (709) 772-8808
Fax: (709) 772-8693

International:

Marvin Hough
Regional Director for Mexico & Central America
Calle Schiller 529
Rincón del Bosque
Colonia Polanco
México, D.F. 11560
Tel: (525) 5387 9316
Fax: (525) 5387 9317
Email: mhough@edc.ca

Claudio Escobar
Regional Director for Brazil & Southern Cone
Av. das Nações Unidas 12901
Cenu Torre Norte, Andar 16
CEP 04578-000
São Paulo - SP
Tel: 55 (11) 5509 4320 Ext. 3320
Fax: 55 (11) 5509 4275
Email: cescobar@edc.ca

Alison Nankivell
Regional Director for China
c/o Canadian Embassy
19 Dongzhimenwai Street
Chaoyang District
Beijing, 100600
Tel: 86 (10) 6532 3536 Ext. 3357
Fax: 86 (10) 6532 4072
Email: anankivell@edc.ca

CZECH REPUBLIC
CZECH EXPORT BANK

I. INTRODUCTION

Created in 1994, the Czech Export Bank supports the Czech economy with over CZK 1.5 billion (USD 48 million) in capital. Four government ministries and EGAP own all shares.

II. PRODUCTS

CEB offers credits to buyers and sellers, and also offers refinancing of credits to banks. Most products require insurance or guarantees from EGAP.

Medium and Long Term

Direct Supplier's Credit
This credit is offered to support exports of capital goods, complete plants, and machinery, particularly to developing countries. The export must be insured by EGAP.

Specifications
Financing is available for up to 85 percent of the contract value, and is available for terms over two years. At least 60 percent of the value must be goods of Czech origin.

Direct Buyer's Credit
This credit is nearly identical to direct supplier's credit, except the credit is issued to the buyer of the Czech goods, rather than the exporter. These exports must also be insured by EGAP.

Specifications
Specifications, including terms, financing available, and eligibility, are identical to those for direct supplier's credit.

III. CONTACTS

Export and Project Finance
Mr. Jindrich Kostalek
Director
Tel: 420 (2) 2284 3264
Fax: 420 (2) 2423 7788

Vodickova 34
P.O. Box 870
111 21 Praha 1
Czech Republic
Tel: 420 (2) 2284 3111
Telex: 121 285 CEBC
Internet: www.ceb.cz
Email: ceb@ceb.cz

CZECH REPUBLIC
EXPORTNI GARANCNI A PJIST OVACI SPOLECNOST, A.S. (EGAP)
ENGLISH: EXPORT GUARANTEE AND INSURANCE CORPORATION

I. INTRODUCTION

Czechoslovakia created EGAP in 1992 as a government-sponsored export credit agency. The purpose of the company is to promote Czech exports by providing exporters and banks with cover to increase competitiveness. When Czechoslovakia split in 1993, EGAP became the public export credit insurer of the Czech Republic. With capital of CZK 1.3 billion (USD 42 million), EGAP operates from both a commercial account and from a government-sponsored account. EGAP is completely owned by four government ministries, with the Ministry of Finance being the largest shareholder.

II. PRODUCTS

EGAP offers numerous products to insure and guarantee Czech exporters and their foreign buyers. These programs are structured similarly; the differences focus primarily on which party is insured, what risks are covered, and how many parties are involved. Many programs are offered as a package with credits from Czech Export Bank.

Short Term

EGAP generally considers short term to extend up to 24 months.

"B"—Insurance of Short-Term Export Credits against Political Risks

This insurance for political risks is available to the exporter. A bank as a beneficiary is also permitted. This insurance can be purchased independently or in conjunction with insurance for commercial risks.

Specifications

Insurance of short-term export credits is offered for terms of up to two years, covering up to 95 percent of the political risk. Premiums are determined by the country risk category; length of risk; and whether a sovereign, public, or private buyer contracts with the exporter. Premiums are generally paid in advance, in a single payment.

CKD Vognoka

CKD Vognoka, the passenger railway carriage producer, will supply Finnish railways with 16 diesel carriages by 2006. The deal, signed in August 2001, is worth Kc850m (USD 26.2 million) and included an option of adding another 20 cars. CKD Vogonka's victory in securing the contract was, "thanks to the securing of the financing of the contract, jointly by EGAP, the Czech Export Bank, and CKD Praha Holding," said a CKD spokesman.

Medium and Long Term

EGAP considers terms exceeding two years to be medium to long term.

"C"—Insurance of Medium- and Long-Term Export Supplier's Credits against Commercial and Political Risks

Intended for machine production and investment, this program covers the entire spectrum of nonmarketable political and commercial risks. The Czech exporter is the insured party, but indemnification can be made to the exporter's bank.

Specifications

Terms are available for up to 12 years, with similar premiums to short-term insurance against commercial risks. Coverage is available for up to 95 percent of the risks.

"D"—Insurance of Export Buyer's Credits against the Risk of Nonpayment

This program covers loans provided by an exporter's bank to a foreign buyer or a buyer's bank. Standard cover, or 95 percent, is available for terms of up to 12 years.

"E"—Insurance of the Bank Confirming the Letter of Credit

Insurance is available for credit lines to cover political and commercial risks. The insured party is the bank confirming the letter of credit.

Skoda Engero-General Electric

In 2002, EGAP helped to insure a Kc2bn (USD 64 million) contract for the supply of two turbo-sets by Skoda Engero for a gas and power plant in Istambul, Turkey. The power plant will be under the chief contractor General Electric, a contract with an estimated worth of USD 180 million.

III. CONTACTS

P.O. Box 6
110 00 Praha 1
Czech Republic

Vodickova 34/701
111 21 Prague 1
Tel: 420 (2) 2284 1111
Fax: 420 (2) 2284 4001
Internet: www.egap.cz
Email: parizek@egap.cz
        sinsky@egap.cz

Rovna Jirina
Director, Political Risks Insurance Department
Tel: 420 (2) 2284 2310
Fax: 420 (2) 2284 4130
Email: rovna@egap.cz

DENMARK
EKSPORT KREDIT FONDEN (EKF)

I. INTRODUCTION

EKF is a state-guaranteed agency established on March 1, 1996, as a successor to the Danish Trade Fund. On November 19, 1999,

EKF became an independent state-guaranteed public agency. EKF's mission is to ensure competitive conditions for Danish exports, primarily using guarantees and insurance. EKF operates through a fund with capital provided by the state, and the state ultimately is responsible for the fund remaining solvent. Upon its creation in 1996, EKF's net capital was approximately DKK 900 million (USD 118). The total guarantee exposure at the end of 2000 was DKK 14.8 billion (USD 1.94 billion), which is an increase of 17 percent over the total exposure at the end of 1999.

II. PRODUCTS

EKF offers three basic programs to support exports. Its guarantee programs allow exporters to confidently market their goods and services abroad. Generally, products are offered for terms exceeding one year. Specifications for most products are similar. With increased premiums, a company can receive greater coverage of the commercial risks, while political risks are not affected. Special risk insurance, project financing guarantees, mixed credits, and an interest tax scheme are also offered. Investment guarantees in developing countries are available as well. Eligibility for all products requires the foreign content of the good to not exceed 50 percent, although small transactions and better risks may include as much as 80 percent foreign content.

Sprout-Matador
Sprout-Matador exports substantial quantities of machines for the manufacture of fodder. In recent years, foreign customers in particular have requested financing. In order to retain this market the company looked for a financing model that would be able to meet the requirements of its customers. By collaborating with EKF as guarantor for the payments on these projects the company was able to cooperate with a bank, which took on the remainder of the risk and granted its customer a loan at a fixed interest rate.

Medium and Long Term

Supplier Credit Guarantee
This guarantee program is offered to Danish exporters who sell their goods to a foreign buyer on credit. EKF covers the supplier's risk that the credit will not be repaid due to commercial or political conditions.

Specifications
Coverage is available for up to 90 percent of commercial and political risks, up to eight years, with up to DKK 80 million (USD 10.5 million) being the maximum credit under this program. Credit payments are made on a quarterly or semiannual schedule, in equal amounts. A minimum of 15 percent must be paid in advance. The payment claim does not include the part of the contract sum that consists of local deliveries, interest during the disbursement period, bank charges, and EKF's guarantee premium. As a general rule, the maximum credit period for export credits to "rich countries" is five years.

Buyer Credit Guarantee
The buyer credit guarantee is offered to banks that lend to foreign buyers of Danish goods and services.

Specifications
EKB grants buyer credit guarantees to banks that make loans to buyers, covering up to 95 percent of commercial and political risks. Terms range from two to eight years, with DKK 200,000 (USD 26,000) to DKK 80 million (USD 10 million) being the recommended credit amounts under this program. Credit payments are to be made on a quarterly or a semiannual schedule, in equal amounts. A minimum of 15 percent must be paid in advance. The payment claim does not include the part of the contract sum that consists of local deliveries, interest in the disbursement period, bank charges, and EKF's guarantee premium.

Financing Guarantee
When Danish exporters or their overseas buyers request loans from banks, these lending banks can request a financing guarantee from EKF.

Specifications
The terms are similar to those previously described.

Haldor Topsoe
With an annual export of DKK 1.6 billion (USD 210 million) to more than 60 countries, Haldor Topsoe requires EKF's services regularly, in particular in connection with large deliveries to countries outside the OECD. It is often difficult, or sometimes even impossible, to obtain local financing and acquire satisfactory bank guarantees to cover payment. This is where EKF comes in. They issue guarantees so that the company is able

to obtain the financing. EKF also provides interest equalization, which means that customers are able to acquire financing at fixed interest rates that often lie well below the level in the customer's home country.

III. CONTACT INFO

Lars V. Kolte
Managing Director and Head of the Guarantee Department
Tel: 45 (35) 46 61 01
Fax: 45 (20) 19 45 03
Email: lvk@ekf.dk

Jan Vassard
Department for Credit and International Relations
Tel: 45 (35) 46 61 03
Fax: 45 (20) 19 45 04
Email: jvs@ekf.dk

Dahlerups Pakhus
Langelinie Allé 17
2100 København Ø
Tel: 45 (35) 46 61 00
Fax: 45 (35) 46 61 11
Internet: www.ekf.dk
Email: ekf@ekf.dk

FINLAND
FINNVERA PLC

I. INTRODUCTION

Owned by the Finnish state, Finnvera plc is a specialized financial company that offers financial services to support the operations of Finnish businesses. Finnvera was set up in 1999 when two Finish institutions, the export credit guarantee agency, FGB, and the state domestic financing company, KERA Ltd., were merged. Finnvera has over 27,000 clients and 396 employees. The share capital is EUR 188.2 million (USD 183.7 million) and its outstanding commitments total EUR 31 million (USD 30.2 million). The two major products provided by Finnvera are loans and guarantees.

II. PRODUCTS

Short Term

Guarantees

The guarantees offered cover risks related to the buyer or the borrower (commercial risks), or to the buyer's or borrower's country (political risks). The most typical commercial risks are bankruptcy, other kind of insolvency, or default. The most common political risks are restrictions on transfer of the currency, rescheduling of debts, expropriation, and war or insurrection.

Buyer Credit Guarantee

A buyer credit guarantee is a security to the lender in case of a credit risk caused by a foreign buyer, the buyer's bank, or the buyer's country. The exporter receives payment in cash for goods sold on credit, while the credit risks are transferred from the exporter to the lender and further to Finnvera. Furthermore, the guarantee covers both commercial and political risks. The coverage provided is normally 85 percent (buyer risk) or 90 percent (bank risk) for commercial risks and 100 percent for political risks. The short-term guarantee premium is charged as a flat fee based on the guaranteed receivables.

Credit Risk Guarantee

A credit risk guarantee covers the exporter against credit loss related to an export. The guarantee covers either the risks due to cancellation of the delivery contract prior to the delivery or the credit risk arising from the buyer or buyer's country. The guarantee normally covers 85 to 90 percent of commercial risks and 100 percent of political risks.

Medium and Long Term

Capital Loan

Capital loans are available to small- and medium-sized limited liability companies that have a maximum of 250 workers and a maximum turnover of FIM 250 million (USD 41 million) or a balance sheet total of maximum FIM 165 million (USD 27 million). Capital loans may be used to improve growth, achieve financing eligibility, and aid corporate structuring. The loans have a maximum of ten years, with a grace period to be negotiated on a case-by-case basis.

Development Loans

Development loans are intended to help finance significant SME development projects. Financing can be geared towards product and process development, upgrading information and quality management systems, product commercialization, or launching exports. The loan can be used to finance production activities, tourism, and enterprises providing services for these sectors. Except for basic agriculture, small enterprises (less than ten employees) in other sectors can also be funded.

III. CONTACTS

Head Office:
Finnvera plc
Helsinki
Visiting address: Vuorimiehenkatu 1
P.O. Box 1010
FIN - 00101 Helsinki
Tel: 358 204 6011
Fax: 358 204 60 7220
Internet: www.finnvera.fi

FRANCE
COMPAGNIE FRANCAISE D. ASSURANCE POUR LE COMMERCE EXTERIEUR (COFACE)

I. INTRODUCTION

COFACE has been a world leader in export credit insurance and it also leads the way in credit information and trade receivables management. COFACE was established in 1946 by the French government, and has now become a private joint stock company. It offers a full range of credit-related services: domestic and cross-border credit insurance, insurable ratings with rating, investment insurance, research into prospective buyers, credit information, customer monitoring, and receivables management. COFACE has broadened its product and service offering while continuing to build its international reach. It presently operates in 99 countries and offers more than 83,000 companies protection and services. COFACE has 3,700 employees representing 40 nationalities. In 2001, COFACE had a turnover of USD 925 million. The COFACE group is rated AA by Fitch IBCA and is listed on the Paris Bourse.

II. PRODUCTS

Medium and Long Term

Since 1946 COFACE has supported exports covered by "major contracts," which entail medium- or long-term financing. The activity is limited to risks that are not insurable in the private market.

Guarantees

The main guarantees administered by COFACE are a market survey cover, medium- and long-term export credit insurance, foreign investment insurance, and exchange risk cover. COFACE coverage of guarantees applies to political, extended political, and commercial risks. (Extended political risk protects the insured group, which is most likely the bank, against nonperformance by a public authority of obligations written in the project contracts.) Commercial risk covers two specific events: one is the payment default of the debtor and the other is insolvency in law of the debtor consisting of its proven incapacity to meet its financial obligations. Terms are generally 95 percent for political and extended political coverage and between 70 to 95 percent for commercial risk coverage.

Medium- and Long-Term Export Credit Insurance

COFACE coverage fluctuates according to the nature of the project and the risks involved. It generally includes political risk and extended political risk. It can cover commercial risks during the repayment period. When dealing with the length of the credit repayment profile, COFACE seeks to define the most favorable conditions compatible with project fundamentals and the international regulations to which France is held. Risk sharing between the different partners (sponsors/investors and commercial banks) is still one of the most essential elements of this kind of transaction. COFACE tries to share risk equitably between all parties.

Project Finance

The project finance team at COFACE is part of the medium- and long-term departments and it participates in limited recourse project financing. As of 2001, COFACE's project finance portfolio consisted of 27 covered deals. The main areas of a COFACE-backed project financing are finance, legal, engineering, economics, and credit insurance. The team is made up of eight people with a project finance manager dedicated to a specific sector. COFACE's coverage varies according to the nature of the project and the risks involved. It usually consists of political risk and extended political risk. It can manage commercial risks during the repayment period and, in exceptional conditions, the same throughout the construction phase as well. Project finance transactions are subject to a specific premium calculation.

In May 2002, COFACE and French aluminium producer Pechiney signed a contract to expand Bauxilum's production. Bauxilum is the bauxite-to-alumina wing of Venezuela's state heavy industry holding. The credit line worth USD 230 million will cover the costs of engineering, equipment to improve technology and environmental improvement works. With the financial backing of COFACE, Bauxilum plans to expand its production from 1.7M to 2M per/year.

IIII. CONTACTS

Head Office:
COFACE
12 cours Michelet
La Défense 10
92065 Paris La Défense Cedex
France
Tel: 33 (1) 49 02 20 00
Fax: 33 (1) 49 02 27 41
Internet: www.coface.com
           www.cofacerating.com
Email: webmaster@coface.fr

Mme Marie-Laure Mazaud
Head of the Project Finance Department
Tel: 33 (1) 49.02.24.44
Fax: 33 (1) 49.02.20.10
Email: marie-laure_mazaud@coface.fr
Mme Mazaud's secretary: (00.33)1.49.02.15.65, which will
    transfer you to the project finance manager in charge of
    the section
Communication Department
Tel: 33 (1) 49 02 19 72
Fax: 33 (1) 49 02 27 13
Email: bernard_blazin@coface.com
International Department
Tel: 33 (1) 49 02 18 58

GERMANY
HERMES KREDITVERSICHERUNGS-
AKTIENGESELLSCHAFT AG (HERMES)

I. INTRODUCTION

Hermes was founded in 1917 as a specialist for all branches of credit, guarantee, and fidelity insurance in Germany. In 1949, Hermes and PwC Deutsche Revision began administering the federal government's export credit guarantee scheme. Hermes now has 1,800 employees and operates 18 branches throughout Germany. There are also representative offices in other European countries. Hermes covered EUR 19.5 billion (USD 18.4 billion) in exports in 2000, over 90 percent of which were medium- to long-term contracts.

II. PRODUCTS

Germany supports exports of goods and services with insurance, guarantees, and loans. Hermes offers insurance and guarantees on a single transaction, revolving transaction, and comprehensive basis. In addition, Hermes offers insurance and guarantees on leases, construction work, investment risk, and exchange rate fluctuation.

Airbus
Nine of the largest transactions covered by Hermes are Airbus Industrie aircraft orders. Airbus arranged for 7-, 10-, and 12-year terms for their sales, which range from EUR 15 million (USD 14.6 million) to EUR 200 million (USD 195.6 million).

Short Term

Hermes considers short term to be six months to two years.

Official Export Guarantee Scheme
Single, revolving, and comprehensive insurance are available in the short term under the official export guarantee scheme. Insurance for revolving transactions covers multiple transactions with a single buyer, while comprehensive insurance covers multiple transactions with multiple buyers.

Specifications

In general, the exporter will assume 10 percent of the political risk and 15 percent of the commercial risk. An exporter may, however, apply to assume a larger share of the risk in return for reduced premiums. In principle, all types of goods and services may be insured. To be eligible, goods and services may include no more than 30 to 40 percent EU content, 30 percent Japanese or Swiss content, or 10 percent from other nations. The remaining content must be German. Hermes offers guarantees to banks along the same lines as insurance to exporters. In general, banks will bear 10 percent of the political risk and 15 percent of the commercial risk. Premiums are the same for buyer credit cover and supplier credit cover.

Long Term

Long-term coverage is only available for single transactions under the official export guarantee scheme. Exporters of aircraft such as Airbus Industrie and companies building power plants abroad use this program primarily to cover the extended period of time needed to construct their products.

Tehri Hydro Project

A major project Hermes has covered is the switching plant for Tehri Hydro Project. The project is to connect the hydroelectric plant to the local power grid. The Indo-Russian project is using primarily German equipment, and thus is eligible for Hermes insurance. The German government wants to promote more trade by helping exporters to establish a reputation in the region and allow it to do more business.

III. CONTACTS

Postfach 50 07 40
D-22746 Hamburg
Tel: 49 (40) 88 34 91 92
Fax: 49 (40) 88 34 91 75
Internet: www.hermes-kredit.com
Email: 09inet@hermes-kredit.com

PwC Deutsche Revision AG
Wirschftsprüfungsgesellsachft
Postfach 60 27 20
D-22237 Hamburg
Tel: 49 (40) 63 780
Fax: 49 (40) 63 78 15 10

10117 Berlin
Jägerstraße 71
Tel: 49 (30) 20 28 43-00
Fax: 49 (30) 20 28 43-01
Contact: Reinhard Kirwa -23
Contact: Marco Paul -25
Email: aga.nl.berlin@hermes-kredit.com

60311 Frankfurt
Große Gallusstr. 1-7
Tel: 49 (69) 13 48-0
Fax: 49 (69) 13 48-160
Contact: Frank Popp -159
Contact: Klaus Preißler -158
Email: aga.nl.frankfurt@hermes-kredit.com

80339 München
Ridlerstr. 35
Tel: 49 (89) 5 43 09-0
Fax: 49 (89) 5 43 09-166
Contact: Anton Kress v. Kressenstein -143
Email: aga.nl.muenchen@hermes-kredit.com

GERMANY
KREDITANSTLT FÜR WIEDERAUFBAU (KFW)

I. INTRODUCTION

The Federal Republic of Germany created KfW to distribute Marshall Plan aid. Today it provides loans to finance exports of investment goods and related services, primarily to developing countries. In 2000, KfW provided EUR 39.7 billion (USD 37.6 billion) in project and export financing.

II. PRODUCTS

KfW deals primarily with long-term loans for capital goods, with a special fund dedicated to ships and aircraft.

Export Financing Program

KfW manages the export financing program for Germany. KfW finances the delivery of capital goods to developing countries. In general, Hermes must insure the transaction. Loans are made either to buyers or banks. Suppliers receive credits only in exceptional cases.

Specifications

In accordance with OECD agreements, the maximum amount financed depends on the size of the contract. KfW can finance 85 percent of the eligible contract value. For those up to EUR 25 million (USD 23.6 million), KfW will finance 85 percent of the actual contract. For contracts between EUR 25 million and EUR 50 million (USD 47.2 million), KfW will finance 85 percent of EUR 25 million, which comes to EUR 21.25 million (USD 20 million). For contracts over EUR 50 million, 85 percent of half the order is financed, with a traditional maximum of EUR 85 million (USD 80.3 million). Loans can be disbursed in Euros or U.S. dollars. Interest rates for loans are fixed, but variable rates are available upon request.

Peru

KfW recently announced a loan of EUR 15.6 million (USD 14.8 million) to support three community projects in Peru. These projects will repair and expand the city water system in Huancavelica, and promote the involvement of private corporations in public water supply and sanitation programs. Another part of the project involves an agro-ecological program that will improve crop and land management.

III. CONTACTS

Postfach 11 11 41
D-60046 Frankfurt
Tel: 49 (69) 74 310
Fax: 49 (69) 74 31 29 44
Internet: www.kfw.de

Charlottenstrasse 33/33a
10117 Berlin
Tel: 49 (0) 30 2 02 64-0
Fax: 49 (0) 30 2 02 64-5188

Belgium
KfW Liaison Office to the EU
50, rue Wiertz
1050 Brussels
Tel: 32 (2) 2 33 38 50
Fax: 32 (2) 2 33 38 59
Email: kfw.brussels@skynet.be
Director: Stephan Sellen

Bolivia
KfW Office La Paz
Avenida Ecuador 2523
Edificio Dallas, piso 10
Casilla 645
La Paz
Tel: 591 (2) 41 33 37
Fax: 591 (2) 41 17 68
Email: kfw@ceibo.entelnet.bo
kfwbolivia@gmx.net
Director: Michael Wehinger

Bosnia and Herzegovina
KfW Office Sarajewo
Hasana Kikica 18
71000 Sarajevo
Tel: 387 (33) 2 66 610
387 (33) 2 66 611 or 21 30 17
Fax: 387 (33) 2 66 612
Email: kfwsaraj@bih.net.ba
Director: Frank Bellon

Brazil
KfW Office Brasilia
SCN Quadra 01-Bloco C-No. 85
Edificio Trade Center
Sala 1706
CEP 70711-902 Brasilia DF
Tel: 55 (61) 328 00 49
Fax: 55 (61) 328 07 49
Email: kfwbrasil@uol.com.br
Director: Dr. Gregor Wolf

China
KfW Office Beijing
1170, Beijing Sunflower Tower
No. 37, Maizidian Street
Chaoyang District
Beijing 100026
Tel: 86 (10) 85 27 51 71-3
Fax: 86 (10) 85 27 51 75
Email: kfwbeij@public3.bta.net.cn
Director: Dr. Karl-Joachim Trede

Côte d'lvoire
KfW Office Abidjan
01 B.P. 7172
Abidjan 01
Tel: 225 (22) 43 35 80
Fax: 225 (22) 43 35 81
Email: kfw-abj@globeaccess.net
Director: Bruno Schön

Egypt
KfW Office Cairo
4D, El Gezira Street
Zamalek 11 211
Cairo
Tel: 20 (2) 7 36 95 25
     20 (2) 7 36 74 96
Fax: 20 (2) 7 36 37 02
     20 (2) 7 38 29 81
Email: kfwcairo@gega.net
Director: Jan Blum

Guatemala
KfW Office Guatemala City
5a Avenida 15-11, Zona 10
Ciudad de Guatemala
Tel: 502 367 55 02
     502 367 00 11
Fax: 502 367 55 03
Email: kfw@gold.guate.net
Director: Helge Jahn

India
KfW Office New Delhi
21, Jor Bagh
New Delhi 110 003
Tel: 91 (11) 4 64 12 02
    91 (11) 4 64 71 13
Fax: 91 (11) 4 64 12 03
Email: kfwindia@vsnl.com
Director: Andrea Johnston

Indonesia
KfW Office Jakarta
Deutsche Bank Building 20th FL
Jalan Imam Bonjol No. 80
Jakarta 10310
Tel: 62 (21) 32 78 75
Fax: 62 (21) 31 90 78 85
Email: kfw@cbn.net.id
Director: Jens Clausen

Jordan (also in charge of operations in Palestinian Territories)
KfW Office Amman
P.O. Box 926 238
Issam Al Ajlouni Street 8
Shmeissani
Amman
Tel: 962 (6) 5 67 40 83
Fax: 962 (6) 5 67 40 87
Email: kfw@go.com.jo
Director: Reinhard Schmidt

Kenya
KfW Office Nairobi
Lenana Road, Kilimani
P.O. Box 52074
Nairobi
Tel: 254 (2) 57 21 22
    254 (2) 57 21 11
Fax: 254 (2) 57 21 03
Email: kfw@nbnet.co.ke
Director: Andreas Holtkotte

Kosovo
German Office for Reconstruction and Development (GORED)
Xhemal Kada 7
Pristina
Tel: 381 (0) 38 50 06 38
Fax: 381 (0) 38 54 90 11
Email: kfwkosovo@compuserve.com
Director: Dr. Johannes Feist

Nicaragua
KfW Office Managua
Optica Nicaraguense 2 c. arriba
20 vrs. al lago
Managua
Tel: 505 268-56 15
Fax: 505 268-56 22
Email: kfw@cablenet.com.ni
Director: Helge Jahn

Palestinian Territories
KfW Office Al Bireh
8/1 Omar Ben Abdul Aziz Street
Al Bireh/West Bank
Tel: 972 (2) 2 40 07 30
Fax: 972 (2) 2 40 07 31
Email: kfw-pal@palnet.com
Director: Reinhard Schmidt

Peru
KfW Office Lima
Avenida Inca 172, piso 6
San Isidro
Lima 27
Tel: 51-1-222-5137/-9178/-2233
Fax: 51-1-222-0242
Email: kfw-peru@tsi.com.pe
Director: Michael Wehinger

Serbia
KfW Office Belgrade
Zupana Vlastimira 6
11000 Belgrade
Tel: 381 (11) 66 65 44
     381 (11) 36 71 27 3
Fax: 381 (11) 66 65 44
Email: kfwbelgr@eunet.yu
Director: Marc Engelhardt

Tanzania
KfW Office Dar es Salaam
65, Ali Hassan Mwinyi Road
P.O. Box 1519
Dar es Salaam
Tel: 255 (22) 2 12 81 89
Fax: 255 (22) 2 12 81 92
Cell: 255 742 6039 08
Email: kfw@africaonline.co.tz
Director: Oskar von Maltzan

Vietnam
KfW-office Hanoi
Regus Centre, Ltd.
#5+6, 2/F, 63 Ly Thai To
Hoan Kiem
Hanoi
Tel: 84 (4) 934 53 55
Fax: 84 (4) 934 53 56
Email: kfw-vietnam@hn_vnm.vn
Director: Dr. Klaus Müller

GREECE
EXPORT CREDIT INSURANCE
ORGANIZATION (ECIO)

I. INTRODUCTION

The Export Credit Insurance Organization (ECIO), established in 1988, is an independent legal entity. ECIO's headquarters in Athens has about 36 employees; its branch in Thessaloniki has 3 employees. ECIO is a nonprofit organization that is governed by a nine-member Board of Directors and supervised by the Ministry of National Economy. Guarantee capital today amounts to GRD 500 billion (USD 1.4 billion). ECIO insures against commercial and political risks of nonpayment those export credits granted by Greek exporters to foreign buyers abroad who buy Greek products, services, or projects. ECIO also insures against political risks the investments undertaken abroad by Greek businesses.

II. PRODUCTS

Short-Term Insurance and Guarantee Programs

ECIO provides insurance against political and commercial risks, as well as natural catastrophes. An exporter can be covered for all exports under a global insurance policy for short-term and long-term credits or be covered on a case-by-case basis. Coverage is considered either from the date of the sales contract or the date of shipment.

Eligibility: In order to be eligible, at least 25 percent of the export value must be of Greek origin. The following are credit terms covered: for consumer goods, up to 3 months; for consumer durables, up to 24 months; for investment goods, usually up to 3 years and in some exceptions up to 5 years.

Premiums: Premiums are paid in advance and the rates usually range from 0.3 to 3.5 percent.

Guarantees for Banks

Banks usually are not given guarantees directly, rather, the insurance from ECIO assists them in covering export risks for their customers.

Export Credit Insurance Programs

ECIO's most important purpose is to insure commercial and political risks of nonpayment for short-term export credits. ECIO provides Type A and Type B export credit insurance programs. While Type A relates to insurance coverage of particular goods for specific clients and countries, Type B offers a yearly insurance contract and relates to all shipments. Type B's premium amounts are supplied at a much lower rate than Type A (50 percent less), but the insured exporter is required to present all invoices to ECIO despite any agreed terms of payment.

Percentage of Cover: ECIO can cover up to 90 percent of an insured shipment value; however, the percentage of cover on each incident depends on the foreign buyer's credit rating and the current political and economic circumstances in the country.

Credit Limit: The insured exporter can prolong a credit limit to a particular foreign buyer up to the amount for the agreed credit period.

Premium: The premium is established on a case-by-case basis as a certain percentage of the shipment value. Generally, the premium depends on the number of commercial and political risks the exporter wants to have covered.

Bond Insurance

ECIO can issue insurance policies to commercial banks covering risk arising from bonds issued by them to overseas customers on behalf of Greek contractors. Coverage is for bid bonds, performance bonds, bonds covering advance payments, and bonds covering exemption of customs duty on machinery imported into the customer's country. ECIO can cover up to 90 percent of the issuer's loss, and up to 50 percent of the loss where the forfeiture is due to a mistake of the Greek contractor. The ECIO and the banks retain the right of recourse to both the exporter and buyer.

III. CONTACTS

Head Office:
Export Credit Insurance Organization
Athens57 Panepistimiou Street, 105-64.
Tel: 30 (01) 331-0017 / 20
Fax: 30 (01) 324-4074.

Branch Thessaloniki: THESSALONIKI,
51 Politechniou St. & V.Hugo St., 546 25
Tel: 30 (031) 548718
Fax: 30 (031) 548762
Email: grammateia@oaep.gr

HUNGARY
HUNGARIAN EXPORT CREDIT
INSURANCE LTD. (MEHIB)

I. INTRODUCTION

MEHIB began operations in 1994. Owned by the Hungarian state, the purpose of MEHIB is to aid exports by assuming some of the financial risks and to encourage "external economic relations," especially those exports of Hungarian commodities and services.

II. PRODUCTS

MEHIB offers ten insurance policies that provide cover for many exporting situations.

Three policies worth noting are:

1. Comprehensive cover for the whole turnover (including manufacturing risk)
2. Comprehensive cover for the whole turnover (post-shipment risk only)
3. Cover for small- and medium-sized exporters with the same risks and terms

Specifications
These policies cover insolvency and protracted default as well as imminent loss. ("Any fact and condition that may result in loss regarding the business relations between the Insured and the Buyer, any commercial contract between them or the policy.") Insolvency of the buyer includes bankruptcy, court-ordered insolvency, suspended payments, or an ordained moratorium, etc. Protracted default occurs when the buyer does not pay all/part of the debt at the date of payment.

Terms: The policy period is an indefinite amount of time to be specified based on yearly insurance periods.

Supplier Credit Insurance for the Post-Shipment Period
Specifications
This particular policy covers political events abroad, including war, riot, etc., and government measures due to these events; unjustifiable, unilateral termination by the buyer; refusal, specifically unjustified refusal, by the buyer to accept goods; protracted default by the buyer; and insolvency.

Terms: A premium payment is decided based on the specifics of the agreement and includes a 10 percent deductible. The period of cover begins no earlier than the signing date of the commercial contract and extends to the time when the insured has any valid credit limits.

III. CONTACT

Hungarian Export Credit Insurance Ltd.
1065 Budapest
Nagymezõ str. 46-48
Tel: +36-1-374-9200
Fax: +36-1-269-1198
Internet: www.mehib.hu/english/
Email: info@mehib.hu

ITALY
INSTITUTO PER I SERVIZI ASSICURATIVI DEL COMMERCIO ESTERO (SACE)

I. INTRODUCTION

There are two Italian agencies that provide insurance, guarantees, and export credit. SACE insures short-, medium-, and long-term export loans made by banks (buyer credits) and by exporters (supplier credits) to finance Italian exports. SIMEST is the institution that provides financial support.

SACE is the insurance, guarantee, and reinsurance organization that provides backing to Italian firms that want to export, and to foreign banks that finance such operations. SACE insures political, commercial, catastrophic, economic, and exchange rate risks. SACE was established in 1977 as a public institution operating as an autonomous section of the state-owned insurance group Instittuto Nazionale delle Assicurazioni (INA, the National Insurance Institute). In 2000, SACE's insurance guarantees amounted to 525 billion lire (USD 266 million) for short-term transactions and 9,654 billion lire (USD 4.9 billion) for medium-to long-term transactions.

SIMEST was created in 1991 as a joint stock company controlled by the Ministry of Foreign Trade. Its shareholders include banks, businesses, and sectoral associations. It promotes direct investment by Italian companies outside the European Union and administers various forms of public support for exports and the internationalization of the Italian economy. SIMEST had a staff of 153 in the year 2000. In 2000, SIMEST funded 146.1 billions of lire (USD 74 million) in new projects.

II. PRODUCTS

Short Term

Short-term projects are considered those with terms of less than two years. Comprehensive policies are available for covering an exporter's entire short-term business. Coverage varies on a case-by-case basis, but commercial coverage may not exceed political coverage.

Comprehensive Policy for SME

The comprehensive policy is a tool that was created to allow small and medium enterprises to easily access credit insurance for their exports.

Eligibility: The European Union considers small or medium enterprises those that have a staff of less than 250 people, an annual turnover not exceeding EUR 40 million (USD 39 million), or assets not exceeding EUR 27 million (USD 26.3 million). There are limitations to coverage for exports to the European Union countries, as well as to Australia, Canada, Japan, New Zealand, Norway, Switzerland, and the United States.

Terms: The risk covered by this policy is credit risk, which occurs when the exporter does not receive the partial or total payment. No application fee is required for small or medium enterprises according to the European Union standards. The maximum insurable percentage is 95 percent.

Fees: The insurance premium is calculated based on annual sales forecasts, and it is paid in two installments: 50 percent when signing the contract and the other 50 percent at a fixed date within the first six-month period of validity.

Contact Information
Tel: 39 (06) 6736320
Fax: 39 (06) 6792430
Email: Acc.plgl@isace.it

Medium and Long Term

SACE considers medium-term projects those with repayment terms between two and five years; long-term projects have repayment terms above five years. SACE has an annual ceiling for medium- to long-term commitments that are set by the State Budget law. In 2000 the ceiling was 9,500 billion lire (USD 4.8 billion).

Investment Policy

This policy insures foreign direct investments abroad relating to contributions of capital, capital goods, technologies, licenses, patents, and management contracts. The political risks covered are loss of the invested capital.

Terms: For the investments made up of capital goods, technologies, licenses, patents, consulting, management, and commercialization, SACE covers up to 95 percent of the investment value. (SACE's coverage is always 95 percent.)

SIMEST

Export Incentives

This program is designed for Italian businesses to supply foreign buyers with machinery, plant, and related services at deferred medium- to long-term (at least two years) payment on competitive terms against those offered by other EU and OECD exporters. SIMEST grants subsidy or stabilization for export credit loans and will cover the difference between the market rate demanded by the lending bank and the subsidized rate (established by international agreements) charged to the foreign buyer. The loan may be granted in euros or in any other major currency.

Specifications
Broker sales and commissions may be up to 5 percent. SIMEST covers up to 85 percent of the contract amount. The request may be presented to SIMEST by the financing bank or directly by the exporter. The applicant must fill out the "Modulistica per la richiesta di agevolazione." SIMEST then examines the request and presents to the loan committee for approval within 90 days of the date of the request.

Contact Information
Antonello Ciccotti,
Simona Ortolani
Carlo de Simone
Email: buyerscredit@simest.it

Paola Carducci
Maria P. Bonanni
Email: supplierscredit@simest.it

Financing for Market Penetration Programmes
This is designed to help Italian companies become established in non-EU countries by setting up permanent branch offices abroad, or sales and customer service networks, or specific promotion outlets (e.g., market research and advertising). Costs covered are market studies, promotion, advertising, and expenses related to the implementation of business abroad.

Specifications
Financing will cover up to 85 percent of the program's estimated costs to a ceiling of ITL 4 billion (USD 2 million). In certain cases the amount can be ITL 6 billion (USD 3 million) for Consortia of Italian Companies. The maximum duration of the loan is seven years, including a pre-amortization period of no more than two years.

Contact Information
Rosa Guarnieri e Carla Di Placido
Email: legge394@simest.it

Short, Medium, and Long Term

Guarantees for Banks

SACE grants short-, medium-, and long-term cover to Italian banks that finance domestic producers for the purchase of foreign goods involved in export transactions.

Specifications

The percentage guaranteed is established on a case-by-case basis depending on the information available on the buyer or guarantor. However, SACE may cover up to 95 percent of the amount financed. SACE may accept liabilities and pay out claims in foreign currencies.

Supplier Credit Policy

The supplier credit policy can be used for short-, medium-, and long-term transactions. The supplier credit policy, concerning single exports, insures several risks pertaining to the same transaction.

Terms: The maximum insured percentage is 95 percent. The insurance premium must be paid upon accepting the guarantee. A 15 percent down-payment is required. Repayment is made in six-month installments. The risks that may be insured are manufacturing, credit, nonrepayment, unfair calling of bonds, destruction or damage of goods, and requisition or confiscation of goods.

Buyer Credit Policy

The buyer credit policy covers a credit institution's risk in extending a loan to an importer for products shipped by an Italian exporter.

Specifications

Terms: The following terms apply to all of SACE's policies. SACE accepts a foreign content of up to 15 percent of the contract value. The exception is for foreign content from EU countries that have concluded reciprocity agreements with Italy, in these cases up to 30 percent of the contract value is accepted. If the 15 percent general rule is exceeded, the normal percentage of cover is reduced.

Fees: Transactions exceeding EUR 250,000 (USD 244,000) shall be equipped with a nontransferable and nonrefundable banker's draft to the order of SACE for the following amounts:

- EUR 500 (USD 488) fee for amounts at risk not exceeding EUR 2.5 million (USD 2.44 million)

- EUR 2,500 (USD 2,440) fee for amounts at risk from EUR 2.5 million (USD 2.44 million) up to EUR 12.5 million (USD 12.2 million)
- EUR 5,000 (USD 4,881) fee for amounts at risk from EUR 12.5 million (USD 12.2 million) up to EUR 50 million (USD 48.8 million)
- EUR 12,500 (USD 12,200) fee for amounts at risk exceeding EUR 50 million (USD 48.8 million)

III. CONTACTS

Casella Postale 253 Roma Centro
00100 Rome
Tel: 39 (0) 6 673 61
Fax: 39 (0) 6 673 6225
Internet: www.isace.it
Email: relazioni@isace.it

Societa Italiana per le Imprese All'Estero (SIMEST)
Corso Vittorio Emanuele II, 323 00186 Roma (Italia)
Tel: 39 (0) 6 686351
Fax: 39 (06) 68635220
Internet: www.simest.it
Email: info@simest.it

Head of Underwriting
Mr. Gianluca Bravin
Tel: 39 (06) 6736226
Email: g.bravin@isace.it
David Mizoule
Tel: 39 (06) 6736213
Email: d.mizoule@isace.it

Structured Finance and
    Direct Investment Division
Tel: 39 (06) 6736 213
Fax: 39 (06) 6793413
Email: div.fsie@isace.it

Informational Systems Division
Tel: 39 (06) 6736217
Fax: 39 (06) 6794489
Email: div.sinf@isace.it

Legal Division
Tel: 39 (06) 6736240
Fax: 39 (06) 6794761
Email: div.leg@isace.it

Accounting Division
Tel: 06 (39) 6736201
Fax: 06 (39) 6794792
Email: div.cont@isace.it

JAPAN
JAPANESE BANK FOR INTERNATIONAL COOPERATION (JBIC)

I. INTRODUCTION

There are two Japanese organizations that offer officially supported export credits: Japan Bank for International Cooperation (JBIC) and Nippon Export and Investment Insurance (NEXI). JBIC offers among other things export credits, import credits, overseas investment loans, untied loans, guarantees, and aid with the objective of assisting Japanese firms to further internationalize their operations. The Export-Import Insurance Division Ministry of International Trade and Industry (EID/MITI), one of world's largest export-import insurers, transferred its function in April 2001 to a newly established, state-owned independent administrative institute called NEXI. However, the government retains the ultimate responsibility to reinsure NEXI.

JBIC was established by merging the Export-Import Bank of Japan (EXIM) and the Overseas Economic Cooperation Fund (OECF) in October 1999. JBIC operations fall into two major categories: the International Financial Operations, which promotes Japanese exports and economic activities overseas, as well as stability in international financial markets; and the Overseas Economic Cooperation Operations, which supports self-reliant development efforts in developing countries. The International Financial Operations markets export loans, import loans, overseas investment loans, untied loans, and equity participations in overseas projects. Official development assistance (ODA) loans, which support the activities of private companies in developing countries, is the major component under the Overseas Economic Cooperation Operations.

In 2002, JBIC had a budget of 1.15 billion yen (USD 9.8 billion) for its International Financial Operations and 760 billion yen (USD 6.4 billion) for its Overseas Economic Cooperation Operation. The bank had a staff of 886.

II. PRODUCTS

Short Term

Short-Term Comprehensive Insurance

NEXI considers short-term contracts those with repayment terms of less than two years. It is designed to cover trade contracts (export contracts and intermediary trade contracts) with a direct credit of two years or less. This insurance is part of the General Trade Insurance Program. It covers losses resulting from nonshipment of export cargoes or from failure to collect proceeds for such shipments or for intermediary trade cargoes and services.

Specifications

This insurance is a comprehensive business insurance policy offered to companies engaged in foreign trade, designed to cover all trade transactions. There are no restrictions on the type of cargo involved. Commercial risk coverage is a maximum of 80 percent before shipment and 90 percent after shipment. Political risk coverage is a maximum of 95 percent before shipment and 97.5 percent after shipment.

Medium and Long Term

JBIC does not provide short-term credit financing. Its products are targeted only at medium- and long-term repayment projects, typically ranging from 2 to 10 years. Some maturities, such as overseas development assistance (ODA) loans have repayment terms of 40 years.

Export Loans

Export loans finance Japanese exports to developing countries. The loans take the form of supplier's credits extended to Japanese exporters, buyer's credits to foreign importers in developing countries and bank-to-bank loans to financial institutions in developing countries. The principal items eligible for these credits are power products, machinery, and petrochemicals. The financial terms and conditions are set in accordance with OECD guidelines.

Specifications

The maximum repayment term depends on the country to which the borrower is exporting. For exports to middle-income countries, the maximum repayment term is five years; for developing countries it is ten years. The minimum down payment should be 15 percent of the export contract. The applicable interest rate is the Commercial Interest Reference Rate (CIRR) or Japanese government bond yield, plus 100 basis points that depend on the repayment terms of the export loan. For 5-year loans, it is the 3-year Japanese government bond yield plus 100 basis points. For 5 to 8.5-year loans, it is the 5-year Japanese government bond yield plus 100 basis points, and for loans over 8.5 years, the rate is the 7-year Japanese government bond yield plus 100 basis points. The loan can be denominated in yen or dollars.

Coverage: JBIC does not finance the down payment portion.

Bolivia-Brazil Gas Pipeline Project

Bolivia is a land-locked country in South America that is blessed with an abundance of natural resources. Its geographical isolation has meant that Bolivia has been slow in modernizing its transportation infrastructure, thereby hindering economic growth. In contrast, Bolivia's neighbor, Brazil, has a rapidly growing economy. A major economic issue in Brazil is how to respond to new energy demands. Bolivia has an abundance of natural gas, but had financial difficulty in developing the supply routes. Brazil had an energy supply problem resulting from its rapidly growing economy. Out of these compatible concerns, the Bolivia-Brazil gas pipeline project was born.

Petrobras (Petroleo Brasileiro) took responsibility for the construction and financing through JBIC of a 35 billion yen (USD 298 million) export loan. In this project, Japanese steel manufacturers received orders for 540,000 tons of steel pipes. Given the current recession in the steel industry, this total shipment of steel pipes will account for some 20 percent of the annual export volume of major steel manufacturers.

Import Loans

JBIC provides long-term funds to Japanese importers for natural resources that are vital for the development of the Japanese economy. The funds provided are utilized by importers to make advance payments. Import loans may be denominated in yen or dollars.

Specifications
Items eligible for this program are energy resources; mineral resources; other raw materials such as salt, lumber, cotton, and wood chips. The borrower may only be a Japanese importer or foreign exporter. For importers of products other than natural resources, guarantee facilities are available when JBIC identifies the irreplaceable need for a particular product.

Contact Information
Energy and Natural Resource Finance Department
Tel: 81 (3) 5128-3061

Overseas Investment Loans
Overseas Investment Loans support Japanese direct investments in developing countries by providing financing for Japanese investors, joint ventures where Japanese firms have equity interests, and government or financial institutions in developing countries that make equity investments in or external loans to the joint ventures. JBIC also provides information and advice on the investment climate in other countries primarily for small- and medium-sized enterprises (SMEs). As an official lender, JBIC also makes an effort to mitigate such risks through dialogues with host country governments and government agencies.

Contact Information
Corporate Finance Department
T: 81 (3) 5218-3062

Untied Loans
These loans aim to create an external environment conducive to Japan's global economic activities, including trade and investment, and supporting structural adjustment in developing countries. These loans are not tied to the procurement of goods and services from Japan but are utilized for the specific purposes designated for each loan. These loans help resolve a wide range of economic problems such as external debt arrears, underdeveloped infrastructure and capital markets, and environmental pollution.

Thailand
Under heavy pressures from large-scale speculative selling of the baht, Thailand's currency began floating in 1997, triggering a sharp drop in the baht and leading to the Asian currency crisis. The Thailand government

requested assistance from the IMF for the structural adjustment of its economy. The IMF subsequently approved a USD 4 billion loan, conditional on the implementation of an agreed-upon economic adjustment program. To help deal with the situation, an international assistance package (totaling USD 17 billion) was put together, with countries in Asia and the Pacific region as well as international organizations participating in the agreement. Japan co-financed with the IMF in the form of untied loan a total of USD 4 billion equivalent yen, which was one of the largest contributions.

The co-financing aimed to support Thailand's international balance of payments by providing funds to finance Thailand's general imports. Fostering exports also became an urgent issue. Consequently, an untied two-step loan [totaling 80 billion yen (USD 667 million) co-financed with private financial institutions] was provided to the Industrial Finance Corporation of Thailand and the Export-Import Bank of Thailand. At the same time, the financing also aimed to ease financing difficulties of Japanese affiliates in Thailand and to contribute to the recovery of Thailand's economy.

Contact Information for Export and Untied Loans
(Contact person will depend on the country)
International Financial Operations I: Asia
Tel: 81 (3) 5128-3058

International Financial Operations II: Central Asia and the
    Caucasus, Pakistan, Afghanistan, the Middle East, Africa, and
    Europe
Tel: 81 (3) 5128-3059

International Financial Operations III: North America, Latin
    America, and the Caribbean.
Tel: 81 (3) 5128-3060

ODA Loans (Aid Finance)
JBIC cooperates with commercial banks to extend concessional aid credits to developing countries. ODA loans account for 40 percent of Japan's economic and social development assistance. These loans are designed for economic and social infrastructure projects such as roads, power plants, urban water supply and sewerage systems, and educational facilities. Their purpose is to spur sustainable economic growth, which in turn will contribute to poverty reduction. There are various types of ODA loans, depending on the needs of the developing countries.

- *Project loans* are the principal form of ODA loans. They provide funds for facilities, machinery, civil work, consulting services, and other project needs.
- *Engineering services loans* provide funds for engineering services such as project information.
- *Financial intermediary loans* (two-step loans) provide funds to small- and medium-sized enterprises involved in manufacturing and agriculture.
- *Commodity loans* are designed for countries facing a shortage of foreign currency reserves needed to import commodities. The goal is to stabilize the recipient's country's economy.

Specifications

As a general rule, ODA loans are provided at a low interest rate, below 2 percent. ODA loans must be requested by the government of the country in which the project will be financed. The grace period is typically between 7 and 10 years, and the repayment term is 40 years. For environmental projects the interest rate may be 1.7 percent. The majority of the loans are provided for Asian countries. Ninety-five percent of ODA loans are not tied to a foreign content requirement.

Chinese Thermoelectric Power Project

Shenyan is located in the northeast Province of Liaoning, China. Shenyang's old industrial district has been developed in the process of rapid urbanization, and this has had an adverse effect on the environment. The city relies on coal for more than 70 percent of its energy. Hence, air pollution from soot and sulfur dioxide is a serious problem. In an effort to reduce pollution, Sheyang has adopted policies to reduce industrial emissions, including altering manufacturing processes and promoting the relocation of industry outside the city.

The city is also implementing a project to supply thermoelectric power for both industrial and residential use. This project falls into the three priority areas set out in JBIC's Medium-Term Strategy for Overseas Economic Cooperation Operations; environment, food, and poverty, and a focus on inland regions to reduce regional disparities. In Phase I, Y5 billion (USD 41.5 million) in ODA loans were provided in December 1996 to construct power supply facilities. The current loans Y1.2 billion (USD 10 million) are provided as Phase II. The proceeds of the loan will be used to produce boilers, power generators, and other equipment to supply thermoelectric power, as well as goods and materials required to address pollution sources at industrial plants.

Guarantees

JBIC provides guarantees for loans made by private-sector financial institutions and public bonds issued by governments in developing countries. Loans to developing countries involve, among others, currency conversion and transfer risk and country risk. JBIC's guarantees, covering such risks, will enable Japanese private financial institutions to make medium- and long-term finances to developing countries to draw private capital and private firms to expand international finance activities.

Project Finance

Project finance refers to the form of financing in which revenue generated from development projects is applied to the repayment of the loan. The key to success for these projects is the control of political and commercial risks. Political risks refer to those risks originated in the host country government, such as expropriation, war, and restrictions on foreign exchange and transfers; commercial risks are those originated by the project developer, such as delays and the failure to achieve the projected level of operations. JBIC's project finance is available for export loans, overseas investment loans (OILs), and guarantees.

Terms: For an export loan, JBIC will support 60 percent of the financing requirement in accordance with OECD Guidelines, while the remaining 40 percent will be financed by commercial banks with NEXI cover. For OIL, JBIC will support a portion not exceeding 60 percent of the debt financing requirements of the project, while the remaining portion will be financed by commercial banks. A guarantee may be provided for the co-financing commercial bank's portion to cover political risks when JBIC provides OILs.

Application Process: Once JBIC receives the information on the transaction, the Project Finance department focuses on the risks inherent in the project. Then it determines whether the project may be bankable under JBIC's risk evaluation criteria, such as project risks, political risk, and country risks. Upon receiving an application for project finance, JBIC cooperates with other potential senior lenders, which may include NEXI, other ECAs, multilaterals, and/or commercial banks. Independent external advisers such as independent engineers, market consultants, and insurance advisers, depending on the nature of the project as well as legal counsel, will likely be needed.

Contact Information
Project Finance Department
Tel: 81 (3) 5218-3070

III. CONTACTS

Headquarters:
Japan Bank for International Trade
4-1 Ohtemachi 1 –chome
Chiyoda-ku, Tokyo 100-8144
Japan
Tel: 81 (3) 5218 3100
Fax: 81 (3) 5218-3956
Email: www.jbic.go.jp/english/

Osaka Branch
13th Floor
Aqua Dojima East 4-4
Dojimahama 1-chome
Kita-ku, Osaka 530-0004
Japan
T: 81 (6) 6346-4770
F: 81 (6) 6346-4779

Division I
Power (Asia and Oceania)
Non-energy resources
Director Kentaro Tsuboi
Tel: 81 3 5218 3812
Email: k-tsuboi@jbic.go.jp

Division II
Power (Europe, Africa, the Middle East, and Central Asia)
Telecommunications
Transportation
Director So Horikiri
Tel: 81 3 5218 3813
Email: s-horikiri@jbic.go.jp

Division III
Director Hideo Naito
Power (The Americas)
Water Treatment
Manufacturing
Petrochemical
Energy Resources
Regional Development
Tel: 81 3 5218 3812
Email: h-naitou@jbic.go.jp

Contact Information For Investment and ODA Loans
Corporate Finance Department
Tel: 81 (3) 5128-3062

KOREA
KOREA EXPORT INSURANCE CORPORATION
KOREA EX-IM BANK

I. INTRODUCTION

There are two important Korean agencies involved in supporting exports: the Korean Export Insurance Corporation and the Korea Ex-Im Bank. The Korea Export Insurance Corporation (KEIC), Korea's official export credit insurance institution, was established in July 1992 to provide insurance against the risk of nonpayment by buyers and issuing guarantees to banks that provide export financing. KEIC operates ten domestic branches and four overseas representative offices, with a total of 311 employees. During 1998, its export insurance amounted to USD 20 billion, and supported 16.3 percent of Korea's total exports.

The Export-Import Bank of Korea is a governmental financial institution. It was established on July 1, 1976. The Bank extends financial support for export and import transactions, overseas investment projects, and the development of natural resources abroad by providing loans, guarantees, trade refinancing, and other financial facilities. The Bank's lending programs are operated in two ways: Loans to domestic suppliers and loans to foreign buyers. Loans to domestic suppliers include export loans, technical service credits, overseas investment credits, overseas project credits, major resources development credits, import credits, short-term trade finance, small business export credits, rediscount on trade bills, and forfeiting. Loans to foreign buyers include direct loan, project finance, relending facilities, and overseas business credits.

II. PRODUCTS

Short Term

KEIC considers short-term transactions those with repayment periods within two years. Out of the total amount underwritten, short-term insurance accounts for 81 percent of all its business. By sector this short-term coverage went towards steel products and machinery (31.2 percent), followed by electric and electronic products (24.1 percent), plastic and rubber products (15.9 percent), and chemical products (11.3 percent). Korea Ex-Im considers transactions with repayment terms and production periods from six months to two years.

KEIC's Products
Short-Term Export Insurance
This insurance provides against losses from failure to export or nonpayment due to the political risks of the importer's country, or commercial risks related to the importer. There are no particular restrictions imposed on the type of payment or transaction.

Export Bill Insurance
This policy insures the negotiating banks against the risk of dishonor on a bill of exchange at maturity by the overseas buyer. Hence, this service is limited to transactions where a documentary bill of exchange is issued.

Specifications for Short-Term Export Insurance and Export Bill Insurance
These policies cover 95 percent of the contract value for most enterprises, and 97.5 percent for small and medium enterprises. Both political and commercial risks are covered. The period of coverage is two years.

Pre-Shipment Export Credit Bank Guarantee/Import Credit Bank Guarantee for Raw Materials for Export
This guarantee is designed to provide joint and several liabilities for Korean exporters who are competent enough to fulfill their obligations regarding export contracts, but have difficulty obtaining funds required for production and purchase of goods for export due to insufficient security.

Specifications
This policy covers 100 percent of the contract value. However, it is limited to the small- to medium-sized enterprise exporter's risks.

Post-Shipment Export Credit Bank Guarantee
Designed to assist in the short-term export transactions of small- to medium-sized enterprises, this guarantee provides an unconditional repayment guarantee against a bank's inability to receive payment from the overseas buyer after negotiating bills of

exchange or shipping documents. Coverage is 100 percent of political and commercial risks.

Korea Ex-Im's Products

Short-Term Trade Finance

These loans are designed for Korean exporters who manufacture exporting goods. They can be denominated in foreign currency or Korean won.

Specifications
Repayment terms are up to 30 days after the last payment date of the export contract. KEIC covers up to 100 percent of the export contract value, less the amount that the borrower has already received.

Contact Information
Trade Finance Group
Joong-ouk Shin
Executive Director
Tel: 82 (2) 3779-6474
Email: trade@koreaexim.go.kr

Import Credit

Import credit is provided to Korean importers for the import of essential materials, whose stable and timely supply is required for the Korean economy. The funds provided should be used to pay the exchange bills of imported goods, but in certain cases may be used to make a payment up front.

Eligibility: Among the eligible items are iron, copper, lead, aluminum, nickel, tin, stainless steel, diamonds, gold ore, white gold ore, bismuth ore, lumber and semimanufactured goods, raw cotton, raw sugar, graphite, mica, asbestos, and equipment for academic study.

Terms: Maximum two-year period for the import of eligible items specified herein and a maximum ten-year repayment period for the import of both equipment and machinery and major resources developed in foreign countries.

Small Business Exporter

This credit is provided to small- and medium-sized companies who manufacture export goods or supply materials needed by their primary exporters on the basis of past export performance. Eligible items are all goods and services that are not prohibited for export by applicable laws and international conventions. The loan is typically in Korean won.

Terms: Up to 90 percent of the contract (100 percent for small companies). Repayment term is for six months and can be extended on a six-month basis as long as the company has continuous exports.

Financial Guarantee

Korea Ex-Im provides guarantees to Korean commercial banks, local branches of foreign banks, and foreign banks that participate in transactions. It also provides domestic or foreign financial institutions with an interest rate support program to compensate for the difference between CIRR and their floating rates. Korea Ex-Im's financial guarantee provides repayment protection for co-financing banks' loans to transactions that satisfy eligibility requirements. Korea Ex-Im guarantees that, in the event of default, it will repay all of the principal and interest on the loan. The applicant may be domestic companies, foreign governments, or companies who are borrowers of the related credit.

Project-Related Guarantees

Korea Ex-Im provides a foreign importer with a 100 percent guarantee that a Korean exporter will perform as contracted. Project-related guarantees include bid bonds, advance payment bonds, performance bonds, and retention bonds. The repayment period and the amount are as stipulated in the contract.

The beneficiary of the guarantee varies with each type of bond:

- Bid bond: Company ordering the related contract
- Advance payment bond: Foreign contractor extending advance payment
- Performance bond and retention bond: Foreign contractor who has concluded the related contract

Fees (per annum): Determined on a case-by-case basis, depending on the risk of the related transaction and credit risk of the borrower:

- Bid bond: 0.2 percent + Margin
- Advance payment bond: 0.3 percent + Margin
- Performance bond and retention bond: 0.4 percent + Margin

Specifications for all products
A bank guarantee, insurance certificate of KEIC, pledge, or mortgage on the borrower's local assets may be required.
Currency: In a foreign currency or Korean won.

Medium and Long Term

Medium- and long-term projects are those with repayment periods of more than two years. The amount of insurance underwritten for medium- and long-term insurance is 11.6 percent. Medium- and long-term insurance typically has been used for shipping vessels, steel pipes, telecommunication facilities, and power generation facilities.

KEIC's Products

Medium- and Long-Term Export Insurance

This is for an export contract whose payment terms are for more than two years. It covers losses arising from failure to receive payment for exported goods or failure to go ahead with a planned export shipment due to either political or commercial risks. Most of the customers using this insurance are exporters of capital goods such as industrial plants, machinery, vessels, etc.

Specifications
Covers up to 100 percent of the contract.

Overseas Constructional Works Insurance

This insurance provides protection against losses arising from three events: failure to proceed with the planned export of construction equipment after a contract has been signed for an overseas construction or engineering project, failure to receive payment for the construction works already completed, or forfeiture of property rights for equipment brought onto the construction site.

Specifications
Coverage is up to 90 percent of the contract (97.5 percent for small- to medium-sized enterprises).

Overseas Investment Insurance

This insurance overs the financial losses of Korean investors who provide surety for obligations of their overseas offices or who fail to recover their investment funds or dividends due to a deterioration in the political circumstances of the host country. It covers political risks such as expropriation, transfer restriction, breach of contract, war, or civil disturbance.

Specifications
Coverage is up to 90 percent of the contract (97.5 percent for small- to medium-sized enterprises). The period of coverage is within 15 years.

Export Bond Insurance

This insurance covers the financial institution that issues bonds guaranteeing a Korean exporter carrying out a contract against the risk to be called for its security obligations. This insurance helps Korean exporters increase their competitiveness in winning overseas project orders, while helping the financial institutions enhance their capital adequacy ratio.

Specifications
Coverage is 95 percent of the contract, and 100 percent with a counter guarantee.

Foreign Exchange Risk Insurance

This insurance was adopted in February 2000 as a means of hedging against foreign exchange risks. Although the contract structure is similar to that of futures, KEIC foreign exchange insurance charges cheaper transaction costs and the procedure is simpler. It also offers cover during the bidding period prior to an actual contract being settled.

Korea Ex-Im's Products

Export Loans

Export loans are extended to Korean exporters as a supplier credit, in order to provide them with the required funds to finance export transactions with repayment terms of two years or more. It is mainly designed to encourage the export of capital goods such as industrial plants, ships, and industrial machinery involving larger credits and longer repayment terms. These loans are for projects whose goods and services are not prohibited for export by applicable laws and international conventions. The borrower may only be a Korean exporter.

Terms: Loans cover up to 100 percent of the export contract value, less the required 15 to 20 percent cash payment. The maximum repayment terms vary depending on the products.

Maximum Repayment Terms:

- Ships: 12 years
- Conventional power plants: 12 years
- Nuclear power plants: 15 years
- Aircraft (large passenger airplanes): 12 years
- Other products: 5~10 years, pursuant to the OECD guidelines

Coverage and Fees: Up to 90 percent of the export contract value, less the amount that the borrower has already received (i.e., cash payment). The exposure fee will be equal to or higher than the minimum premium in the OECD guidelines. A management fee or administration fee may be charged up-front on a project-by-project basis.

Overseas Investment Credit

Overseas investment credit is provided to Korean companies that invest abroad in the form of capital subscription, acquisition of stocks, and long-term credit. This credit is extended when prospective projects are considered as contributing to the sound development of the national economy, and promoting economic cooperation. However, investments by individuals who do not engage in business, as well as investment in foreign stocks and bonds for speculative purposes, or in banking, insurance, and leisure businesses, are not eligible for this credit. The borrowers may be Korean companies that make capital subscription to acquire shares of foreign companies and/or make long-term loans (longer than one year) to foreign companies, or Korean companies that conduct investment projects outside Korea.

Types of Loans: Loans to Korean companies for equity participation in foreign companies and loans to Korean companies for re-lending to foreign companies, in which the Korean companies have equity share, as long-term funds for ventures operating outside Korea.

Specifications

Maximum ten-year repayment period including a three-year grace period.

Coverage: Financing ratio is up to 90 percent of the funds required for major resources development projects, and 80 percent (90 percent for small- and medium-sized companies) of the funds required for other investment projects.

Direct Loans

Direct loans are an export credit service that helps foreign buyers purchase Korean goods and services with repayment terms of two years or more. Under this program, Korea Ex-Im directly enters into loan agreements with foreign buyers and provides them with loans that are used to pay the Korean exporters when the shipping schedule is fixed.

Eligibility: The same as that applied to the export loan program; the borrower may be a foreign importer or a foreign government. The borrower must submit a letter of guarantee, irrevocable L/C, and a promissory note issued or confirmed by the importer's government, the central bank of the country, or creditworthy financial institutions. The borrower may choose to disburse the loan in three different ways: through a letter of credit, direct payment, or reimbursement.

Coverage: Over USD 1 million (except for mixed credit with EDCF or Korean exporters of small- and medium-sized companies).

Fees:

- An exposure fee will be equal to or higher than the minimum premium in the OECD guidelines.
- A management fee or administration fee may be charged up-front on a project-by-project basis.

Relending Facility

Relending facility, a type of buyer credit provided by Korea Ex-Im, is a line of credit extended to creditworthy banks in foreign countries to help foreign buyers obtain loans for the purchase of manufactured goods from Korea. Under the Relending Facility Agreement, a borrowing bank (relending bank) provides loans to foreign importers on its own. The buyer who wants to import eligible goods from Korea through the relending facility should contact the relending bank to confirm the availability and terms and conditions of the loan.

Project Finance

Project finance is extended to a foreign project company that intends to import plants, facilities, and technical services from Korea. The repayment of this financing depends on the project cash flows with limited recourse to the sponsors. This form of financing does not need the typical export finance security package.

Terms: Financing terms and conditions depend on the construction period, size, and life of the project. The maximum repayment period is flexibly applied up to 14 years, depending on the nature and economic feasibility of the project and the weighted average life of the financing. There is a required minimum 15 percent cash down payment. Korea Ex-Im covers up to 100 percent of foreign contents.

Eligibility: The project should include export transactions with a legally and economically independent project company. More than 25 percent of the total project cost should be financed with equity from the sponsors and/or shareholders. Not more than 50 percent of the total project cost may be co-financed by other export credit agencies or multilateral development agencies.

Repayment of Principal: Principal is repaid on the basis of semiannual installments, with the first repayment date of the principal within 6 months from the project completion date.

Also, the alternative repayment could be considered subject to economic feasibility and nature of the corresponding project.

Fees: The exposure fee is equal to or higher than the minimum premium in the OECD Guidelines.

Management fees or administration fees may be charged upfront on a project-by-project basis.

Hyundai and Kia Motors Company

The Korea Ex-Im Bank will extend a USD 31.4 million loan to the Dominican Republic Government to import motor vehicles from Hyundai Corporation of Korea. This is the second time the Bank has supported this type of transaction. Korea Ex-Im disbursed a USD 20.4 million direct loan and approved a financial guarantee and interest rate support of USD 14.3 million. Hyundai will export 1,718 buses and 117 trucks manufactured by Hyundai Motor Company and Kia Motors Corp. This is part of the Dominican Republic's strategy to modernize its mass transit system and strengthen its tourism industry, the major source of foreign currency. The Government is also planning to purchase about 5,000 vehicles worth USD 500 million over the next four years.

III. CONTACTS

Korea Export Insurance Corporation
16-19, 23F, Young Poong BLDG 33
Seorin-Dong, Chongro-gu
Seoul 110-752, Korea
Tel: 82 (2) 399-6800
Fax: 82 (2) 399-6597
Internet: www.keic.or.kr
Email : keicb04@keic.or.kr

911 Wilshire Boulevard, Suite 1640
Los Angeles, CA 90017, USA
Tel: 1 (213) 622-4314
Fax: 1 (213) 622-5316

Korea Ex-Im
16-1, Yoido-dong, Youngdungpo-gu, Seoul 150-873
Postal Address : Yoido P.O. Box 641, Seoul 150-606
Tel: 82 (2) 779-6114
Fax: 82 (2) 784-1030
Telex : K26595 EXIMBK
Cable : EXIMKOREA.SEOUL

Young Kim
Chief Representative
460 Park Ave. 8th Floor
New York, N.Y. 10022, U.S.A.
Tel: 1 (212) 355-7280/2
Fax: 1 (212) 308-6106
Email: exnewyork@earthlink.net

Ship Export Credit Office
Pyung-ku Lee
Tel: 82 (2) 3779-6319
Email: ship@koreaexim.go.kr

Overseas Economic Research Institute
Jea-min Lee
Tel: 82 (2) 3779-6679
Email: oiri@koreaexim.go.kr

Small Business Exporter Credit
SME Export Credit Group
Kyung-suk Hong
Tel: 82 (2) 3779-6301
Email: smallbiz@koreaexim.go.kr

Export Loans
Export Credit Group
Tae-dong Park
Tel: 82 (2) 3779-6410
Email: buyer@koreaexim.go.kr

Overseas Investment Credit
Overseas Investment Credit Group
Young-moon Kim
Tel: 82 (2) 3779-6432
Email: overinv@koreaexim.go.kr

The Netherlands
Nederlandsche Credietverzekering Maatschappij N.V. (NCM)

I. INTRODUCTION

NCM was founded in 1925 in Amsterdam by a number of Dutch banks and insurance companies, as well as a German bank. In

2000, the NCM's turnover was EUR 501 million (USD 487 million) and they protected EUR 172 billion (USD 167 billion) of global trade. NCM has their headquarters in Amsterdam and operates in Belgium, Canada, Germany, Finland, France, Denmark, Sweden, Norway, Spain, Italy, Ireland, Malaysia, the United Kingdom, and the United States of America. Worldwide NCM has a staff of 1,840 and can provide information about 26 million companies.

NCM insures more than 17,000 companies, ranging from multinational conglomerates to small enterprises requiring straightforward low-cost credit insurance. Through the insurance programs, businesses can cover their trade receivables against political and commercial risks. Political risks include war or natural disaster, government moratorium, and transfer delay, while commercial risks include buyer insolvency, protracted default, and non-acceptance of goods in breach of contract.

II. PRODUCTS

Short Term

Short-Term Insurance
For short-term transactions (under 360 days repayment terms), cover is given for consumer goods, raw materials, and semi-finished goods as well as services. Normal credit terms are up to 6 months; consumer durables may be covered up to 12 months. Cover is generally given on a whole turnover basis. In some cases, cover is possible for one or more countries or for special business sectors. Cover is usually 75 percent; the maximum covered is 95 percent for political risks and 90 percent for commercial risks.

Medium and Long Term
For medium-term transactions, coverage is available for capital goods, construction work, and services. For capital goods the maximum maturity is 5 years; capital goods and construction work contracts may be covered on credit terms of up to 10 years, depending on the size of the contract and the country of destination. Cover may be given to a maximum of 95 percent. NCM requires a minimum cash payment of 15 percent on or before delivery, of which 5 percent is to be paid at the date the contract becomes effective.

Specifications
Foreign content requirement: For medium-term business the maximum foreign content accepted is 30 percent. Occasionally, a

foreign content of up to 50 percent can be accepted (e.g., if the respective content is not available in the Netherlands and cannot be substituted by Dutch content).

Coverage: Percentage of cover may go up to 95 percent both for political and commercial risks.

Eligibility: NCM examines the creditworthiness of the buyer and the buyer's country. In some cases a particular transaction can be covered only if an exporter obtains additional guarantees from the buyer or a guarantee from the central government. NCM's products can be for short-, medium-, and long-term transactions. However the coverage for each of these varies.

Global Policy
Designed for multinational corporations, whose requirements are inherently complex, NCM's global policy offers a total credit management solution. It covers global trade from anywhere to anywhere in the world. The policy insures against buyer insolvency, protracted default, political risks, war, and the failure of a publicly owned buyer to perform its obligations.

International Policy
This NCM corporate program is designed specifically for the needs of companies based in the United Kingdom and Ireland with an annual turnover typically of GBP 5 million (USD 7.8 million) or more. It covers the export and sales risks within the United Kingdom and Ireland. Specifically, it covers buyer insolvency and default, and has the most complete political risk cover available. Political risks include any action by a foreign government that prevents payment, political events that delay the transfer of funds from the buyer's country, any law that releases the buyer from the obligation to pay beyond the deposit of local currency, war or natural disasters that prevent the completion of the contract, and the refusal of a government-owned buyer to pay the amount owed.

Guarantees For Banks
NCM provides buyer credit policies to financing banks and covers the risk of nonpayment of a loan. NCM also offers direct guarantees to banks for drafts or promissory notes discounted by them, provided that each underlying transaction is covered by a supplier credit risk policy.

Loans
Private banks exclusively provide loans in the Netherlands. Exports of Dutch goods and services, whether sold on short-,

medium- or long-term credit conditions, are financed and refinanced by exporters and commercial banks at market rates only. These banks can lend at floating rates or fixed rates without any state support.

Aid Programs

The Export Transactions Program (known as ORET) and the Program for Environment and Economic Self-sufficiency (Miliev) offer grants that can be combined with export credit. This program was designed to enable developing countries to buy Dutch goods and services, and Dutch companies to participate in projects aimed at increasing employment in developing countries. In 2000, NLG 330 million (USD 146 million) were available as grants.

Eligibility: Requests have to be submitted to the Ministry for Foreign Affairs. Transactions are evaluated for their contribution to the long-term development of the recipient country and for their compatibility with Dutch policy on development cooperation.

NCM Support of UK Construction Industry

Over the past two years more than 2,600 UK construction companies have gone into liquidation, and 2,500 self-employed contractors have become bankrupt. Suppliers caught up in the ripple effect of these insolvencies have themselves been faced with huge losses that they have been unable to recoup. Previously, standard credit insurance policies were not designed to meet the trading and contractual needs of the construction industry.

NCM's solution to the problem is a tailor-made credit insurance policy that acknowledges the trading and contractual practices of the industry, delivering payment and cash flow security in a risky trading environment. In the event of buyer insolvency, the policy also covers losses relating to retention payments up to 10 percent of the contract value, and expenses incurred for work in progress. If the contract in progress is binding, NCM will also continue to cover the client for an additional three months after normal cover is withdrawn, to allow completion.

III. CONTACTS

In Netherlands:
NCM N.V.
Keizersgracht 281
1016 ED Amsterdam
(P.O. Box 473, 1000 AL Amsterdam)
The Netherlands
Tel: 31 (20) 553 9111
Fax: 31 (20) 553 2811
Internet: www.gerlingncm.com
Email: info@ncmgroup.com

In USA:
NCM Americas
5026 Campbell Blvd, Suites A-D
Baltimore MD 21236
USA
Tel: 1 (410) 246 5524
Fax: 1 (410) 246 5530

Ministry of Economic Affairs
P.O. Box 51
Bezuidenhoutseweg 30,
2594 AV Den Haag
The Netherlands
Tel: 31 (70) 3081986
Email: ezinfo@postbus51.nl

Mark Felmar
VP of Underwriting; CURE
Tel: 1 (410) 246-5482
Email: mark.felmar@ncmamericas.com

Rose Gore
Account Manager
Tel: 1 (410) 246-5484
Email: rose.gore@ncmamericas.com

Dorothy Kliphouse
Administrative Account Manager
Tel: 1 (410) 246-5580
Email: dorothy.kliphouse@ncmamericas.com

Thomas Beckwith
VP of Finance
Tel: 1 (410) 246-5506
Email: thomas.beckwith@ncmamericas.com

NORWAY
THE NORWEGIAN GUARANTEE INSTITUTE FOR EXPORT CREDITS (GIEK)

I. INTRODUCTION

The Guarantee Institute for Export Credits (GIEK) was established in 1929. It is the central governmental agency responsible for furnishing guarantees and insurance for export credits. GIEK's primary function is to promote export of Norwegian goods and services, as well as Norwegian investment abroad, primarily by covering exporters' commercial and political risks. GIEK, through the subsidiary GIEK Credit Insurance Ltd., primarily services exporters who are unable to secure satisfactory short-term export credit offers in the private market. GIEK offers long-term guarantees for export of capital goods to most countries, including emerging markets. GIEK's guarantees also cover the export of ships, a major Norwegian export.

Eksportfinans was established in 1962 on the initiative of the Ministry of Finance and the Norwegian Bankers' Association. The Norwegian commercial banks founded Eksportfinans as their specialized institution for long-term export financing. Since 1978 Eksportfinans has handled the official Norwegian export financing scheme on behalf of the government. New loans in 2001 totalled USD 2 billion.

II. PRODUCTS

Specifications
Foreign content up to 30 percent of the contract value is accepted. In some cases, up to 50 percent of the contract value is accepted. Percentages of cover are up to 100 percent for political risks and up to 90 percent for commercial risks.

Short-Term Insurance

Short-term insurance is provided by GIEK Credit Insurance Ltd, a wholly owned subsidiary of GIEK. This company is the new issuer of whole turnover policies formerly provided by the Commercial Section in GIEK. The company has a solid capital base. GIEK Credit Insurance Ltd has ten employees.

Whole Turnover Policy

A whole turnover policy protects the exporter against losses on short-term export credits (up to 360 days). The policy covers risk in connection with nonpayment by foreign buyers for ongoing exports. The policy normally covers 100 percent of the exports, however, an upper limit is set for the amount that the exporter may be owed by any individual buyer at any given time. Those who may apply are exporters who have themselves granted credit to a debtor and financial institutions that have granted a loan to an exporter. The premium is calculated on the basis of the value of the export that the whole turnover policy is intended to cover.

Medium- and Long-Term Guarantees

GIEK offers guarantees for the export of capital goods to over 150 countries, including emerging markets. The guarantees are issued on behalf of the Norwegian government and can be used as security for banks and other financial institutions to facilitate funding. The guarantees may encompass a single transaction or a series of transactions and cover not only commercial risk (i.e., bankruptcy on the part of the debtor or nonpayment for other reasons) but also political risk (i.e., war, expropriation, and actions by the public authorities that prevent payment). Contracts covered by GIEK may involve up to 30 percent foreign components and up to 40 percent with components of Swedish or Finnish origin.

An exporter is required to provide sufficient credit information before application for coverage is processed.

Individual Policies

This program covers the risk associated with individual deliveries of goods and services, and coverage is normally furnished for long-term credits (beyond two years). There are two types of individual guarantee policies: buyer's credit guarantees and supplier's credit guarantees. The buyer's credit guarantees secure repayment of loans granted to a foreign buyer in connection with the purchase of Norwegian goods or services. The supplier's credit guarantees provide protection from losses on credits extended by the exporter to a foreign buyer in connection with purchase of Norwegian goods or services. The buyer and supplier guarantees normally cover both commercial and political risks.

Coverage: GIEK will cover up to 90 percent of the total credit amount in connection with commercial risks and up to 95 percent for political risks.

Terms: For these individual policies, the conditions of sale and borrowing must comply with the OECD Consensus Agreement as regards cash payment, term, installment plan, etc. Terms specify that for credits in excess of two years there must be a cash payment of at least 15 percent, in other words, the maximum financing must not exceed 85 percent. The loan must be repaid in equal semiannual instalments from the time of consolidation.

Bond Guarantees

These guarantees are normally issued by the exporter's bank in favor of the purchaser, and GIEK may cover up to 50 percent of the bank's risk. The exporter is required to repay any disbursements by the bank and GIEK in the event of calling.

Investment Guarantees

These guarantees cover political risks associated with investments outside Norway. The guarantee may cover Norwegian investments abroad in the form of equity capital, borrowings, production equipment, or other deliveries connected with the establishment of a company or participation in ventures outside Norway. This guarantee scheme is restricted to political risks.

Pre-Shipment Guarantee

This policy protects the exporter during the production period against noncompletion or nonfulfillment by the purchaser of concluded contracts as a result of the purchaser's bankruptcy, insolvency, or political events.

Eksportfinans

Norwegian export contracts can be financed with medium- and long-term export loans—those exceeding 365 repayment day terms—to foreign buyers. The credits are given by Eksportfinans on government-supported terms, or on commercial terms. Loans on market terms are extended to finance initiatives aimed at promoting Norwegian exports or other international activities involving Norwegian enterprises.

Government-Supported Export Financing

Government-supported export financing is available to buyers of Norwegian capital goods and services. The minimum loan period is two years; the maximum loan period is up to five years for high-income countries and normally up to ten years for low-income countries. However, it is possible to apply for a 8.5 year maturity for large projects in high-income countries. Loans are repayable in semiannual installments in arrears, the first time six months after the final disbursement.

Terms: Loan collateral in the form of a guarantee from GIEK, a Norwegian bank, or major international bank.

Export Financing on Commercial Terms

This program is an alternative to government-supported export financing that provides flexibility and financial solutions tailored to the Norwegian export contracts. Up to 100 percent of the contract is viable for financing. The loan period is at least two years. The maximum available maturity is determined depending on the size of the loan, the currency, and the guarantee availability. Loan collateral in the form of a guarantee from GIEK, a Norwegian bank, or major international bank is required.

Aid Finance

GIEK also runs a separate national program for exports to and investments in developing countries. It may provide interest subsidies for commercial bank credits or cash grants. In the former case, the credit will usually be in a pre-mixed form and extended either by Eksportfinans or another financial institution. Eligible recipients are low-income (including LLDs) and lower middle-income countries. The grants can be used for matching and are normally tied to a benefit from Norway. In addition, a third party may be subcontracted for up to 30 percent of the gain.

SHIP EQUIPMENT TO RUSSIA

Norwegian Partners Marine AS has signed a contract for the delivery of ship equipment packages to two ships in a series of five oil tankers that are being built in Russia for LUKoil Arctic Tankers Ltd. The equipment packages consist of equipment from several Norwegian and foreign producers, and each package has a contract value close to USD 17 million. Eksportfinans ASA has provided a five-year loan that covers 85 percent of the contract sum. The loan is guaranteed by GIEK under the SUS/Baltic scheme. Norwegian Partners Marine AS has delivered ship equipment packages to the other three ships in the series. These ships were also financed with a loan from Eksportfinans ASA together with a guarantee from GIEK. There is also a guarantee from the Russian state.

III. CONTACTS

P.O. Box 1763
Vika, N-0122 Oslo
Tel: 47 (22) 87 62 00
Fax: 47 (22) 83 24 45
Internet: www.giek.no
Email: giek@giek.no

Contact Information
A/S Eksportfinans
Dronning Mauds gate 15
0250 Oslo
Tel: 47 (2) 283 01 00
Fax: 47 (2) 283 22 37
Internet: www.eksportfinans.no

The Norwegian Agency for Development Cooperation (NORAD)

Postboks 8034 Dep
0030 Oslo
Tel: 47 (22) 24 20 30
Fax: 47 (22) 24 20 31
Email: postmottak@norad.no

Additional Contacts

Fredriksen Arne
Senior Underwriter
Tel: 47 (22) 876212
Fax: 47 (22) 837358
Email: arne.fredriksen@giek.no
Regarding Product
Whole turnover scheme

Aasbo Arild
Senior Adviser LT - Project Finance
Tel: 47 (22) 876214
Fax: 47 (22) 832445
Email: arild.aasbo@giek.no
Regarding Product:
Bond guarantees
Individual policies—buyer's credit
Individual policies—supplier's credit
Investment guarantees
Pre-shipment guarantee

Regarding Region/Country:
Eastern Europe

Ajer Øyvind
Ass. Dir. General, GAR
Tel: 47 (22) 876231
Fax: 47 (22) 822445
Email: oyvind.ajer@giek.no
Regarding Product:
Individual policies—buyer's credit
Individual policies—supplier's credit

Krogh Tore
Senior Adviser LT
Tel: 47 (22) 876215
Fax: 47 (22) 832445
Email: tore.krogh@giek.no
Regarding Product:
Bond Guarantee

Toset Cathrine
Adviser JUR
Tel: 47 (22) 876233
Fax: 47 (22) 832445
Email: cathrine.toset@giek.no
Regarding Product:
Bond guarantees
Individual policies—buyer's credit
Individual policies—supplier's credit
Investment guarantees
Pre-shipment guarantee
Whole turn-over scheme

Regarding Export Financing on Commercial Terms

Finance Department
Direktør Olav Tore Breilid
Tel: 47 (22) 01 22 11
Email: otb@eksportfinans.no
Anniken Amundsen
Tel: 47 (22) 01 23 40
Email: ana@eksportfinans.no

Consulting Department
Finn O. Bjerke
Tel: 47 (22) 01 22 75
Email: fob@eksportfinans.no
Tor Østbø
Tel: 47 (22) 01 22 60
Email: toe@eksportfinans.no

Investor Relations and Long-Term Funding
Søren Elbech
Tel: 47 (22) 01 22 10
Email: soe@eksportfinans.no
Elise Lindbæk
Tel: 47 (22) 01 22 64
Email: el@eksportfinans.no

POLAND
EXPORT CREDIT INSURANCE
CORPORATION KUKE

I. INTRODUCTION

KUKE S.A. has been in existence since 1991. Its objective is to provide export credit commercial and noncommercial insurance and reinsurance to cover all exporters regardless of the scale of their operations or directions of exports. KUKE insures export receivables from over 180 countries worldwide, and acts in close cooperation with other export credit agencies. KUKE's initial share capital was USD 2 million. By a decision of the shareholders the capital was increased to USD 79.8 million by 2001.

KUKE's insurance products allow companies to reduce risk inherent in their export business, provide sales security, expand export sales, and enter new markets. KUKE offers its insurance products to large, medium, and small exporters, including domestic sales and the import of raw materials for export-oriented production. KUKE also provides specialized insurance-related services, such as risk examination and analysis and assessment, for businesses and undertakes recovery actions on behalf of domestic and foreign companies. KUKE's objective is to cover goods and services of Polish origin, but it does accept a non-Polish component on a case-by-case basis. Both exporters and banks financing transactions with buyer credit may apply for an insurance policy.

II. PRODUCTS

Specifications
Eligibility: Eligible entities are those registered and operated in Poland according to Polish Commercial Code rules. Both Polish and foreign banking institutions financing Polish exports under buyer credit facilities can apply for insurance cover.

Foreign content requirement: Foreign content is accepted up to 50 percent of the transaction value of the export final product. However, foreign content up to 90 percent is accepted for certain products.

Short-Term Insurance

KUKE provides insurance to cover short-term commercial and noncommercial risks for up to one year. There are two major types of short-term insurance programs: short-term domestic credit insurance and short-term export credit insurance. There are several policies under each of these subdivisions. The commercial risks covered are bankruptcy, insolvency, and protracted default. The noncommercial coverage applies to losses due to moratorium on payments, non-transfer, war, revolution, prolonged mass strikes, natural disasters, protracted default of a public buyer, and decisions of Polish authorities that prevent the carrying out of an established export contract.

Insurance of Short-Term Export Credits
Insurance of short-term export credit is provided to those exporters who are involved in transactions with deferred payment for a period of up to one year. The insurance covers receivables for the goods or services delivered. Exporters may cover themselves against failure to receive payment from debtors because of commercial, political, and nonmarket risks.

Turnover Policy—Commercial Risks
This policy is issued to exporters realizing cyclical sales on credit terms; the insurance covers receivables under export contracts for the delivery of goods and services due from private customers and payable within a period of up to one year. The agreement is signed for a period of 12 months and may be automatically extended for the following year.

Specifications
This policy protects the exporter against the risk of failure to receive payments because of the deterioration or loss of financial liquidity by the importer, the result of which is legally declared

insolvency, actual insolvency, protracted default by the foreign customer (default occurs when the customer fails to pay the receivables within 180 days from the due date specified in the contract), in the case of receivables payable by documentary collection, failure to accept goods because of the customer's insolvency, arbitrary refusal to accept goods (in this case the payment of claim depends on the recognition of claim by court or as a result of arbitration proceedings).

Turnover Policy—Political and Catastrophic Risks

This policy is issued to exporters realizing cyclical sales on credit terms who want to cover themselves against the risks relating to the political situation in the debtor's country and the occurrence of catastrophic events. The insurance covers receivables under export contracts for the delivery of goods and services due from private and public customers and payable within a period of up to one year.

Specifications

The policy covers the exporter against political risks, such as a ban on the transfer of receivables, general moratorium on payments, proclamation of nationalization acts, war operations, revolutions, massive strikes, and other legal acts preventing the foreign customer from meeting his contractual payment obligations; and catastrophic risks such as the occurrence of natural disasters (earthquakes, cyclones, floods, volcanic eruptions, etc.)

Europolicy for Small- and Medium-Sized Exporters

This policy is specifically designed for the operations of small- and medium-sized exporters. It provides an opportunity to seek new customers, enhances competitiveness on the international market, and offers transaction security according to international standards.

Specifications

This policy is issued to exporters realizing export sales in the amount of USD 1 million annually. The maximum credit limit for one customer must not exceed USD 60,000. The insurance covers receivables due for the goods or services delivered payable on the credit terms of up to 180 days from the date of the delivery, and it covers receivables from 26 OECD countries (with the exception of Turkey) and from Mexico, Slovakia, Lithuania, Latvia, and Estonia.

Specifications for all short-term products:
Coverage: KUKE covers up to 90 percent for political and catastrophic risk, and up to 85 percent of commercial risks.

Medium-Term Insurance

KUKE provides insurance for export contracts financed with medium- and long-term credits (supplier's credit, buyer's credit) against commercial and political risks. This insurance enables Polish exporters to deliver capital goods and receive payment while providing financing to buyers for a term of two or more years.

Specifications
For all the medium- and long-term policies, the following specifications apply.

Credits for financing export contracts submitted for insurance must not exceed 85 percent of the contract value, or in other words, the contract terms have to provide for 15 percent cash payment; credit should be repaid in equal amortization installments payable at regular intervals not longer than six months.

Supplier Credit Insurance
Supplier credit insurance covers the exporter's risk of extending traditional vendor credit to a foreign customer.

Specifications
The insurance covers production risk—the risk that occurs prior to the dispatch of goods or delivery of services, and the risk of no payback of costs incurred by the exporter in connection with signing and preparation. The insurance also covers credit risks— the risks of the contract in case its performance was stopped for a period of at least six months, and the risk of not getting paid for the executed deliveries. The insurance covers receivables due under an export contract for the delivery of domestic goods and services, financed with a credit granted for two years or more.

Buyer Credit Insurance
This is a credit directly offered to the foreign buyer or to the foreign bank in order to finance the Polish export contract. The buyer credit facility is a convenient way to finance the export transaction without using the exporter's own financial resources. The facility enables exporters to receive payments for the delivered goods and the services performed immediately after presentation of the documents to the financing bank, confirming

that the contract has been fully or partially completed. By using buyer credit, the risk of nonpayment is transferred to the bank or another institution financing the export contract.

Contract Guarantees

This policy protects the exporter against the importer's insolvency, while at the same time accommodating the importer's need for protection against improper performance of the contract. From the exporter's point of view, the contract guarantee confirms the company's credibility in the international market, the guarantor being the measure of this credibility, and allows it to meet the importer's requirements.

The exporter may obtain from KUKE:

- Advance payments bond—a written obligation to pay to the importer (beneficiary) the amount specified in the bond in case the exporter (orderer) fails to perform the contract and refuses to return the advance. The guaranteed amount is the amount of the advance transferred by the importer to the exporter. The bond becomes effective upon the advance having been received in the orderer's account.
- Performance bond—an obligation of KUKE to pay the amount specified in the bond in case the orderer (exporter) fails to perform or improperly performs the contract and refuses to repair the damage, make up for the loss, or pay contractual penalties. The importer (beneficiary) uses this type of guarantee to protect against any negative consequences of improper performance of the contract.
- Bid bond—a written obligation of KUKE to pay the amount specified in the bond in case the orderer (bidder) who won the auction refused to sign the contract on terms specified in the bid offer, or in any other way failed to meet the obligations under the bidding procedure. The bid bond is submitted as a security by the bidder.

Re-guarantees

KUKE also provides re-guarantees as a security for guarantees issued by a bank. A re-guarantee may be used by the exporter as a security for the bank issuing a contract guarantee for the benefit of the importer.

Customs Bonds

KUKE provides guarantees to secure payment of customs duty. With such a bond the Customs Office makes it possible to bring goods into the Polish customs area without the need to make advance payment of applicable duties and to submit them to customs procedure (admission to trading, free importation for processing, bonded storage, temporary clearance). KUKE is a guarantor that is accepted by all customs offices. KUKE issues customs bonds following the filing of an order and risk acceptance.

Loans
Financing in Poland is provided by commercial banks. There is an agreement between KUKE and several banks on how they will use KUKE policies as collateral when granting credits to exporters.

III. CONTACTS

Widok 5/7/9, 00-023 WAR-SZAWA
Tel: 48 (22) 827 78 84
Fax: 48 (22) 827 35 87
Internet: www.kuke.com.pl
Email: inform@kuke.com.pl

Zbigniew Buczek
Tel: 48 (22) 55 68 44
Email: zbigniew.buczek@kuke.com.pl

Barbara Plotzke
Tel: 48 (22) 55 68 427
Email: barbara.plotzke@kuke.com.pl

Filip Myszak
Tel: 48 (22) 55 68 445,
Email: filip.myszak@kuke.com.pl

Stanisław Kłyk
Tel: 48 (32) 253 05 28
Fax: 48 (32) 253 85 09
Email: stanislaw.klyk@kuke.com.pl

Jolanta Czekalska
Tel: 48 (32) 253 05 28
Fax: 48 (32) 253 85 09
Email: jolanta.czekalska@kuke.com.pl

Tomasz Wojnarski
Tel: 48 (71) 783 75 82
Fax: 48 (71) 783 75 83
Email: kuke_wroclaw@poczta.gnet.pl

Tomasz Wojnarski
Tel: 48 (58) 321 72 05
Fax: 48 (58) 321 72 06
Email: kukegdpa@gdansk.multinet.pl

Andrzej Rasiński
Tel: 48 (61) 843 07 43,
Fax: 48 (61) 843 47 24,
Email: arank@wlkp.top.pl

PORTUGAL
COMPANHIA DE SEGURO DE CREDITOS, SA (COSEC)
CONSELHO DE GARANTIAS FINANCEIRAS (CGF)

I. INTRODUCTION

COSEC initiated its operations in 1969 as a joint stock company owned by the Portuguese government. However, in 1992 COSEC became fully privatized. COSEC provides credit insurance for Portuguese export and domestic credit insurance, it also covers financial credits, bonds, factoring, leasing contracts and Portuguese investments abroad. In addition, it provides commercial risk cover for its own account and is responsible for the management of state guarantees to cover political and extraordinary risks.

Conselho de Garantias Financeiras (CGF) is a specialized state body operating in the area of officially supported export credits. It examines and decides on transactions submitted by COSEC whenever the granting of risk insurance on behalf of the state is involved. The CGF must also be consulted on general matters related to insurance and cover policy for political and extraordinary risks. The Chairman of the CGF is appointed by the Ministries of Finance and of Economy. The other members are representatives of the Banco de Portugal (the central bank), the Ministry of Finance, the Ministry of Economy, ICEP (Investment, Trade and Tourism of Portugal), BPI Group, and COSEC.

II. PRODUCTS

Specifications for all products
Foreign content up to 40 percent of the contract value is accepted.

Percentages of cover for commercial risks are up to 90 percent for OECD countries, and up to 85 percent for other countries. Political and extraordinary risks are covered up to 90 percent for low-risk countries; this percentage is lowered gradually to 70 percent for more risky countries.

Short Term

Short-term programs are granted to companies with maximum credit terms of one year. Programs are categorized depending on where the products are being sold, either in the domestic or in the export markets. Short-term insurance covers credit risks, such as the failure to pay outstanding credit due to the customer's bankruptcy or insolvency, approval of any creditor's agreement or moratorium, insufficient means of payment or payment default, and pre-credit risks. Fees are established on the basis of the sales turnover, the nature of the goods or services, the customer's quality and sector of activity, payment terms and conditions, and the risks covered.

Short-Term Export Credit Insurance
This insurance covers the nonpayment of goods and services sold on credit in the export market. Credit repayment terms can be up to one year, and coverage up to 90 percent. The policyholder may be indemnified within 60 days. In case of "protracted default," the claim is admitted 6 to 12 months after the maturity date of the invoice.

Small Business Export Credit Insurance
This insurance is tailored for small and medium businesses selling on credit terms in the export market, with sales turnover of up to USD 2.36 million. The suspension or discontinuance of manufacture (i.e., the pre-credit risk) can also be covered. Credit terms should not exceed 90 days, and are covered up to 90 percent. Fees are based on the insured's estimate of annual sales turnover.

Medium and Long Term

COSEC protects the exporter against losses on medium- and long-term export credits with repayment terms of over one year.

Specific Policy
This insurance covers nonpayment by the importer/buyer who undertakes a transaction of good or services exported from

Portugal. It is designed to protect those companies established in Portugal that sell goods or services on the export market, and for public and private buyers or for political risk countries. This policy may cover up to 99 percent commercial and political precredit risks, and the nonpayment of the credit granted to the importer.

Bond Insurance
Covers accurate and timely execution of construction contracts or the supply of goods, payment to the customs authorities, and compliance with any other legal or contractual obligations.

Guarantees
These are special policies for bank credits related to supplier and buyer credits. Guarantees cover the failure to reimburse the export financing. It has the guarantee of COSEC. Covers up to 99 percent of nonpayment of credits form the importer (individual transactions or lines of credit) or the exporter (pre-financing), caused by commercial, political, or monetary events or natural catastrophes.

Eligibility: For supplier credits, coverage depends on the basis of a country-grading table and detailed analysis of the political and economic situation of the importing country. For buyer credits and lines of credit, cover decisions are taken mainly on the basis of criteria used for credit insurance of extraordinary risks or commercial risks depending on the nature of the borrower.

III. CONTACTS

COSEC
Avenida da República, 58
1094-057 Lisboa
Tel: 351 (1) 791 37 00
Fax: 351 (1) 791 37 20
Internet: www.cosec.pt
Email: cosec@cosec.pt

CGF
Avenida da República 58-13
1069-057 Lisbon
Tel: 351 (1) 791 38 96
Fax: 351 (1) 791 37 20

SPAIN
COMPANIA ESPANOLA DE SEGUROS DE CREDITO A LA EXPORTACION, S.A. (CESCE)
ENGLISH: SPANISH EXPORT CREDIT INSURANCE COMPANY

I. INTRODUCTION

CESCE was established in 1970. It was created to provide Spanish exporters with the insurance they need to successfully confront the political and commercial risks of foreign commerce. CESCE provides a wide variety of insurance. The majority of CESCE is currently owned by the public sector (50.25 percent), with the remainder (49.75 percent) held by private sector banks and insurance agencies. CESCE has approximately USD 99 million in capital funds and USD 90 million in accumulated reserves. There are no nationality requirements as long as the goods exported are Spanish. Foreign content is generally limited to 10 percent of the contract value. Higher percentages may be accepted on a case-by-case basis.

II. PRODUCTS

Short Term (Sales with delayed payment of up to 360 days)

Open Insurance Policy for Exports
Designed for exporters that maintain a constant flow of sales to different importers and markets or companies that are considering beginning regular activity in the global marketplace. This policy indemnifies exporters for unpaid credits.

Specifications
Commercial risks: Coverage up to 90 percent. Covers insolvency on behalf of the importer to repay the debts owed to the exporter.

Political risks: Coverage up to 99 percent. Covers any situation outside the scope of the importer that originates in government policy and that makes it impossible for the importer to repay its foreign debts.

PYMES 100 Export Insurance Policy (Medium or Small Business)
This policy is intended for small-to medium-sized companies that maintain a constant flow of sales to different importers and markets or that are planning to have regular international sales.

Specifications
Commercial risks: 85 percent
Political risks: 99 percent

Individual Supplier Credit Insurance Policy
This policy was created to cover the exports of companies that do not maintain a constant flow of sales abroad. At the same time, this policy is also designed for cases in which the activity involved is part of a more complex transaction. It covers the risks of nonpayment, unjustified contract termination, and/or political causes.

Specifications
Commercial: 85 percent
Political: 99 percent

Individual Short-Term Guarantee
With this guarantee, CESCE insures financial institutions from the inherent risks of confirming a guarantee from a foreign institution. The insured in this case is the institution offering confirmation for a letter of credit. It generally covers political and extraordinary risks. In case the debtor is a public entity, the risk of nonpayment by the debtor can be included in the risks covered.

Specifications
Political: 99 percent

Medium and Long Term (Sales with delayed payment of over 360 days)

Buyer Credit Insurance Policy
Insures financial institutions for the repayment of credits granted to foreign buyers for the purchase of Spanish goods and services in case of nonpayment.

Specifications
Commercial: 94 percent
Political: 99 percent

Medium-and Long-Term Supplier Credit Insurance Policy
Two main risks, credit and contract termination, are covered. Credit risk: When the exporter grants the importer a deferment on payments, CESCE insures the risk of nonpayment once the goods and services have already been delivered. CESCE indemnifies the exporter for the losses derived from nonpayment.

Contract termination risk: CESCE covers the exporter for the net definitive loss suffered (prior to the credit risk) when the completion of the contract is impossible or interrupted due to unjustified reasons stemming from unilateral decisions from the buyer or from political risks.

Specifications
Commercial: 94 percent
Political: 99 percent

Overseas Civil Works Insurance Policy

Conceived for businesses that perform services abroad (constructions, assemblies, installations, etc.), this policy insures against the risks present when performing and executing the project. Spanish contractors are covered from the net definitive loss that arises from risk of termination of a contract, negative certification, nonpayment of certifications, nonpayment of credits (deferred payment); risk of confiscation or nonrepatriation of machinery; and risk of non-transfer of working capital.

Specifications
Commercial: 94 percent
Political: 99 percent

Insurance Policy for Guarantors for the Performance of Guarantee Deposits

This policy is designed for operations in which the exporter must guarantee a deposit for an export transaction to the buyer or authorities of the importing country. It insures the institution that issues the guarantee in the name of the exporter against the risks involved. A loan is created between the Spanish financial institution and the exporter where the financial institution backs the guarantee in the name of the exporter. The insurance policy covers the nonpayment of this loan.

Specifications
Commercial: 99 percent
Political: 99 percent

Insurance Policy for Exporters for the Performance of Guarantee Deposits

Similar to the insurance policy for guarantors for the performance of guarantee deposits, this policy covers exporters from the risks of improper performance of the deposits by the foreign contractor.

Specifications
Commercial: 99 percent
Political: 99 percent

Working Capital Bank Guarantee
This guarantee is devised for operations in which a financial institution grants a loan to the exporter for working capital during the manufacturing stage or for the cash discount in foreign currencies. CESCE covers the financial institution from the net definitive losses that arise as a consequence of a partial or total lack of repayment of the pre-financing or financing by the exporter.

Specifications
Commercial: 94 percent

Barter Exchange Insurance Policy
This policy insures the exporter against nonpayment for political reasons in barter exchange operations. These operations are where the buyer pays the exporter by the delivery of products instead of cash or credit.

Specifications
Political: 99 percent

Project Finance Operations Insurance Policy
CESCE provides insurance against political and commercial risks for projects whose guarantee are the project's assets and cash flow.

Specifications
Commercial: Depends on the project
Political: Depends on the project

International Investment Insurance Policy
There are four political risks that CESCE can insure: property rights, lack of conveyance, noncompliance with agreements or breach of contracts, and revolution or war by the authorities in the host country.

Specifications
Political: 99 percent

InterGen Chinese Power Project

The Fujian Province in China witnessed economic growth of 19.2 percent per year between 1991 and 1996 and a power demand increase of approximately 12.6 percent. The rapidly expanding economy outpaced the growth in power-generating capacity. Fujian Pacific Electric Company Limited is a special purpose company formed in China as a wholly foreign-owned enterprise to finance, build, operate, and own its own 720 MW power-generating facility in the Fujian Province. The facility is partly owned by InterGen (70 percent), Lippo China Resources Limited (25 percent), and the Asian Development Bank (5 percent), and has a total cost of over USD 755.2 million.

Acting as sponsors of the project, InterGen and Lippo secured over USD 566 million in loans. CESCE provided a USD 75.7 million export credit supported by political risk insurance. The strategic combination of ECA and ADB support allowed the sponsors to obtain economical financing during times of financial uncertainty in the Asian markets.

Export Financing

As of December 31, 1992, no Spanish government agency provided export financing directly. The financing of exports is entrusted to the private sector. However, the Spanish government does ensure sufficient funding by the private sector by providing interest rate insurance. This is done by the Ministry of Economy through the Institute of Official Credit.

III. CONTACTS

Headquarters:
CESCE
Velázquez, 74
28001 Madrid, Spain
Tel: (34 91) 423-4800
Fax: (34 91) 576-5140
Information: (34 0) 211-1010
Internet: www.cesce.com
Email: estudios@cesce.es

Instituto de Credito Oficial (ICO)
Paseo del Prado 4
28014 Madrid
Tel: 34 (91) 592-1600

Ms. Carmen Vara-Martin
Operations with America
Tel: 34 (91) 592-1600
Ext: 1510
Email: vara@cesce.es

Ms. Victoria Arauzo
Project Finance Operations
Tel: 34 (91) 592-1600
Ext. 1538
Email: arauzo@cesce.es

SWEDEN
EXPORTKREDITNÄMNDEN (EKN)
THE SWEDISH EXPORT CREDIT
CORPORATION (SEK)
THE SWEDISH INTERNATIONAL DEVELOPMENT
COOPERATION (SIDA)

I. INTRODUCTION

Sweden has two main corporations that support Swedish exports and imports. EKN concentrates on insurance and guarantees while SEK focuses on export finance. Sida concentrates on issuing aid and grants. The Swedish Export Credit Guarantee Board (EKN) is a government agency established in 1933 to promote Swedish exports by issuing guarantees. For 2001, EKN guarantee commitments were over SEK 27 billion (USD 2.87 billion). Its guarantee exposure amounted to SEK 120 billion (USD 12.7 billion). EKN strongly supports Swedish exports by providing guarantees on a short-, medium-, and long-term basis. SEK was established in 1962 specifically to finance exports of Swedish capital goods and services on commercial terms. Standard & Poor rated the SEK long-term foreign debt AA+ and Moody gave it an Az2. Sida administers the concessionary credit scheme and is responsible for administering the bilateral aid programs (on a grant basis) for the main recipient counties.

II. PRODUCTS

Short, Medium, and Long Term

EKN Guarantees
Short-term products are usually extended to the export of consumer durables for a maximum credit period of 12 months and

raw materials and semi-manufactured goods for a maximum of 6 months. Medium-term credits are extended to the export of capital goods for a period of between two to five years. Long-term credit is extended for the export of larger scale plants for up to ten years. The guarantee's term depends on the amount of the contract. If the credit contract amounts to USD 80,000, the period of credit will be for three years; if USD 175,000, then four years; if USD 350,000, then five years.

Guarantees cover buyer and borrower losses from commercial events and buyer losses due to unforeseeable political upheaval in a buyer country. By combining guarantees for different purposes, guarantees provide a complete package of protection. For example, a guarantee covering the default of payment can be combined with a production loss or cancellation guarantee. At EKN, war, natural catastrophe, confiscation, nationalization, transfer constraints, etc., in a foreign buyer country qualify as a political risk. On the other hand, a commercial risk involves a situation where a foreign buyer has lost its capability to pay. If the company goes into bankruptcy or experiences a suspension of payments, a commercial risk guarantee will apply.

Guarantee for Loss on Claim for Exporters
Covers the risk of an exporter or leasing company from defaults on payments in individual transactions.

Guarantee for Loss on Production and Loss on Claim for Exporters
Covers the risk of an exporter for costs incurred up to the time that a contract is wholly or partly canceled, or execution of the contract is interrupted for a continuous period not shorter than six months, and for defaults on payment.

Guarantee for Bonds
Covers risks related to a Swedish exporter issuing a bond on behalf of a foreign buyer for the fulfillment of an offer or contract. The guarantee covers inequitable calling of such a bond.

Guarantee for Physical Loss
Covers the risk of property used in work abroad being confiscated, lost or damaged because of political events such as war or revolution. Normally, this guarantee is issued only with a guarantee for loss on production and loss on claim for the export transaction in question.

Combined Guarantee

Guarantee to an exporter for costs incurred and guarantee to a lender for nonpayment, for risks in one and the same export transaction.

Terms: Each guarantee can be offered short, medium, or long term. EKN normally covers 100 percent of political risks, but in higher risk guarantees, EKN may reduce this amount. With commercial risk coverage, EKN covers 90 percent and requires that the policyholder have 10 percent of the risk. If the EKN feels that responsibility for 90 percent of the risk is too high, then it can increase the level of excess held by the policyholder. EKN compensates its customers in four months if the loss was due to political events, but will take six or more months to indemnify its customer if a commercial event that produces insolvency occurs.

Fees: EKN does not charge its customers for applying for or receiving a guarantee. It charges a premium that is based on participants' credit ratings, country risk, period of risk, and amount of guarantee. The minimum base premium is SEK 750 (USD 87).

Eligibility: Eligible companies are those that are domiciled in Sweden. Foreign companies can also be eligible for EKN support if 50 percent of their product content originated in Sweden. In principle, Sweden will guarantee any product, new or used. For example, EKN guarantees:

- exports of goods and services
- plant and contract work
- leasing and risks accrued while presenting bond loans
- banker's financing
- confirmed letters of credit
- Swedish companies' investments abroad against political risks

---

Ericsson Telecom

In April 2002, EKN signed a guarantee for Ericsson Telecom for SEK 77.5 million (USD 9 million). The guarantee facilitated the export of mobile telephony to Telefonos de Mexico (TELMEX). This guarantee was one among many that EKN organized for Ericsson Telecom.

EKN has also arranged guarantees for Ericsson Telecom in the Philippines and Germany. These guarantees for Ericsson come to a total of SEK 202 million (USD 21.5 million).

Export Credits

SEK makes a loan to a commercial bank or to a company through a commercial bank. Therefore, the application and evaluation is handled by the commercial lender. SEK has, however, on occasion extended credit in its own name. Mostly it works from a Swedish network of credit lines. It has two systems under which it provides export support, the market rate system (the M system) and the state support system (the S system).

Specifications

Under the S system, SEK uses the Arrangement on Guidelines for Officially Supported Export Credits. The credit terms must comply with the EKN. SEK relies on a commercial bank to prepare, assess, and document the credit to determine its eligibility. Under the S and M systems, SEK will charge an annual commitment fee of 0.25 percent.

III. CONTACTS

EKN

Box 3064
S-10361 Stockholm
Tel: 46 (8) 788-0000
Fax: 46 (8) 411-8149
Telex: EKN S 17657
Internet: www.ekn.se
Email: info@ekn.se

SEK

Box 16368
S-10327 Stockholm
Tel: 46 (8) 613-8300
Fax: 46 (8) 203-894
Telex: 12166 SEKs
Internet:www.sek.sk

Sida

S-10525 Stockholm
Tel: 46 (8) 698-5000
Fax: 46 (8) 208-8640
Internet:www.sida.se
For Aid finance:
S-10525 Stockholm
Tel: (46 8) 698 50 00
Fax: (46 8) 20 88 64
Internet: www.sida.se

SWITZERLAND
INVESTMENT RISK GUARANTEE (IRG)

I. INTRODUCTION

The IRG is an organization designed to facilitate investment projects in developing countries by insuring the investor when no adequate insurance exists in the commercial or private market. Guarantees will cover equity investments and loans. Income or return from equity or loans can be insured within the IRG guarantee if the payments were transferable when the IRG agreement was reached.

II. PRODUCTS

Specifications
Private persons with a Swiss citizenship or legal companies controlled and domiciled in Switzerland are eligible. If a company has a close relationship to the Swiss economy, then eligibility will be reviewed. IRG guarantee coverage is limited to 70 percent of the investment capital or loan. Political upheaval, nationalization, and transfer complications are the risks for which IRG will indemnify its customers. IRG guarantees will not cover the losses due to an incapable or unwilling private capital recipient, currency depreciation, or voluntary disinvestments. Terms have a maximum of 15 years, but longer periods can be arranged. Standard premium rates are 1.25 percent in equity investment cases, 1.75 percent in case of loans (if a sovereign payment guarantee exists, this will be reduced to 1.25 percent), and 4 percent in case of a guaranteed annual income. These rates can be increased or decreased according to the risks mitigated or excluded from the guarantee. The premiums are due within 30 days.

III. CONTACTS

Investment Risk Guarantee (IRG)
Kirchenweg 8
8032 Zurich
Tel: 41 (1) 384-4777
Fax: 41 (1) 384-4787
Internet: www.swiss-irg.com
Email: office@swiss-irg.com

General
Tel: 41 (1) 384-4777
Fax: 41 (1) 384-4787
Internet: www.swiss-irg.com
Email: office@swiss-i rg.com

Peter W. Silberschmidt
Tel: 41 (1) 384-4780
Email: Peter.Silberschmidt@swiss-irg.com

Bohumil Matousek
Tel: 41 (1) 384-4790
Email: Bohumil.Matousek@swiss-irg.com

Hans R. Wuethrich
Tel: 41 (1) 384-4783
Email: Hans.Wuethrich@swiss-irg.com

SWITZERLAND
SECO (AID FINANCE)

SECO provides concessionary funds with a mixed financing system that consists of funds from the Swiss government (grants) and funds from a network of six private banks (commercial loan). The government has the authority to provide 35 to 50 percent of the financing. The percentage awarded depends on the agreement that the Swiss government has with the host country. This process is completed with the close cooperation of SECO, ERG, and the participating commercial banks. The ERG communicates with the commercial banks because ERG coverage is mandatory for mixed financing.

II. PRODUCTS

Specifications for procurement tied to Switzerland
The mixed financing that SECO makes possible is under the condition that at least some of the procurement from the financing will be tied to Switzerland. For example, SECO allows a 15 percent coverage of local costs, but it also subtracts the total local cost from the maximum 50 percent of each credit that can be subcontracted to foreign enterprises. The project participants from the recipient country choose Swiss suppliers, but SECO specifies that their rates must be internationally competitive.

Specifications for projects in developing countries
The aim of SECO is to provide grants to developing countries to build infrastructure. The recipient country must have a per capita income of less than USD 3,030, the project must be development oriented, and the recipient country must have approved and marked the project as a priority investment. In addition, the project must have a competitive international bidding and the Swiss bid must have been the lowest bid in cash without taking the financing offered into consideration.

Terms and Costs: These are in accordance with the Arrangement.

Von Roll
Since 1985, the State Secretariat for Economic Affairs has granted China mixed credit packages of a total of CHF 350 million (USD 233 million) for industrial goods and infrastructure projects. Since the late 1990s priorities have increasingly shifted to environmental protection, the transfer of environmental technology, and to measures aimed at promoting the development of the private sector and boosting investment.

Concessionary credits, which combine a nonrefundable credit from the Swiss Confederation and a commercial credit from a bank group, will enable China to acquire the Swiss technology and equipment it requires. An initial project in early 2002 provided a mixed credit package of CHF 20 million (USD 13 million) for a trash incineration plant from the Swiss company Von Roll for the city of Xiamen. This plant will be able to dispose of a significant part of the waste generated in this city of 1.7 million inhabitants.

III. CONTACTS

General Information
Tel: 41 (31) 322-5656
Fax: 41 (31) 322-5600

SWITZERLAND
SWISS EXPORT RISK GUARANTEE AGENCY (ERG)
STATE SECRETARIAT OF ECONOMIC
AFFAIRS (SECO)

I. INTRODUCTION

There are three Swiss agencies that arrange insurance guarantees, investment guarantees, and aid financing. These organizations aim to create and safeguard employment opportunities and promote foreign trade. ERG issues export insurance in the form of guarantees; IRG issues investment insurance in the form of guarantees; and SECO, with six cooperating commercial banks, provides aid financing. Switzerland, however, does not have a government organization that provides export credit financing (lending). Commercial banks provide export credits on market terms.

II. PRODUCTS

The ERG provides insurance guarantees and coverage that goes beyond the normal commercial and noncommercial export credit agency coverage. Guarantee coverage is as follows:

- Political risks include political events abroad that destroy the merchandise which the exporter still owns, or makes a private importer incapable of fulfilling contractual obligations due to war, revolution, or civil unrest.
- Transfer risks include problems with currency transfers due to a government action that infringes on the buyer's ability to pay. For example, a buyer deposits his payment in a local bank, but the bank cannot transfer that payment into the foreign currency.
- Commercial risks include the risk of insolvency or a refusal to pay by public bodies, private entities, or ERG-approved banks. (The commercial risks of the project finance structure cannot be insured. However, the commercial risks that can be covered are the project participants, suppliers, and purchasers.)
- Pre-delivery risks are designed for situations in which delivery of goods becomes impossible due to an increase in risk or a change negatively affecting the transport facilities.
- Contingent currency risk coverage is designed for situations where an unforeseeable, but insured, loss occurrs and redemption for financing or forward exchange contracts is needed in a foreign currency. It does not cover fluctuations in a foreign currency.

Short, Medium, and Long Term

ERG programs can be offered for short, medium, or long term, but the terms decided on are based on the buyer country and the amount agreed to in the contract. In general, short term is from 180 to 360 days, medium term is 1–5 years, and long term is over 5 years, but not exceeding 10 or 14 years. If the contract value is CHF 100,000 to 150,000 (USD 66,000 to 100,000), then the credit period will be 2 years; if CHF 150 000 to 250,000 (USD 100,000 to 166,000), then 3 years; if CHF 250,000 to 500,000 (USD 166,000 to 333,000), then 4 years; and if over CHF 500,000 (USD 333,000), then 5 years or more.

Guarantees

The ERG has a number of guarantee programs. Some of their most common ones are guaranteeing goods, work, services, licensing, and bonds. Specifically, the guarantees may be extended to:

- Exports of consumer and capital goods
- Construction, engineering, and other services
- Licensing and know-how agreements
- Goods on consignment abroad or on exhibition at trade fairs (cover against seizure of goods or inability to re-export)
- Bid bonds, down payment guarantees and performance bonds

The ERG has more customized products that fit special situations such as guarantees for banks or guarantees for investments abroad.

Guarantees for Banks

The process for guaranteeing banks begins with an exporter. The exporter must submit an application for a guarantee. It is first issued to the exporter, but the exporter can then request that the ERG guarantee be assigned to domestic or foreign banks or another third party.

Specifications

These guarantees can have short, medium, or long terms. The ERG offers commercial, political, pre-shipment, transfer, and contingent currency risk coverage with up to 95 percent of the delivery value guaranteed if a default in payment should occur. Delivery value is the sum of the value of goods, the ERG premium, interest accrued, credit interest, and some local costs. The prevailing rules of the Berne Union and the Arrangement are applied. Eligible applicants must be Swiss residents or listed with the Register of Commerce. Most products are pure Swiss, but foreign content will be accepted on a case-by-case basis. Products with over 50 percent foreign content will be accepted. However, if the product's foreign content exceeds 50 percent, then additional fees should be expected.

Guarantees for Investments Abroad

This program was designed to encourage Swiss investment abroad by insuring against foreign commercial and political risks.

The program insures foreign investors against loss through dispossession of their direct investments in developing countries.

III. CONTACTS

Swiss Export Risk Guarantee Agency (ERG)
Kirchenweg 8
8032 Zurich
Tel: 41 (1) 384-4777
Fax: 41 (1) 384-4787
Internet: www.swiss-erg.com
Email: office@swiss-erg.com

State Secretariat of Economic Affairs (SECO)
Bundesgasse 8
3003 Berne
Tel: 41 (31) 322-2944
Fax: 41 (31) 311-3981
Email: seco@seco.admin.ch

Jean-Denis Baumberger
Tel: 41 (1) 384-4786
Email: Jean-Denis.Baumberger@swiss-erg.com

René Dubs
Tel: 41 (1) 384-4789
Email: Rene.Dubs@swiss-erg.com

Max Hänggi
Tel: 41 (1) 384-4792
Email: Max.Haenggi@swiss-erg.com

Hans R. Wuethrich
Tel: 41 (1) 384-4783
Email: Hans.Wuethrich@swiss-erg.com

TURKEY
EXPORT CREDIT BANK OF TURKEY
(TURK EXIMBANK)

I. INTRODUCTION

In 2001, the Turk Eximbank supported exports of USD 5.6 billion accounting for 18 percent of Turkey's exports. Turk

Eximbank strongly supports exports with export finance, insurance, and guarantee programs.

II. PRODUCTS

Short Term

Turk Eximbank has many short-term financing options that provide support throughout the export process.

Pre-Shipment Export Credits

This program is designed to support businesses at the front-end of the export process, manufacturers, exporters, and manufacturer-exporters of all sectors from the early stages of production. These credits can be offered in foreign currency or in the Turkish lira.

Pre-Shipment Export Credits for Small- to Medium-Sized Businesses (SMSE)

This program does not differ from the above pre-shipment export credit program other than its special focus is on small- and medium-sized businesses. Many Turkish Banks have a mandate to reserve 30 percent of their credit limit for on-lending to SMEs.

Pre-Shipment Export Credits for Priority Development Areas

This program does not differ much from the other pre-shipment export credit programs except that it is aimed at the eastern and southern provinces of Turkey. The Turkish government has declared these areas a priority for development. In addition, intermediary banks are mandated to reserve at least 5 percent and extend up to 25 percent of their credit to exporters in these areas.

Specifications

The above-mentioned pre-shipment export credit programs have the same term limitations, up to 180 days, with a choice of credit in either Turk lira or foreign currency. The export credits will cover 100 percent of the FOB (free on board) export commitments (i.e., it will cover the supplier's cost of transporting the supplies to the ship or transportation vessel). Costs for Turk Eximbank's assistance and export credit vary by case. Market interest rates, loan repayment periods, and the costs of funding make up the total cost. Eligibility for using the SME product depends on the business classification; to qualify the business must be an exporter that has 200 or fewer employees.

Export Credit Insurance

With export credit insurance, the buyer can defer payment on a shipment of goods and services and the exporter can receive payment from a commercial bank upon shipment. Export credit insurance provides insurance that the buyer will not default on his deferred payment and it promises to indemnify the exporter or a bank if an eligible situation arises preventing the buyer from making payments. Eligible commercial risks include a protracted default, insolvency, and repudiation. Eligible political risks include nonpayment of a public buyer, war, civil disturbance, currency transfer problems, seizure, cancellation of import license, etc.

Specifications

The payment term for export credit insurance is a maximum of 360 days. During this period, the Turk Eximbank will cover 90 percent of the commercial and political risks. Cost of cover involves the sum of the premium, interest rates, and administrative fees charged for the application process. Premiums vary from 0.05 to 4 percent and must be paid in cash. The risk class of the buyer's country, the tenor, the payment term, and the buyer's credit status all factor into the total cost of cover and the premium charged. Interest rates are flexible—fixed or floating rates can be arranged. Turk Eximbank does not specify a minimum content requirement for short-term export credit insurance.

Post-Shipment Export Credit Discount

This program was designed to increase the proportion of commercial banks' funds toward export financing. To achieve this aim, Turk Eximbank came to an agreement with two commercial banks in Turkey. If these banks discount export receivables tied to shipments covered under short-term export credit insurance, then Turk Eximbank indemnifies them on the unpaid amount if the buyer defaults on post-shipment payments.

Medium and Long Term

Turk Eximbank medium-term agreements last anywhere from one to five years. Long-term agreements are for more than five years.

Export Credit Insurance

This program was designed for a single buyer multi-transaction arrangement in which the export would be either capital or semi-capital goods. Generally, Turk Eximbank will cover commercial and/or political risks for up to five years, but it may extend payment terms if special conditions apply. This program can also be extended to long-term overseas investment, but in this case only political insurance is available.

Specifications
Export credit insurance for capital and semi-capital goods covers 95 percent of 85 percent of the export credit value if an eligible commercial or political event occurs. The premium, paid in cash, varies from 0.05 to 4 percent and depends on the risk class of the buyer's country, the tenor, the payment term, and the buyer status. Interest rates are flexible—fixed or floating rates can be arranged. The only fee charged is an administration fee at the beginning during the application phase. Turk Eximbank specifies that an export must have at least 60 percent domestic content.

National Bank of Kyrgyzstan
Kyrgyzstan and Turkey have signed a framework agreement in order for Turk Eximbank to extend a credit line to National Bank of Kyrgyzstan for USD 75 million (guaranteed by the Government of Kyrgyzstan). Due to the heavy burden on the budget after the global economic crisis combined with the natural disasters in the south region of the country, the debt of National Bank of Kyrgyzstan was rescheduled in 1998.

III. CONTACTS

Main Headquarters:
Müdafaa Cad. No. 20/B
06100 Bakanliklar Ankara
Tel: (90 312) 417 13 00
        45 106 EXBN-TR
Fax: (90 312) 425 78 96
Telex: 45 080 EXMB-TR
Internet: www.eximbank.gov.tr
Email: ankara@eximbank.gov.tr

Istanbul Branch:
Muallim Naci Cad. No. 121 Sifa Yurdu Duragi
80840 Ortaköy Istanbul
Tel: (90 212) 227 29 04
Fax: (90 212) 259 04 08
Email: istanbul@eximbank.gov.tr

Izmir Branch:
Cumhuriyet Bulvari, Emlakbank Konak Is Merkezi, No. 34/4
35200 Konak Izmir
Telephone: (90 232) 445 85 60
Telefax: (90 232) 445 85 61
Email: izmir@eximbank.gov.tr

Ahmet Kilicodlu
CEO

Opsman Aslan
Assistant General Manager
Export Credits

Alev Arkan
Assiatant General Manager
Buyer's Credit & Insurance/Guarantee

Ertan Tanriyakul
Assiatant General Manager
Treasury & Funding

Cuneyt K. Baky
General Secretary

UNITED KINGDOM
EXPORT CREDITS GUARANTEE
DEPARTMENT (ECGD)

I. INTRODUCTION

Established in 1919, ECGD was the world's first export credit
agency. It facilitates UK exports and development by providing
insurance and guarantees to UK exporters against the risks of
nonpayment by buyers, to banks against nonpayment of the
financing that they advance for exporters, and to overseas borrowers for the purchase of exports. In 2000–2001, its 380 employees supported UK exporters worth GBP 5.6 billion (USD 8.7
billion). ECGD had a net contribution of GBP 205 million (USD
319 million) with premium income, net recoveries, and interest
exceeding expenditure.

II. PRODUCTS

The five broad and comprehensive products that ECGD offers are:

- Tender to contract/forward exchange supplement (TTC/FES)
- Bond insurance policy (BIP), contract bonds and guarantees
- Export insurance policy (EXIP), insurance for exporters
- Lines of credit
  - Supplier credit finance facility (SCF)
  - Buyer credit, flexible finance for project exports
- Long-term
  - Overseas investment insurance
  - Project finance

Short-, Medium-, and Long-Term

ECGD does not limit its programs by their terms of payment. In fact, long-term investment in development and trade is one of its main functions. ECGD offers two products that are generally reserved for long-term purposes: overseas investment insurance and project finance. ECGD offers four other broad programs that can be customized for the particular ECGD customers. Terms are broken into three categories, short term (up to 360 days), medium term (from one to five years), and long term (over five years). Normally, ECGD will assess an application and determine which payment plan would be most appropriate.

Tender to Contract (TTC) / Forward Exchange Supplement (FES)

This program was designed for businesses that "tender" or bid for contracts and need concrete foreign currency prices to win. If the business quotes a price for the work contract and the price of sterling goes down, the business is still liable to commit to the contract. If the business has TTC, it can put a claim on ECGD to cover the net loss in procurement from the value of sterling and the quoted foreign price.

Specifications
The payment term depends upon the difference in the value of sterling as to whether the tenderer either pays or is charged. There are three premiums charged at three progressive stages. The first premium is 0.01 percent of the amount covered with a minimum premium of GBP 5,000 (USD 7,700). It is a nonrefundable fee that will be charged shortly after the application is made, when the first schedule of guaranteed exchange rates are issued. The second premium is a nonrefundable premium of 0.4

percent of the amount guaranteed. It must be paid upon entering the forward exchange supplement (FES). The third premium ranges from 2.5 to 4.1 percent. Eligibility rests on the basis that the value of the UK content in the contract must be at least GBP 10 million (USD 15.5 million). There is no limit on the value of UK content that is insurable. Once the value exceeds GBP 80 million (USD 124 million), however, only UK content will be covered.

Bond Insurance Policy (BIP)—Contract Bond and Guarantee Insurance

This program was designed to insure exporters when an unfair claim or unforeseen political event arises against an exporter's interests in a bond or guarantee. The bond insurance will protect the exporter under the bond or under any related counter-guarantee (a situation where an importer, exporter, and more than one bank are involved in indemnification) by insuring the exporter's particular terms.

Specifications
The payment term will depend on the value and life of the bond. Advance payment, performance bonds, on demand bonds, and counter-guarantees and counter-indemnities are all eligible for cover. Unfair calls and political events are covered, but BIP only complements the basic ECGD coverage for the underlying contract. On the positive side, BIP may come into effect sooner than ECDG's issuance of the basic guarantees because it is issued separately. BIP is charged separately and in addition to the basic guarantee insurance. The cost of cover depends on bond value, duration, and the ECGD's interpretation of risk.

Export Insurance Policy (EXIP), Insurance for Exporters

This program provides insurance if the unexpected occurs and the exporter does not receive payment on a shipment of goods or services under contract. ECGD insures the exporter's direct interests or the parts in the contract where the exporter may suffer losses.

Specifications
ECGD offers flexible terms—short, medium, or long—for export credit insurance that covers purchaser risks and/or political risks. An exporter may purchase both or one of the categories of risks covered. The maximum percentage insured is 95 percent, but choosing a lower percentage of cover will lower the premium. The cost of cover depends not only on the percent of coverage,

but also on the credit of participating parties and the risk rating of the recipient country.

Lines of Credit—Buyer and Supplier

These programs were designed for either the supplier or buyer who ECGD promises to guarantee payment for a trade transaction, but the contractual relationship is between two banks, rather than between a bank and either the supplier or buyer. These lines of credit can come in the form of a supplier credit from the supplier credit facility (SCF) or in the form of a buyer credit guarantee from the BCG. There can be two purposes to either line of credit, a general-purpose line of credit (GPLOC) or a project line of credit (PLOC) that is reserved solely for a buyer credit guarantee. The situations for which PLOCs were designed involve purchases from a number of UK exporters for the purposes of a common project. The buyer or borrower will then nominate the individual contracts that will be financed under the allotted financing.

Specifications

The payment term is from two to five years or more with coverage of 85 percent of the contract value. The buyer will be required to pay 15 percent directly to the supplier before the credit period begins. The interest rates will usually be given in fixed interest rate terms and the premium will be assessed on a case-by-case basis. Supplier and buyer credits are evaluated on a case-by-case basis so ECGD does not specify particular eligibility requirements.

Angloco

ECGD helped Angloco Ltd., an independent family-owned British company, export equipment to the fire department in Barbados. The order included 15 fire engines, major water/foam tender appliances, three front-line airport fire fighting and rescue vehicles, and a 32m hydraulic ladder/platform aerial rescue appliance. The order totaled GBP 2.5 million (USD 3.89 million).

ECGD guaranteed the credit extended to the government of Barbados. It is also extended insurance to further reduce the risk of loss due to nonpayment for political or commercial risks.

Overseas Investment Insurance (OII)

This program was designed for UK businesses that make investments abroad, but need political insurance against expropriation, war/political violence, transfer and inconvertibility restrictions, and breach of contract. This program does not provide protection against commercial risks. Three types of transactions can be insured with OII: foreign direct investment, shareholder loans, and bank loans. For the first 15 years, ECGD has to cover the risks for the original terms at the original premium rate to encourage the investor to keep the capital in the developing market. If the investor voluntarily withdraws capital, ECGD is not responsible for any loss that may occur.

Specifications
Cost of cover varies with the creditworthiness of buyer and supplier and with the recipient country's risk rating. ECGD can cover foreign investment as small as GBP 20,000 (USD 31,000).

III. CONTACTS

London:

P.O. Box 2200
2 Exchange Tower
Harbour Exchange Square
London E14 9GS
Tel: 44 (207) 512-7000
Fax: 44 (207) 512-7649
Internet: www.ecgd.gov.uk
Email: buecgd@ecgd.gov.uk
      help@ecgd.gov.uk

Cardiff:

Lamborne House
Lamboune Crescent
Llanishen
Cardiff
CF14 5GG
Tel: 44 (292) 032-8500
Fax: 44 (292) 032-8600
Internet: www.ecgd.gov.uk

Executive Directors:
Vivian Brown
Chief Executive
Email: vbrown@ecgd.gov.uk

Tom Jaffray,
Group Director, Resource Management
Email: tjaffray@oecgd.gov.uk

John Weiss
Group Director, Underwriting
Email: jweiss@oecgd.gov.uk

Victor Lunn-Rockliffe
Group Director, Assistant Management
Email: Vlunn-rockliffe@oecgd.gov.uk

John Ormerod
Director, Strategy and Communications Division
Email: jormerod@oecgd.gov.uk

Nicholas Ridley
General Counsel
Email: nridley@oecgd.gov.uk

Ian Dickson
Director of Finance
Email: idickerson@oecgd.gov.uk

Steve Dodgson
Director of Personnel
Email: sdodgson@oecgd.gov.uk

Non-Executive Directors:
Tony Davies, Former Senior Banking Advisor, Financial Services
     Authority
John Wright, Former Director, Clydesdale Bank PLC and
     Yorkshire Bank PLC
David Harrison, CBE, Group Advisor, Lloyds TSB Group Plc

For business inquiries and to request ECGD publications:
Email: Help@ecgd.gov.uk

For general policy inquiries:
Email: publicenquiries@ecgd.gov.uk

UNITED STATES
U.S. EXPORT-IMPORT BANK

I. INTRODUCTION

The Export-Import Bank of the United States (Ex-Im Bank) is an independent U.S. government agency chartered by Congress to facilitate the financing of exports of U.S. goods and services. By neutralizing the effects of export credit subsidies from other governments and by absorbing credit risks the private sector will not accept, Ex-Im Bank enables U.S. firms to compete fairly in overseas markets on the basis of price, performance, delivery, and service.

Ex-Im Bank provides export credit support to either U.S. exports or to foreign purchasers of U.S. products. Through loan guarantees and insurance, Ex-Im Bank fosters exports by making working capital available to U.S. exporters. Through similar mechanisms, as well as direct loans (and on occasion grants), Ex-Im Bank provides credit at attractive interest rates to foreign buyers to encourage their purchase of U.S. goods and services.

In 65 years, Ex-Im Bank has supported more than USD 300 billion in U.S. exports. In 2000, it supported USD 15.5 billion dollars in U.S. exports and 2,500 export transactions.

Ex-Im Bank reviews requests for financing based on the financial and technical aspects of a transaction, as well as the degree of foreign government-subsidized export credit the U.S. exporter faces from competitors. Ex-Im Bank also considers the impact the transaction will have on the United States economy. Because of its mandate to create economic benefits in the U.S., Ex-Im Bank will not support transactions where less than 50 percent of the contract value is of U.S. origin. In all but a few exceptions, Ex-Im Bank is also prohibited from financing military sales.

Types of Commitment

Depending on the stage of the transaction, Ex-Im can issue a letter of interest, a preliminary commitment, or a final commitment.

Letters of Interest (LI). These letters indicate financing terms offered to exporters by Ex-Im Bank for a specific transaction. The LI was developed to greatly improve the efficiency and shorten response time (an LI is normally issued within seven days of a request). It is used when the U.S. exporter needs a financing indication from Ex-Im Bank in the early stages of negotiations. Engineering, economic policy, and credit analyses are not performed by Ex-Im Bank prior to issuing the LI.

The LI will indicate that Ex-Im Bank is open for business in that foreign market, the maximum repayment term for the potential sale, the assigned risk category for the proposed obligor and/or guarantor, the indicative exposure fee, commitment fee, interest rate, and the program options (loans or guarantees) that may be available. The LI is valid for six months from the date of signing. There is no obligation for the Ex-Im Bank to convert the

LI to a final commitment. When the appropriate application is submitted, Ex-Im Bank charges a one-time processing fee of USD 100 for an LI or final commitment.

Preliminary Commitment (PC). Preliminary commitments outline the terms and conditions of the financial assistance Ex-Im is prepared to offer on a specific transaction. Consequently, a PC requires Ex-Im Bank to underwrite the credit prior to issuing a commitment. PCs are used only in special situations to enable suppliers to provide financing offers in response to transactions requiring financial commitments. All applications must contain the information requested in the Small Business Administration/Ex-Im Bank Joint Applications. If the loan amount is less than USD 833,333, then the exporter needs to apply to the SBA. Otherwise the applicant must apply directly to Ex-Im Bank. A PC is usually valid for six months. The applicant may be any responsible party, the foreign buyer, the U.S. exporter, a financing institution, or a firm representing either the buyer or the exporter. There is a processing fee of USD 500 to obtain a PC for working capital guarantees and a USD 200 processing fee for direct loans or guarantees.

Final Commitment. A final commitment is a formal authorization of Ex-Im Bank support and is issued after the buyer has signed a contract with a U.S. supplier. It is not necessary to have a letter of interest or preliminary commitment before a final commitment can be authorized. Application for final commitments must be submitted by the prospective borrower for a direct loan and can be submitted by either the borrower or lender for a guarantee. Unlike PC allocations, in which Ex-Im Bank may waive some of the informational requirements due to the early stage of the transactions, applications for a final commitment must include all appropriate information for Ex-Im Bank to appraise the financial, economic, and technical elements.

II. PRODUCTS

A. Short-Term Products

Short term means that the payment or contract will not be less than 180 days and not exceed 360 days (six months to one year). The products that Ex-Im offers short term are:

- Working capital guarantees: export-related working capital guarantees for U.S. exporters to obtain loans
- Credit insurance: foreign accounts receivable financing for U.S. exporters

Working Capital Guarantees (WC)

This product helps small- to medium-sized exporters who have potential to expand their exports, but need additional working capital to purchase inventory, manufacture products, and extend terms to buyers overseas to make that expansion. The loan amount cannot be for less than USD 833,000 or the Ex-Im Bank delegated authority lenders or U.S. Small Business Administration will review the application.

Working capital guarantees can be used for the following:

- Acquisition of inventory
- Payment of direct or indirect costs
- Support of letters of credit that function as bid bonds, performance bonds, or warranty bonds (warranty bonds must be approved)
- Indirect exporter, subcontractor to exporter
- Repayment of pre-existing exporter debt (this use must be pre-approved)

It cannot be used for:

- Financing of defense, military, or nuclear items
- Exporting any items to defense or military buyers
- Purchasing life-saving or charitable items without Ex-Im Bank's written consent
- Support of domestic sales
- Support of capital expenditures
- Support of overseas operations
- Repayment of debt unrelated to the loan without prior approval from Ex-Im Bank

The working capital guarantee process involves communication between the exporter, the Ex-Im Bank, and a commercial lending bank. The exporter can apply for a guarantee from the U.S. Ex-Im Bank, receive a preliminary commitment letter, and then explore potential commercial lending banks. The preliminary commitment letter makes making a loan to the exporter more attractive because it indicates interest and a possible guarantee of the exporter's payments. Once an exporter reaches an agreement with a commercial bank, the bank issues a final commitment letter to the Ex-Im Bank indicating that it would like to make a loan to the exporter if Ex-Im will guarantee the loan. The contractual relationship is made between the Ex-Im Bank (the guarantor) and the commercial lending bank in the interest of the exporter. Ex-Im Bank, then, makes a guarantee to a commercial lender for the exporter's benefit. The guarantee will pay up to 90 percent of the exporter's loan payments if the export business becomes incapable of making the payments itself.

Oldenburg Group

Oldenburg Group Inc. (OGI) produces a variety of highly specialized machinery for particular industrial, marine, and mining uses. The firm has manufacturing facilities throughout the Midwest. In March 2002, Ex-Im Bank approved a working capital guarantee of USD 15 million, 12-month export revolving line of credit to support export sales. OGI will use the line of credit to support customers primarily in South Africa and Australia. With domestic sales stagnant or slowing down due to the gradual decline of the U.S. coal mining industry, OGI has increased its reliance on foreign sales.

Specifications

Terms: Working capital guarantees are normally extended for up to 12 months, but may be longer if the loan supports a single export transaction (transaction-specific loan). For multiple export transactions, a lender may extend a revolving loan to three years.

Coverage: Ex-Im Bank's working capital guarantee covers 90 percent of the principal and accrued interest on the loan. The lender must retain 10 percent of the risk in the loan facility and this 10 percent risk cannot be separately collateralized. The lender must be secured with exportable inventory, accounts receivable already exported, or another form of collateral that Ex-Im deems acceptable. In the case of the underserved market, the Ex-Im Bank will guarantee up to 100 percent (see Alternate Funding Source below).

Fees: Ex-Im Bank charges a nonrefundable processing fee of USD 500 for each application for a preliminary commitment, USD 400 of which goes toward the facility fee charged for the processing of the final commitment. Or, the bank will charge a processing fee of USD 100 for a final commitment application. In addition to either initial charge is an up-front facility fee of 1.5 percent of the total loan amount, based on a one-year loan. For example, 180-day loans would have an up-front facility fee of 0.75 percent of the total loan amount.

Eligibility: Exporters must be a commercial entity currently exporting or planning to export and the business must be domiciled in the United States. Single/specific export transactions are eligible as well as multiple export transactions (revolving). Any lender, bank or public or private provider of commercial credit with three years of operating history may apply.

Collateral Requirements: Ex-Im loan guarantees must be collateralized customarily with export-related inventory or accounts receivable. Disbursements are made against a borrowing base, with typical advance rates of 75 percent for eligible inventory and 90 percent for eligible accounts receivable. For service-sector businesses, engineering design and allocable overhead may be treated as collateral. Additional support generally consists of second or junior liens on other exporter assets such as the guarantee of principal shareholders (over 20 percent ownership).

Application Procedure and Information Requirements: Exporters may apply directly to Ex-Im Bank for a preliminary commitment to a guarantee. The information requested consists of:

- Information on the goods to be financed
- A summary of the exporter's business plan and history of activities
- Three years of audited financial statements
- A recent interim financial statement, including aging of accounts receivable and payable
- At least five credit and/or bank references
- A summary of management's experience in related and non-related fields

For newly formed trading companies or other exporters, an opening balance sheet may be submitted in lieu of this information.

Application forms are available from Ex-Im Bank directly or on-line at its Internet site, www.exim.gov. Ex-Im will analyze whether the applicant meets the program guidelines and offers a reasonable assurance of repayment. If approved, then the exporter may approach various lenders to acquire the best loan package. A preliminary commitment is valid for six months. If it is the lender that is applying, it will have to submit its credit analysis of the exporter, describe how it will control disbursement and use of funds, and explain the agreed-upon payment procedures.

Special Programs Associated with Working Capital Guarantees
City/State Partners Program: With this program, exporters or lenders can go to state and municipal institutions whose staff has been trained in Ex-Im Bank programs. These local government agents will guide exporters or lenders through the Ex-Im Bank application process. To locate these government agents, contact Ex-Im directly or look on their website.

Delegated Authority: This program was created to accelerate the process of obtaining a working capital guarantee. An applicant can directly apply through a commercial lender who has been approved as a delegated authority. There are four levels of delegated authority lenders, each with specific loan limits per exporter. The lowest lender level is limited to making loans of USD 2 million per exporter while the highest lender level is able to make loans of up to USD 10 million per exporter and an aggregate of USD 150 million in loans under this program. This permits the lenders to commit Ex-Im Bank to a loan with minimal documentation and provides for a reduction in guarantee fees.

Priority Lender Program: With the priority lender program, a qualified bank is assured faster turnaround for loans of up to USD 5 million. Qualification for this status includes attendance of Ex-Im Bank seminars, completion of at least two working capital loans, and submission of an annual report every year. Under this program, Ex-Im Bank guarantees its priority lenders that it will make a decision on a pending loan within ten business days for standard transactions.

Alternate Funding Source: This source has developed three programs, one for the lender and two for the exporter. The program for the lender was designed to support a lender with an overline/liquidity facility that enables the lender to leverage limited capital resources. Programs for the exporter concentrate on helping them find commercial support. The first program assists exporters who have a preliminary commitment, but cannot find a lender. The second exporter program focuses on the underserved markets, such as businesses owned by minorities or women, businesses located in economically depressed or rural areas, and businesses targeting environmental improvement. In these cases, Ex-Im Bank will provide 100 percent guarantees.

Weather Modification, Inc.

Weather Modification, Inc., of Fargo, North Dakota, a small company that performs atmospheric research and cloud-seeding services, has used an Ex-Im Bank guarantee of a USD 850,000 revolving working capital loan from Norwest Bank for additional capital to fill growing orders from countries including Mexico, Thailand, Greece, and Turkey.

Single Buyer Short-Term Export Credit Insurance

The purpose of this program is to provide foreign credit risk protection for exporters against default of payment due to commercial and political hazards such as political violence, government intervention, or transfer and inconvertibility problems. This program, however, does not cover product disputes or cancellation of contract. It allows the exporter the opportunity to expand its overseas sales by providing comprehensive credit risk protection on the short-term sale of goods to a single buyer.

Terms: Repayment terms are up to 180 days, although it may be extended to 360 days for agricultural commodities, fertilizer, and consumer durables.

Coverage: In general, short-term credit insurance policies cover the gross invoice value for 90 to 98 percent of a commercial risk and 90 to 100 percent for specified political risks. Interest is covered at a specified rate up to a limited time after the due date. Premiums vary according to the terms of the sale and type of buyer. In all cases, however, Ex-Im Bank requires the exporter to pay a USD 500 refundable advance premium. The exporter does not incur a deductible. The following table outlines the maximum coverage available.

Type of Transaction	Maximum Coverage
Transactions with sovereign obligors	100 percent
Transactions with non-sovereign public sector obligors and private sector obligors	90 percent
Letter of credit transactions	95 percent
Bulk agricultural transactions	98 percent

The maximum coverage varies from 90 to 100 percent according to the type of transaction or according to the buyer's public or private association. For a single buyer multi-transaction, the first shipment as well as subsequent shipments will be insured until the maximum volume has been reached. Any shipments made after the maximum volume has been met will no longer be insured. It is customary for the insurance on a single transaction to have a 3-month period in which the shipments can be made. If, however, multiple shipments must be made and the period of time will be longer, the Ex-Im Bank will extend the period of coverage to 12 months.

U.S. Content Requirement: For short term, there is a minimum of at least a 51 percent U.S. content requirement (labor and material including mark-up).

Eligibility: In order to be eligible for this insurance program the exporter must show at least one year of successful operations, a positive net worth, at least one principal engaged full-time in the company, and no more than USD 500,000 in average annual credit sales over the prior two years.

Eligible Exports: Consumables, agricultural commodities, raw materials, consumer durables, spare parts, and services.

Interest Rates: Cover and principal are at the same percentage and are limited to the lowest rate of interest agreed to in the buyer obligation or legal interest rate in the approved country for the currency of the buyer. The interest rate for buyers using the U.S. dollars is the prime rate minus one-half percent.

Deductible: There is no deductible per se, but the policy-holder is at risk for the amount that exceeds the maximum percentage insured or the amount specified in the policy declarations.

Premiums: The premium is paid on the principal of the insured amount, but the Ex-Im Bank has minimum premium rates according to the exporter's size and classification of transaction participants.

Type of Transaction	Minimum Premium	Small Business
Transaction with sovereign obligors or guarantors	USD 750	USD 500
Transactions with non-sovereign public sector obligors, bank obligors or guarantors, and letter of credit transactions	USD 1,500	USD 750
Transactions with private obligors	USD 2,500	USD 1,000

Minimum premiums should be paid by the last business day of the month following shipment to make the insurance enforceable. Short-term single buyer policies, therefore, require premiums to be paid before shipment. The premiums applicable for small business come from the table above but may vary with repayment terms and other pertinent factors. Pre-shipment insurance can be added to the premium upon request if there is an existing or foreseeable risk to the goods before shipment and delivery is supposed to take place. Actual premiums are methodically calculated with a set of rules that lead to regular and fair premium pricing. Country risk classification (official levels of 1–7 set by the OECD), buyer credit quality, number of buyers, and exporter experience are all taken into account.

Short-Term Multi-Buyer Export Credit Insurance

This plan provides comprehensive (commercial and political) risk insurance on the sale of goods and services from one exporter to a number of buyers.

Eligible companies:

- U.S. corporations, partnerships, or a group of privately organized individuals
- Foreign corporations
- Foreign sales corporations

Premium: For the multi-buyer policy, the premium amounts are calculated with the insured's sales profile, export credit loss history, length of payment terms, countries involved, and the number and types of participating buyers. Premium rates are calculated per USD 100 of the gross invoice on the sale value. Generally, the Ex-Im Bank gives a composite amount including the entirety of the shipments. The exporter, however, must pay a refundable minimum advance premium of USD 500.

After paying the advance premium payment of USD 500, the exporter must submit a monthly report of the number of shipments made, indicate the amount of premiums payable, and enclose the premium payment. If the insured fails to submit a monthly premium report, makes a premium payment past due, or does not declare a shipment, then the Ex-Im Bank can terminate the policy, deem certain shipments uninsured, or continue the policy, but hold the exporter liable for the premium due.

Deductible: All exporters are charged a first-dollar deductible for losses on all eligible transactions shipped within 12 months. The minimum first-dollar loss deductible is USD 5,000 and the actual amount is based on total annual export credit sales. The deductibles must be held for the insured's own account.

Option I. The exporter must retain 10 percent of the commercial risk on each transaction, plus absorb the first-dollar loss deductible for commercial losses on eligible transactions shipped within 12 months.

Option II. The exporter must retain 5 percent of the commercial and political risks for each transaction and it must absorb a first-dollar loss deductible for losses on all eligible transactions shipped within 12 months.

Coverage: Under the multi-buyer policy, the percentage of coverage is based on the gross invoice value, but there is variation within the two options:

- Option I has a split coverage plan with 100 percent political risk coverage and 90 percent commercial risk coverage after a commercial loss deductible. Certain bulk agricultural sales can be approved for 98 percent commercial risk coverage.

- Option II is the equalized coverage plan that covers 95 percent of commercial and political risks and a first loss deductible applies rather than a commercial loss deductible. The same extra commercial coverage can be approved for certain agricultural sales.

The Ex-Im liability amount must be equal to or less than the aggregate limit of liability specified in the declarations to the policy.

Interest: If any interest is charged and there is a written statement about interest charged, then Ex-Im will cover the documented interest that has been charged up to 180 days after the due date or the day up to the claim payment, whichever comes first. The interest rates that the Ex-Im Bank will charge have the same restrictions as in the short-term single buyer policy.

Special endorsements may include coverage for sales into consignment, sales from an overseas warehouse, non-acceptance of shipments, pre-shipment risks on select or turnover transactions, foreign currency payments, sales out of foreign trade fairs, used equipment, or dairy/breeding sales.

Small Business Export Credit Insurance Policy
This policy enables small businesses to participate in exporting by insuring their export credits. This program has the same structure as the previous insurance policies. There are, however, a few adjustments.

Eligibility: The exporter must meet the Small Business Policy Standards, have had USD 5 million or less total export credit sales volume over the past two years (excluding cash or irrevocable letter of credit sales), meet the SBA's small business guidelines, have at least one principal working full-time, have a positive net worth, and have one year of successful operating history.

Coverage: There is 100 percent coverage of political risk, but the 95 percent commercial risk coverage remains the same.

Eligible Assignees: Under the Small Business Policy, the insured may assign the amounts payable to a financial institution that will enhance the confidence of payment to the assignee, especially if the exporter has had previous policy violations.

Applicants must

- Have a current bank reference evidencing satisfactory experience (current bank line of credit is preferred)
- Provide two supplier references evidencing credit of at least USD 25,000

- Have a net worth of 20 percent of policy liability, which can include subordinated shareholder debt
- Not have accounts overdue by three months in the amount of USD 10,000, even if the account is attributable to disputes
- Provide the two most recent fiscal year-end financial statements. If the policy is worth USD 500,000 or less, a financial statement signed by an authorized author is sufficient; if the policy is worth between USD 500,000 and a million, the Ex-Im Bank requires a CPA-reviewed financial statement with notes, and if the policy value exceeds USD 1 million, then the Ex-Im Bank requires a CPA-audited financial statement with notes
- Possibly provide personal credit or financial reports of the applicant's shareholders

Deductible: The small business does not have a deductible for commercial or political risks.

Edusystems Export, Inc.

Ex-Im Bank approved a USD 617,832 medium-term loan guarantee to support the USD 672,335 export by Edusystems Export Inc., in Walworth, WI, and other U.S. suppliers of laboratory equipment to Atilim Universitesi, Ankara. Edusystems is a wholesaler of vocational and technical school supplies. Amatrol Inc., located in Jeffersonville, IN, a small specialty manufacturer of assembly line robots, and Lake Shore Cryotronics Inc., located in Westerville, OH, a small business that makes low temperature sensors, cryogenic and magnetic measuring instrumentation, and tachometers, are the suppliers on the export sale. The equipment will be used in the teaching facilities in the university's departments of physics, computer science, and management. Allfirst Bank, in Baltimore, MD, is the guaranteed lender.

Other Short-Term Insurance Programs

The Ex-Im Bank offers other insurance programs that follow the same structure as the previous insurance programs with a few exceptions. These include the following:

- The umbrella policy which covers 100 percent of specified political risks and 95 percent of all other risks. The policy is designed for exporters with little export experience and it extends many of the administrative duties and the minimum annual premium to an administrator. It is renewable annually.

- Financial institution buyer credit policy, which supports financial institutions who encourage exporters by extending a direct buyer credit loan or reimbursement loan to a foreign buyer.
- Bank letter of credit policy, which protects banks against loss on irrevocable letters of credit issued by foreign banks for the purchase of U.S. exports.
- Small business environmental policy, which insures the sale of environmentally beneficial goods without the restriction of the volume of the shipment as a qualifying factor.
- Two leasing policies, an operating lease policy and a financing lease policy. These policies were designed for entities that provide leases for U.S.-manufactured goods and they insure against governmental repossession and against a default on the stream of lease payments.

B. Medium- and Long-Term Products

Medium-term commitments are over 1 year, but do not exceed 4 or 5 years. Long-term commitments are generally over 5 years, but commitments up to 10, 12, or 14 years are customary. The U.S. Ex-Im Bank has an upper limit commitment of 20 years, but that kind of long-term agreement is rare. The main medium- and long-term products that U.S. Ex-Im provides are the following:

- Direct loans: credit extended to foreign buyers of U.S. goods and services at a fixed interest rate for two or more years.
- Insurance/guarantees: guarantees repayment from a foreign buyer to a lender on an export loan that has repayment terms of at least two years. The guarantee has either a fixed or floating interest rate.
- Credit guarantee facility (CGF)
- Project finance
- Grants: special funds set aside to counteract credit subsidies offered by other governments.

Direct Medium- and Long-Term Loans

Ex-Im will make a direct loan to a foreign buyer of U.S. exports. The direct loan program supports U.S. exporters against other exporters. The advantages of a direct loan are its fixed rate financing and that the rate is held in place through the loan's life. The disadvantages are that Ex-Im provides no support for cash payment, the goods must always be shipped on a U.S. vessel: an acquisition list, contract, and credit agreement are required; and the borrower must have a L/C bank or pay cash. The direct loan requirements and restrictions make this program timely to process when compared with the guarantee program.

Specifications
Medium-term financing is available for contracts that have a repayment term less than or equal to seven years and have a contract value of less than or equal to USD 10 million. Long-term financing is available for contracts that have a repayment term greater than seven years and have a value greater than USD 10 million. Ex-Im offers fixed lending rates that will not change from the date the contract begins until the date the contract ends. The Ex-Im Bank can make a loan that is 85 percent of the U.S. export value, but the participants must pass the Ex-Im Bank credit and transaction analysis. The Ex-Im Bank must also approve the receiving country. The buyer must make a cash payment to the supplier for at least 15 percent of the supply contract. Ex-Im will allow the payment to be from a lender, the exporter, or from the buyer's own account. The 15 percent can be paid at once before the loans have been disbursed or the buyer and supplier can settle a payment plan where the buyer pays with installments after the financing has been disbursed.

Medium- and Long-Term Guarantees

With this product, Ex-Im guarantees the repayment of a private sector loan to a creditworthy foreign buyer of U.S. goods and services. Ex-Im Bank guarantees will cover the principal and interest on a loan for 100 percent if the buyer defaults on repayment due to a political or commercial risk. The Ex-Im Bank also offers guarantees that will cover only political risk insurance. In both cases, however, the foreign buyer must make a cash payment for 15 percent of the contract value to the supplier. Guarantees have full support from the U.S. government and notes guaranteed by Ex-Im are freely transferable.

Eligibility: Lenders may be located in the United States or a foreign country. Any financing institution, U.S. bank, foreign bank, the exporter's financial supporter, or any capable party can act as the lender. Eligible exports are U.S. capital equipment, projects, and services. The buyer must be creditworthy and be domiciled in a country eligible for Ex-Im's assistance.

Ex-Im extends guarantees that have foreign government association or support, but private sector buyers will be assessed by their creditworthiness or offer a creditworthy bank as a guarantor.

Terms: Repayment terms can range from one to ten years. The terms depend upon the value of the export contract, the item exported, the recipient country, and the market terms. Lenders can choose a market rate of interest and a 360- or 365-day year for interest calculations. The guarantee is available for fixed or floating rate loans and will cover 100 percent of the interest.

Coverage: Comprehensive guarantees will cover 100 percent of the principal and interest for the eligible content of all risks contributing to the default in payment. Ex-Im will guarantee up to 85 percent of the value of eligible goods. Political risk only guarantees only pay the principal and interest if there is a transfer difficulty, political violence, expropriation, etc. This guarantee is available to private or non-sovereign public buyers. For loans denominated in foreign currencies that are acceptable to Ex-Im, foreign currency guarantees are issued that can be either comprehensive or political risk only.

Costs and Fees: Ex-Im requires a 15 percent cash payment to the supplier. The payment can come from the buyer's own finances, a loan, or even from the supplier. If the payment will not be paid in a lump sum before the finances are to be disbursed, Ex-Im asks that the supplier and buyer negotiate a payment arrangement. Ex-Im charges a commitment fee and an exposure fee, but the Ex-Im customer does not incur these charges until Ex-Im has authorized a final commitment. The commitment fee is 1/8 of 1 percent per annum on the undisbursed balance of a guaranteed loan. Commitment fees are based on a 360-day cycle and they begin to accrue 60 days after Ex-Im's final commitment. Exposure fees may be financed by Ex-Im. They are risk-based and calculated and payable as the guaranteed loan is disbursed or in a lump upfront payment. The party responsible for the exposure fee must be determined and Ex-Im must be notified at the time of the final commitment application.

Credit Guarantee Facility
This program has a line of credit between a U.S. bank and a foreign bank. The foreign buyer can go to the local bank for approval and make purchase payments through the local bank. A U.S. bank will receive the payments from the foreign bank and disburse the payment to the supplier. If there is a default in payment, then the Ex-Im guarantees the U.S. bank the payment from the foreign bank.

U.S. Ex-Im gives an approved financial institution authority to underwrite "a bundle" of transactions in lieu of Ex-Im underwriting individual transactions. U.S. Ex-Im, in turn, guarantees the transactions that the bank guarantees. In this way, Ex-Im shifts many of the time-consuming details to a bank and accomplishes its mission in supporting U.S. exports. Since the lines of credit are pre-approved and the commercial banks are smaller facilities than Ex-Im, smaller creditworthy importers may be more likely to obtain foreign currency credit.

Specifications

Terms of repayment are two to five years long. Coverage is 100 percent of principal and interest for up to 85 percent of the U.S. export value. The credit guarantee facility will lend credit under similar terms and conditions that Ex-Im abides by. The facility has a minimum USD 10 million with which it lends. Various fees will be charged; interest can be either floating or fixed. The interest rate formula depends on the amount of the loan (10 million has three-year Treasury + 100 basis points, 10 to 17 million has five-year Treasury + 100 basis points, or over 17 has seven-year Treasury + 100 basis points). An exposure fee will be charged if the transaction is financed. The buyer must still make a 15 percent cash payment to the exporter outside of the credit guarantee facility.

Ex-Im Bank has provided a credit guarantee facility by Standard Chartered to EDC Venezuela. The guarantee will be used, in part, to buy used generation equipment. The amount of the CGF is in excess of USD 26 million (25 million plus an exposure fee) over a term of five years.

C. Special Programs

Aircraft Finance
Operations and Maintenance Contracts
Engineering Multiplier Program

Insurance

The export credit insurance program helps U.S. exporters develop and expand their overseas sales by protecting them against loss should a foreign buyer or other foreign debtor default for political or commercial reasons. The purpose of this program is to provide foreign credit risk protection for exporters and lenders against commercial and political risks of default, political violence, government intervention, and transfer or inconvertibility risk. Eligible exporters that may apply for insurance programs must be financially liable entities such as U.S. corporations, partnerships, or individuals organized or residing in the U.S.; foreign corporations, partnerships, or individuals doing business in the United States; and foreign sales corporations controlled by United States corporations, partnerships, or individuals organized or residing in the United States.

Medium-Term Insurance Policy

The medium-term policies insure credit sales on terms of one to five years, and in some cases for up to seven years. For medium-term insurance, the ineligible foreign content should be excluded from cost, when there is 0 to 15 percent eligible content the total contract price is eligible for coverage; when 15 to 50 percent is eligible foreign content only the U.S. content is eligible for coverage.

Medium-Term Single-Buyer Insurance Policies

This program is designed for exports of U.S. capital and equipment, so that they can insure their receivables from individual foreign buyers against loss due to commercial and specified political risks and the commercial risks of default, and interest.

Specifications

The foreign buyer must make a 15 percent cash payment before delivery of the products. The buyer must be a creditworthy entity located in an acceptable country. Exports should consult the country limitation schedule for any special conditions that may apply to the importing country. Banks may apply for cover of medium-term lines of credit extended to a foreign buyer. Political and commercial coverage is 100 percent.

D. Project and Structured Finance

Contact Information
Business Development Group
Export-Import Bank of United States
811 Vermont Avenue, NW
Washington, DC 20571
Tel: (202) 565-3946

The Ex-Im Bank has a project and structured finance division that offers limited recourse funding and structured trade finance to large projects mobilizing scarce capital. This department has only been operating for five years, but it has flourished under Vice President Barbara O`Boyle, who coordinates both types of projects.

The Ex-Im Bank funds a small percentage of a larger project and its contribution involves expanding the export of an American product or service in the natural resource and infrastructure sector. The Ex-Im Bank considers greenfield projects and expansions of either production or facilities appropriate projects. There is no limit or minimum on the project size, sector, or country, but an applicant should take in to account the costly nature of project finance.

Limited Recourse Project Finance

With limited recourse project finance, Ex-Im guarantees a created project company or special purpose vehicle (SPV) and relies on future project cash flows for repayment. The term "project finance" implies that a number of sponsors make contributions, agree to a certain amount of risk, draw up interrelated contracts, and depend upon project cash flows for repayment. Contracts clarify repayment plans and distribute financial responsibility and rewards among the sponsors to ensure repayment and project completion. Projects involving natural resources and infrastructure sectors involving hard currency revenues captured off-shore or long-term offtake contracts are the most suitable projects due to the nature of their cash flows.

Ex-Im often shares the risk of large projects with other government agencies such as AID, TDA, or OPIC. The project finance program makes U.S. exporters more competitive in the development of private infrastructure and in the extraction of natural resources.

Generally, Ex-Im Bank uses financial, legal, and technical advisors that assess the viability of a project. This comprehensive approach facilitates project design and builds sponsor confidence of project success, but also accrues costs and takes more time. The Ex-Im Bank, however, might curb the costs on smaller projects by using only internal consultants and the due diligence of an arranging bank. Feasibility studies, however, may reveal that a trade finance structure rather than a project finance structure might be more efficient and less expensive for a small project. In this case, Ex-Im will notify the sponsors and pass the project to the appropriate Ex-Im department. On the other hand, Ex-Im is looking at risk sharing with suppliers and reinsurance in key industry sectors to make project finance more comprehensive and expansive.

Maximum Possible Support. When appropriate, Ex-Im will extend a maximum amount of support that coincides with OECD Arrangements, including:

- Financing of interest accrued during construction that relates to Ex-Im financing
- 15 percent allowance of foreign content in the U.S. package
- Financing local costs of host country up to 15 percent of the U.S. contract value

Increased Flexibility. The new OECD project finance rules allow for more flexibility because they allow Ex-Im Bank to provide loan repayment terms that match the project revenue stream. The project arrangements can be created with each project, customizing repayment, creating flexible grace periods or back-ended repayment profiles, and more laxity on total repayment terms. For example, telecommunication projects are more likely justifiable candidates for extended grace periods than power projects due to the nature of the industry's cash flow.

The program offers flexibility in the design of the assistance, but it limits the maximum average life of the project. It subjects the maximum average life to 5.25 years, but offers an extension of the project's average life by up to 7.25 years. This extension is constrained with a maximum grace period of 2 years and a maximum repayment term of 14 years.

These new flexible terms have additional constraints:

- If the project's repayment term extends beyond 12 years and the project utilized a direct loan, then the bank will add 20 basis points to the CIRR rate of the direct loan.
- After completion, interest rates cannot be capitalized.
- With additional constraints, the flexible terms will be offered in high-income OECD markets.
- The Ex-Im Bank will decide on the allowed average life of the new flexible terms when meeting the minimum premium benchmark fees required as of April 1, 1999.

The Ex-Im Bank offers several financing options, but during construction and operation, only political and comprehensive guarantees are available.

Project Criteria:
- If the project requires, long-term contracts should be in place with creditworthy entities for the purchase of output and/or input for the project. The contract's terms should extend to the terms of the requested Ex-Im financing.
- Project risk should be allocated appropriately so that each entity assuming risk can manage their responsibility.
- Total project costs should be reasonable and should reflect the costs of similar undertakings.
- Pricing for a product unit must reflect market-based pricing.
- Devaluation risks should be mitigated through denominating revenues in hard currencies and using revenue adjustment formulas based on changing currency relationships or other structural mechanisms.

- Project sponsors, off-takers, contractors, operators, and suppliers must be able to illustrate technical, managerial, and financial capabilities needed to complete the project.
- Sponsors must release a description of their operation, history, and relevant experience.
- Three years of audited financial statements must be provided.
- A technical feasibility study needs to be provided to demonstrate that project technology is reliable and proven.
- A detailed estimate of operating costs must be given.

Application Procedure:

Consulting Firm. A meeting with a consulting firm specializing in project finance is advisable. They will be familiar with project finance options from Ex-Im Bank and other government agencies. Their expertise will guide your company through the project finance process efficiently and work with the Ex-Im Bank on a project plan and financing options that will ensure a successful completion.

Business Development. The Ex-Im Bank recommends an introductory meeting with a project finance business development officer. In this meeting, the business development officer will introduce different Ex-Im Bank programs, criteria, and processes. This officer functions as the liaison between the project finance department and the Ex-Im client. They negotiate the project decisions and agreements. It is for this reason that being prepared and informed during the introductory meeting would behoove the Ex-Im project finance candidate.

Project Finance Letter of Interest (LI). The application for the LI gives the Ex-Im Bank basic information to create the range of options that it can offer to a project. The LI application can be filled out and submitted on-line, but attachments such as an executive summary of the project containing project description, location, participating parties, estimated time frame, and total project cost also need to be submitted. The application and processing fee is USD 100. The actual LI informs the client of what Ex-Im sees as the most appropriate programs and outlines its estimated project terms. This preliminary letter also informs the client that Ex-Im will or will not consider the project.

Competitive Letter of Interest (CLI). To qualify for a competitive letter of interest (CLI), the project participants should be in the final stage of a bidding competition with U.S. procurement or already in the Ex-Im Bank process with at least a preliminary finance LI. CLIs cost USD 1000 and they take about two to four weeks to process. In this time, the Ex-Im Bank project finance division conducts a preliminary in-depth analysis of the project using only finance consultants from the project finance division. Essentially the additional information required calls for an expansion on the information requested in an LI. For example, the bank requests more information about off-takers and suppliers, risk mitigation proposals, analysis of project strengths and weaknesses, potential sources and uses of funds, and a copy of project agreements.

For more information about the CLI and prior to filing an application for a CLI speak with a Project and Structured Finance representative at Ex-Im.

Contact:
Kristine Wood
Tel: (800) or (202) 565-3913
Email: kristine.wood@exim.gov.

Cheryl Conlin
Tel: (202) 565-3955
Fax: (202) 565-3695.
Email: Cheryl.conlin@exim.gov

Link to CLI web page: www.exim.gov/ebd-p-06.html

Final Commitment Application Submission. This application includes the standard final commitment application and five copies of the materials requested under "Project Criteria."

Preliminary Review. The project finance business development staff will review the final commitment application and in five to ten business days will ask for further information or determine the application complete. If they decide they need more information, the staff will return the application with a full and complete explanation of the additional information requested.

In addition to analyzing the application's completion and project's viability, the staff considers whether the Ex-Im project finance program is a good match for the project. If they conclude that Ex-Im might have better options in other departments, they will forward the application and notify the applicant.

Phase I: Evaluation

Choice of Financial Advisor. If Ex-Im decides the project is worth further investigation, they will give the customer a choice in the financial advisor outside of Ex-Im that will do the comprehensive financial evaluation of the project. The advisor that Ex-Im tries to find will ideally be experienced in the industry and knowledgeable in the particular market.

Contract and Evaluation Fee. Before the financial advisor begins his review (Phase I of evaluation), the applicant will pay an evaluation fee and complete a contract and indemnity agreement between itself and the financial advisor. The project company has 30 days to complete these three requirements before Ex-Im returns the application.

Evaluation. Once Ex-Im and the customer decide on a financial advisor, they forward the materials to an unbiased financial analyst who then has 45 days to give Ex-Im their opinion of the project.

Other Fees. If after Phase I evaluation Ex-Im Bank wishes to proceed with the project, it will charge the applicant additional fees for the Phase II due diligence in the form of in-house analysis, outside advice, and appropriate administrative costs. Payment of these fees for all projects will depend on the advice of independent outside legal counsel, independent engineers, and insurance advisors. In addition, there may be other fees associated with conducting a suitable study of the project. Payment for these and any other fees will be the responsibility of the project sponsors or the applicant.

Phase I: Preliminary Project Letter. Upon satisfactory completion of the Phase I evaluation process, the structured finance division will issue a preliminary project letter within 45 days from the date evaluation begins by the financial advisor. The PPL will indicate if Ex-Im Bank is prepared to move forward on a financing offer and the corresponding general terms and conditions based upon the information available at the time of application.

Phase II: Evaluation Post-PLL. After issuance of the PPL, Ex-Im Bank will work with the applicant to proceed to a final commitment. Please note that Ex-Im Bank does not issue preliminary commitments for project finance transactions. Ex-Im Bank will continue to utilize the financial advisor for Phase II of the due diligence process.

Financing Forms
Guarantee to a Lender
In most project finance arrangements, Ex-Im will make an agreement with a lender to guarantee a foreign buyer of a U.S. export. The export will be used in a part of a larger project scheme, exporting an essential good to the construction of a power plant. This kind of guarantee requires the most due diligence and in-depth research.

Political Risk Only Insurance (PRO)
PRO insurance provides a guarantee to the lender for the term of debt for a project. The project assessment is a streamlined

process compared with traditional project finance. The more efficient process reduces the time and cost commitment of all participants involved.

The process and information required are the same as traditional project finance, but the project should be at a more advanced stage, making the evaluation and application process shorter. The evaluation period is shortened, but the project undergoes the scrutiny from the outside financial advisor and depends on the preliminary project letter and post-preliminary project letter. The project has pre-arranged the Ex-Im requirements and project negotiations so the information is readily available for Ex-Im to conduct its traditional assessment, but with optimum speed.

With PRO insurance, Ex-Im focuses its traditional assessment on the specific project's potential risk, the industry risk, the project's capability to repay the debt, and additional government support that mitigates Ex-Im's responsibility. Ex-Im asks for issues affecting stakeholder risk sharing, identity of sponsors and their equity interest, financial and technical capability of project participants, and overall financing structure.

Use of a project finance-consulting firm as well as frequent meetings with a business development officer from the Ex-Im Bank would be beneficial in attaining a PRO.

Following the post preliminary project letter, Exim will need evidence of the following requirements, the complete EPC contract, "eligibility documentation," project cost break-down, a current financial model, revised project documents, and reports from all technical consultants.

Pre-Completion Comprehensive Cover During Construction

This program assesses the mitigation of commercial risks through the construction period. Like all project finance candidates, the project risk must be shared and properly disbursed and participating parties must be capable of the responsibility allotted to them. In addition, the co-lenders will have to assume some of the risk-sharing. In this program, commercial banks play a large role because Ex-Im uses resources from the commercial banks to monitor project construction. Ex-Im catalyzes construction by providing either a direct loan or guarantee to a lending bank.

GEOTHERMAL POWER PLANT IN KENYA

As part of the Government of Kenya's efforts to increase the country's electricity supply, Ormat International, Inc., was awarded a build, own, and operate contract to develop the geothermal fields in the Kenyan East Rift Valley. Total project costs are currently estimated at USD 205 million. As financial advisor to Ormat International, Delphos International has arranged political risk insurance for Ormat's equity investment and is arranging complementary insurance for the project's commercial lenders. In addition, Delphos International is also arranging project financing from US Ex-Im Bank, with the transaction currently in Phase II of that lender's due diligence.

E. AID Finance Programs

Congress was expected to pass a bill on May 1, 2002, extending re-authorization to the Exim Bank aid finance programs through 2005. However, the bill is still being disputed and will be settled in conference; treasury's position in the procedure is the essence of dispute between the Senate and House. If the bill should pass, which it most likely will, it will extend the ceilings of bank loans, guarantees, and insurance from USD 75 billion to USD 130 billion and it would authorize a 2.2 percent increase in the Exim Bank's budget to aid programs so it totals USD 412 million. These programs offer financing to support the sale of U.S. exports. Ex-Im Bank financing can match the foreign government offers so that U.S. exports remain competitive. The bank reviews tied and partially untied aid programs on a case-by-case basis in which it consults with both NAC and the Secretary of Treasury.

Tied Aid Program

Tied aid is a government-to-government concessional financing of public division capital projects in developing countries. Tied aid is provided by the aid agencies of affluent-country governments, oftentimes in dual financing packages with their national export credit associations. To certain degrees, tied aid terms are more concessional than the customary credit terms available by Ex-Im Bank and its counterparts. Due to the fact that tied aid typically involves total maturities longer than 20 years, ordinary export credit that comprise terms up to and including 10 to 12 years are not considered tied aid.

Ex-Im bank tries to counter foreign tied aid offers. For example, the Tied Aid Capital Projects Fund is a U.S. trade plan that is aimed at opposing trade- distorting foreign tied aid in select cases.

Interest Rates: Interest rates are equal to one-half to two-thirds of the market rate in the currency of denomination.

Ormat, Inc.
In April 1994, Ormat, Inc., a California energy company, originated and negotiated project financing with the U.S. Ex-Im Bank for USD 173,000,000 million. The funding was used to finance a 118.5 MW power plant in the Philippines and included a political risk guarantee by Ex-Im Bank.

Specifications
Exim Bank compels convincing information about foreign tied aid offers before presenting certain matching terms and they will evaluate the recipient's governments' written or oral (to Exim-Bank or U.S. Embassy) confirmations; and/or duplicates of correspondence or bilateral aid procedure agreements among foreign exporters, donor, and recipient governments. Foreign tied aid must also follow OECD rules.

Budget Cost: Exim-Bank does not habitually acquire budget cost exceeding 50 percent. Exim-Bank will generally not match tied aid credits with average terms surpassing 30 years, or average rates below one-half market rates in U.S. dollars, or involving grants beyond 40 percent of export value.

III. CONTACTS

Headquarters:
811 Vermont Ave., NW
Washington, DC 20571
Tel: (800) 565-EXIM (3946), (202) 565-EXIM (3946)
Fax: (202) 565-3380 FAX
(202) 565-3377 TDD
Telex: 197681 EXIM UT
Internet: www.exim.gov

Official Export Credit Agencies of non-OECD Member Countries

AFRICA
AFRICAN EXPORT-IMPORT BANK

I. INTRODUCTION

The African Export-Import Bank, Afrexim, has a mandate to promote and finance intra- and extra-African trade. In 1993, African public, private, and institutional investors, as well as non-African financial institutions and private investors, met in Nigeria to establish the bank with authorized share capital of USD 750 million. Afrexim is unique in that its signatory countries have financial obligations with the bank that are not subject to the controls of participating member states. The bank's assets are therefore free from regulations, moratoriums, controls, or any other fiscal or monetary restrictions of any single member state. In 2000, Afrexim approved slightly more than USD 1 billion in loans.

Shareholders and nonshareholders importing goods from a participating state are eligible for the services offered by Afrexim. Most goods and services, with the notable exceptions of military goods and narcotics, are eligible for financing. Afrexim defines an African good as one produced in Africa and having 30 percent African added value.

II. PRODUCTS

Short Term

Line of Credit Program

This program provides funded and nonfunded lines of credit to African and non-African banks, which permits small businesses to access Afrexim's resources indirectly. The program is meant for use by central, commercial, and merchant banks as well as other financial institutions in participating countries, and in nonparticipating countries that will facilitate imports from Africa. Lines of credit are offered on renewable terms of up to 360 days.

Afrexim Direct Financing Program

This program includes credit facilities for pre- and post-export financing, import financing, and export credit guarantees. Intended for larger corporations, it is a direct transaction between Afrexim and the exporter.

Specifications

This program is available to companies with a net worth of at least USD 2 million and an annual export turnover of at least USD 10 million. The loan must be used to facilitate African exports, either by an African company exporting a product or importing capital goods that will be used to export goods, or a corporation importing African goods. Financing is available up to 75 percent of the contract for pre-export, and 80 percent of the contract for post-export. Import financing is available for loans up to 70 percent of the contract. Afrexim will guarantee up to 100 percent of the loan.

Special Risk Program

Afrexim offers various credit facilities with different objectives. By offering guarantees and insurance, Afrexim works to help African borrowers establish and enhance their creditworthiness. Currently two types of credit facilities are available, while several others are envisioned for the future.

The Country Risk Guarantee Facility transfers the risk in lending from African countries to Afrexim. This guarantee program allows banks to lend to African countries and corporations with greater security.

Specifications

Coverage is available for up to 100 percent of the lender's exposure with respect to the risks of exchange control regulation, moratorium on debt payment, or a change in law or policy affecting the timing, currency, or manner of debt repayment. However, amounts of exposure are limited to Afrexim's available limit for each country. This facility is normally available for terms of 360 days, which can be extended.

ALSCON

Through the use of Afrexim, Aluminum Smelting Company of Nigeria (ALSCON) has been able to obtain its alumina supplies from Friguia, Guinea, thereby lowering transportation cost and improving greater economic cooperation among the two countries.

The second special risk program Afrexim currently offers is the Joint Bill Discounting/Financing Facility. This facility allows Afrexim to share payment risks of African banks. Letters of credit issued by participating African banks are jointly discounted, purchased, or financed by Afrexim.

Specifications
Afrexim's participation is determined on a case-by-case basis, but the maximum exposure does not exceed 40 percent of the approved bank's shareholders' funds. Afrexim's participation will not exceed 50 percent of the face value of the qualifying instrument. This facility is available for terms of 360 days.

Medium and Long Term

Infrastructural Services Financing Program
This program is expected to become more important with the growth in projects requiring financing. The infrastructural services financing program will provide project financing for African countries that can provide goods and services to these projects.

Specifications
Examples of eligible transactions include port services, electricity, oil field services, and railroads. Afrexim will also co-finance infrastructure projects with other ECAs.

III. CONTACTS

Head Office:
P.O. Box 404 Gezira
Cairo 11568
Egypt
Tel: 20 (2) 578-0281
Fax: 20 (2) 578-0277
Telex: 20003 AFRXM UN
Internet: www.afreximbank.com
Email: info@afreximbank.com

Harare Branch
Eastgate Building
3rd Floor Gold Bridge (North Wing)
2nd Street, Harare
Zimbabwe
Tel: 263 (4) 729 751-5
Fax: 263 (4) 729 756
Telex: 26770 AFXYBK ZW

ARGENTINA
BANCO DE INVERSION Y COMERCIO EXTERIOR (BICE)
ENGLISH: FOREIGN COMMERCE AND INVESTMENT BANK

I. INTRODUCTION

BICE was created in 1991 by Presidential decree and was authorized in 1992 to act as Argentina's export credit agency. BICE promotes exports and the improvement of Argentinean productivity. In 2001, BICE disbursed more than USD 59 million for foreign trade, and held assets of almost USD 1.1 billion. BICE's total disbursements for the year 2001 were mainly concentrated in the industrial and manufacturing sector (42.9 percent), construction (23.4 percent), and agriculture (10.6 percent). All products to be supported by BICE require a minimum Argentinean content of 60 percent.

II. PRODUCTS—SHORT, MEDIUM, AND LONG TERM

Capital Goods Acquisition Financing
This credit support is for the purchase of capital goods, including spare parts and accessories. Up to 20 percent of the amount of the loan can be used on spare parts and accessories, and/or on the installation and assembly of equipment.

Specifications
The loan can be for a minimum of USD 20,000 and a maximum USD 500,000, and can cover up to 90 percent of the cost of the purchase. The length of the term can be for up to five years.

Project Finance Credit
This credit support is designed for investment projects that need domestic or imported capital goods, services, and/or working

capital. This also includes projects for the restructuring or modernization of industry.

Specifications
The loan can be for a minimum of USD 50,000 and a maximum of USD 500,000, and can cover up to 90 percent of the cost of the project or investment. The term length can be for up to five years.

MERCOSUR Trade Agreement Mixed Partnership Financing
This credit program is designed specifically for investments or projects in any of the MERCOSUR agreement countries (i.e., Argentina, Brazil, Paraguay, and Uruguay). It can help finance a portion of the Argentinean goods or services that make up part of the investment or project.

Specifications
The loan amount has no minimum, and can be for a maximum of USD 10 million. It can cover up to 90 percent of the Argentinean component of the investment or project. The term length can be for up to 8.5 years.

Small- and Medium-Sized Business Financing
Targeted specifically at small- and medium-sized businesses, this credit support helps finance the production and commercialization of goods and services in any sector of the economy. The financing can be used to purchase capital goods and durable consumption products.

Specifications
The loan can cover up to 90 percent of the cost of the goods and can be for a minimum of USD 10,000 and a maximum of USD 500,000. The length of the term can be for up to three years.

Leasing Contract Financing
This program assists leasing contracts for the purchase of domestic and imported capital goods.

Specifications
The loan can be for a minimum of USD 10,000 and a maximum of USD 500,000, and can finance up to 100 percent of the cost of the purchase. The term length can be for up to 5.5 years.

Argentinean Milk Industry

The powdered milk industry in Argentina has been facing an uphill battle during the recent economic turmoil. Through a trust fund administered by HSBC BANK, BICE has extended loans totaling USD 7.5 million to aid the Argentinean powdered milk industry. This credit will help this industry finance its exports.

III. CONTACTS

Mr. Rodrigo Mignone
Commercial Division
Tel: (54-11) 4317-6900
Ext: 1108
Email: rmignone@bice.com.ar

Mr. Damian Martin
Foreign Commerce Division
Tel: (54-11) 4317-6900
Ext: 1120
Email: dmartin@bice.com.ar

BRAZIL
BANCO NACIONAL DE DESENVOLVIMENTO ECONOMICO E SOCIAL (BNDES)
ENGLISH: BRAZILIAN DEVELOPMENT BANK EXPORT IMPORT DIVISION

I. INTRODUCTION

BNDES-exim is a division of BNDES (Brazilian Development Bank) and promotes Brazilian exports through pre- and post-shipment working capital financing, buyer credits, and supplier credits. In 2000, disbursements for exports totaled more than USD 3.1 billion, representing 5.6 percent of Brazilian exports. By working as a mezzanine bank, it has access to a vast network of national and foreign banks.

BNDES was created in 1952 and is the chief federal agency in promoting Brazil's development through medium- and long-term financing. It is completely owned by the Brazilian government. Designed specifically for national development, BNDES has many financing options for a variety of Brazilian industries. Some of the financing available includes leasing, industry capitalization, agricultural financing, and guarantees.

II. PRODUCTS

Short Term (Up to 30 months)

Pre-Shipment Financing (Working Capital)

This credit supports Brazilian exporters by financing the pre-shipment phase of the export. This can include many aspects of the production process, from the purchase of equipment to the payment of salaries.

Specifications

The term of the credit is normally 18 months, but can be extended up to 30 months. The loan amount can cover up to 100 percent of the selling price of the goods exported on a FOB basis. The amortization of the principal is done at the end of the term. Interest payments are every three months, beginning three months after the disbursement. The interest rate is LIBOR plus a spread (which depends on the size of the company requesting the loan) and a spread of the agent bank (which depends on the risk involved in each industry). Contracts of almost any value can be financed, and a minimum Brazilian product requirement of 60 percent is needed.

Maxion

The Brazilian automobile engine manufacturer Maxion obtained a pre-shipment credit worth USD 45 million to increase its exports by USD 57 million. After BNDES granted the loan, the company exceeded its own expectations and increased its exports by USD 98 million. The company also increased the national content of its products from 35 percent to 67 percent.

Special Pre-Shipment Financing

This credit has the same purposes as the regular pre-shipment financing, but is designed for exporters who can demonstrate a yearly increase in the volume of their exports. By doing so, exporters are eligible for lower interest rates and more favorable terms.

Specifications

The term of the credit is normally 24 months, but can be extended up to 30 months if the exporter reaches the projected total value of exports. The exporter can have up to 12 months from the disbursement of the loan to the final shipment, and from then another 6 months to begin amortization payments. The loan amount can cover 100 percent of the selling price of the goods exported on a FOB basis. The amortization of the principal can be done in up to twelve installments, while the interest payments are made each trimester. The interest rate is the same as in the pre-shipment financing. Contracts of almost any value can be financed, and a minimum Brazilian product requirement of 60 percent is needed.

Long Term (Up to 12 years)

Post-Shipment Financing (Buyer and Supplier Credit)

Through this financing option, BNDES helps Brazilian exporters and the buyers of Brazilian exports. The buyer credit directly finances the foreign purchasers of Brazilian capital goods, while the supplier credit finances the credit that exporters can extend to their buyers.

Specifications

The credit has a maximum term of 12 years and can cover up to 100 percent of the selling price of the goods on any basis (FOB, CIF, EXW, etc.). Amortization and interest payments are made each semester. The interest rate is LIBOR plus a spread (which depends on the size of the company requesting the loan) and a spread of the agent bank (which depends on the risk involved in each industry). Contracts of almost any size can be financed, and a minimum Brazilian product requirement of 60 percent is needed.

Embraer

In 2000, Brazil's largest exporter, aerospace giant Embraer, made exports worth USD 2.7 billion. Of these exports, 52 percent, approximately USD 1.4 billion, were financed by BNDES under the post-shipment credit lines. The loans were used to fund the sale of EMB-120, ERJ-145, and ERJ-135 aircraft. USD 607 million was used to finance the purchase of Brazilian aircraft by Mesa Airlines (USA).

III. CONTACTS

Head Office:
Av. República do Chile 100 / 18o andar
20139-900
Rio de Janeiro - RJ
Brazil
Tel: (55-21) 2277-7200/7210
Fax: (55-21) 2220-8244
Internet: www.bndes.gov.br/english/
Email: exim@bndes.gov.br

Mr. Renato Sucupira
Director BNDES-exim
Email: sucupira@bndes.gov.br

Mr. Luciano Pires
Executive Manager BNDES-exim (Aircraft, Capital Goods,
   Chemical and Petrochemical Products, Small/Medium
   Business)
Email: ciani@bndes.gov.br

Mr. Henrique Avila
Manager BNDES-Exim (Oil & Gas Products, Textiles, Trading
   Companies)
Email: henavila@bndes.gov.br

COLOMBIA
BANCO DE COMERCIO EXTERIOR DE COLOMBIA (BANCOLDEX)
ENGLISH: BANK OF FOREIGN COMMERCE OF COLOMBIA

I. INTRODUCTION

Created by Presidential decree in 1991, BANCOLDEX serves the Colombian exporters through rediscount transactions with previously authorized banks that act as financial intermediaries. BANCOLDEX also offers financial guarantees and international banking operations. In 2000 BANCOLDEX reported assets of over USD 1.1 billion. BANCOLDEX is essentially publicly owned, with the main shareholders being the Ministry of Foreign Commerce and the Ministry of Finance.

II. PRODUCTS

Short, Medium, and Long Term

Working Capital

The working capital credit provided by BANCOLDEX is designed to help finance the costs of production and/or commercialization of a good or service for export. Additionally, it permits the funding of promotional activities oriented to finding new export markets or the broadening of existing ones.

Specifications

The amount financed depends on projected annual foreign sales. When the resources are needed for promotional purposes, the amount will be calculated based on the total cost of the promotional activity. The financing can be in Colombian pesos or dollars. If in pesos the term can range between less than 12 months or as long as 36 months, the grace period is for a maximum of 12 months, and interest payments are made on a quarterly basis. In dollars the term can be for 12 to 36 months, the grace period is to be agreed upon on a case-by-case basis, and the interest payments are made at the end of each semester. In any of the two currencies, the repayment is made in equal semester installments. The program is designed for direct and indirect exporters, importers, and Colombian businesses abroad.

Credit for the Investment in Fixed and Differed Assets

This credit program is for the investment in fixed and differed assets that are needed for the improvement of the production process and/or the commercializing of goods and services for export. This includes the increase of production capacity, the development of industrial retooling, and the enhancement of existing technology. The credit could be used for financing projects such as late-blooming crops, machinery and equipment, maintenance costs during unproductive periods, and the purchase of terrain for the execution of the project.

Specifications

The credit can be requested for up to 100 percent of the total cost of the project if the amount requested does not exceed the exports during the period of the loan. If in pesos the term can be for up to seven years, the grace period for up to three years, and interest payments made on a quarterly basis. In dollars the term can be for up to five years, the grace period for up to two years, and the interest payments made each semester. In either of the two currencies, the principal repayment is made in equal semester installments. It is designed for direct and indirect exporters, importers, and Colombian businesses abroad.

Leasing

This program supports commercial financing companies with up to 100 percent of the cost of the leasing contracts they sign with companies that are eligible for BANCOLDEX credit. This includes financial, international, and operational leasing, as well as leaseback programs.

Specifications
Similar to those previously stated for other programs.

Business Creation, Acquisition, and Capitalization Credit

This credit helps fund equity contributions to businesses. The funds can be used for working capital, investment in fixed and deferred assets, substitution of debt (except shareholder loans), and the total or partial purchase of companies related to exports. Additionally, the funds can be used for the creation of a new business or for the acquisition of stock or social interest quotas that allow for vertical and horizontal business integration.

Debt Consolidation Credit

This credit finances the debt consolidation process by substituting debt with BANCOLDEX-backed credit. It helps businesses by improving the terms, the interest rate, or the repayment schedule. All debts can be consolidated, with the exception of shareholder loans.

Multipurpose Small and Medium Business Credit

Targeted for small- and medium-sized businesses, this credit can be used for the financing of working capital, the acquisition of hardware and software for the implementation of electronic commerce, and for new technology for the management of information.

Specifications
The credit can finance up to 100 percent of the amount of the exporter's business plan. The amount financed for each business cannot exceed the equivalent of USD 150,000 in Colombian pesos. Terms are similar to those described above.

Transfer of Business Credit

This credit finances the costs of the partial or complete transfer of the physical plant of a business within the Colombian border.

Specifications
Up to 100 percent of the transfer cost, without exceeding 5 billion Colombian pesos (USD 1.82 million), or the total amount of exports during the term of the loan. Similar terms apply to this program.

Buyer and Post-Shipment Supplier Credit
BANCOLDEX offers buyer credit through correspondent banks (previously rated by BANCOLDEX) to the purchaser of Colombian goods and services and for engineering and/or construction projects developed abroad by Colombian companies. Post-shipment supplier credit is also offered.

Specifications
Up to 100 percent of the CIS (cost, insurance, and shipment) cost of the Colombian goods and services. Construction and engineering projects can be financed as follows:

- Up to 100 percent of the Colombian goods and services that make up part of the project
- Up to 50 percent of the components of the project that are imported from other countries
- Up to 85 percent of the local costs and operating expenses for the project's execution

The financing is in dollars. For consumer products the term of the loan can be up to one year, intermediate goods up to 18 months, and for capital goods and engineering projects up to five years. The repayment of the loan is to be done in installments each semester after a two-year grace period.

Small and Medium Business Guarantee
Through a pact between BANCOLDEX and the National Guarantees Fund, small- and medium-sized businesses can attain an instantaneous or a semiautomatic guarantee.

Specifications
The instantaneous guarantee covers up to 50 percent of the loans (for a maximum amount of USD 150,000 or the equivalent in pesos) granted by any bank in any line of credit in favor of a small- or medium-sized business. The semiautomatic guarantee is good for up to 70 percent of the loans (for a maximum amount of USD 100,000 or its equivalent in pesos) granted to small- and medium-sized businesses by the financial intermediaries that operate this program.

Liquidex Dollars and Pesos

BANCOLDEX buys through discount factoring the amounts invoiced for credit purchases and sales for products and services sold abroad or domestically—up to 85 percent if the exchange is in pesos, and up to 90 percent if in dollars.

International Banking Operations

BANCOLDEX has the following banking operation services: confirmation or notice of export letters of credit (at sight, of acceptance, deferred payment), receipt and negotiation of standby letters of credit, discount factoring, import letters of credit, and guarantee rates.

Specialized Credits

BANCOLDEX also offers certain specialized financing options like the young entrepreneur credit, credit for the improvement and development of industrial productivity and technology, and the financing for programs of environmental improvement.

III. CONTACTS

Head Office:
Calle 28 N° 13 A - 15, Pisos 38 al 42
Bogotá, Colombia
Tel: (57-1) 382-1515
Fax: (57-1) 336-6984
Internet: www.bancoldex.gov.co
Email: bancoldex@bancoldex.com

Mr. Gustavo Ardila
Commercial Vice-President
Tel: (57-1) 382-1515
Ext: 2146
Fax: (57-1) 336-7731
Email: gardilal@bancoldex.com

Mr. Alejandro Contreras
Director, Correspondents Abroad Department
Tel: (57-1) 341-0677
Ext: 2342
Fax: (57-1) 336-7732
Email: corresponsales.exterior@bancoldex.com
        acontrerasa@bancoldex.com

COLOMBIA
SEGUREXPO

I. INTRODUCTION

After being suspended by political strife for ten years, the Colombian government reopened the lines for export credit insurance and established SEGUREXPO de Colombia in 1993. By 1995, the government was offering coverage under political and extraordinary risk. Most recently, CESCE, a Spanish export credit insurance group, invested heavily in SEGUREXPO and aided its development and growth in the Colombian market. Today, SEGUREXPO also enjoys major backing from BAN-COLDEX and the private sector.

II. PRODUCTS

Export Credit Insurance
This insurance protects the exporter or his beneficiary, when extending credit to a buyer, from extended default—six months after the invoice has expired. This can be as a consequence of any commercial, political, or extraordinary risk that is not expressly excluded from the contract. The insurance covers:

- The costs incurred during the production process or period of execution of a service contract, up to a term of 180 days (pre-shipment)
- Credits that have a 180-day term (post-shipment)

Specifications
Under the policy, 90 percent of political or extraordinary risk is covered. These risks are described as political circumstances or economic alterations in the country of the debtor, or administrative or legislative measures adopted by the debtor's government, that impede or delay the transfer of currency, or that make it impossible for the debtor to pay the exporter.

Up to 90 percent of commercial risk is covered by SEGUR-EXPO. Commercial risk covers general insolvency of the debtor, or conditions in which credits paid to the exporter are not cashable. Also covers situations in which credits given to the foreign buyer by the exporter go unpaid for more than six months.

III. CONTACT

Head Office:
Segurexpo de Colombia S.A.
Calle 72 No. 6-44 Piso 12
Bogotá, Colombia
Tel: (57-1) 217-0900
    (57-1) 317-6917
Fax: (57-1) 2110218
Email segurexp@col1.telecom.com.co
Internet: www.segurexpo.com/

Mr. Carlos Alberto Silva Mora
Commercial Director
Tel: (57-1) 317-6917
    (57-1) 217-0900
Ext: 126
Email: carlossolva@segurexpo.com

CROATIA
CROATIAN BANK OF RECONSTRUCTION AND DEVELOPMENT (HBOR)

I. INTRODUCTION

The Croatian Bank for Reconstruction and Development (HBOR) was founded in June 1992 and is entirely owned by the Republic of Croatia. The primary mission of the bank is to finance the reconstruction and development of the Croatian economy. The HBOR helps to promote Croatian exports through its loan programs.

II. PRODUCTS

Loans by HBOR are divided into three separate headings. The first is the loan program for the preparation and export of goods. This loan specifically targets monies allocated toward the preparation of exports, export of goods, or the whole cycle from the preparation of exports to the final payment. Export services are not covered except for the export of construction services, export services directly related to the export of goods, the export of final processing, and exports based on international agreements.

The second is the loan program for the export of capital goods by granting loans to foreign banks and buyers. Loans under this heading have the purpose of prompt payment to the Croatian exporter for the capital goods export transaction. This loan is also conditioned with an insurance policy against political and commercial risks. Third is the loan program for suppliers. This loan aids in the prompt payment of export transactions so that the disbursement of loan funds to the supplier starts upon the fulfillment of all stipulated conditions. Both the supplier and the foreign buyer sign an export contract on the purchase of goods, works, or services on credit. The foreign buyer repays the loan to the supplier and the supplier repays the loan to HBOR.

HBOR is also involved in several loan programs to aid small- and medium-sized businesses to help spur entrepreneurship in the country. HBOR offers two options for export credit insurance in the short and long term. The first is an insurance policy for direct delivery of goods and services and the second is a policy for buyer export credit facilities.

III. CONTACTS

Head Office:
Strossmayerov trg 9
10000 Zagreb
Tel: 385 (1) 459-1666
Fax: 385 (1) 459-1721
Internet: www.hbor.hr
Email: info@hbor.hr

Credit Division
Ms. Branka Ivančić
Executive Director
Tel: 385 (1) 459-1680

International Operations Division:
Tel: 385 (1) 459-1819

Small and Medium Enterprises
Ms. Mira Dronjić
Email: mdronjic@hbor.hr
Tel: 385 (1) 459-1672

Export Financing
Preparation of Exports and Export of Goods
Ms. Dora Matošić
Email: dmatosic@hbor.hr
Tel: 385 (1) 459-1609

Export of Capital Goods
Ms. Ivanka Maričković-Putrić
Email: iputric@hbor.hr
Tel: 385 (1) 459-1807

Debt Office
Ms Sanja Gracin
Email: sgracin@hbor.hr
Tel: 385 (1) 459-1804

Export Insurance
Ms Ružica Adamović
Email: radamovic@hbor.hr
Tel: 385 (1) 459-1800

CYPRUS
EXPORT CREDIT INSURANCE SERVICE (ECIS)

I. INTRODUCTION

The Export Credit Insurance Service of Cyprus (ECIS) operates within Cyprus' Ministry of Commerce, Industry and Tourism. It was established in 1974 with the aim of providing cover to Cypriot exporters of certain manufactured goods against risks out of their control.

II. PRODUCTS

ECIS offers insurance to cover goods that have at least 25 percent of the product's value added in Cyprus. Although typically ECIS provides cover for sales to buyers overseas, it is also possible to receive cover for sales to merchants within Cyprus, who then export the goods.

Terms: Cover is usually provided for 90 percent of the loss, and if loss is due to failure of the buyer to accept the goods, then the exporter must endure a loss of 20 percent of the invoice value. Exchange rate fluctuations are not covered under these policies.

Risks: ECIS provides cover for six types of risk:
- Insolvency of the buyer
- Failure of the buyer to pay for goods delivered and accepted
- Failure of the buyer to accept goods which have been dispatched
- Political events, economic difficulties, government action, revolution, riot, earthquake, etc., outside Cyprus that prevent performance of the contract, payment, or transfer
- General moratorium decreed by the government of the buyer's country
- Repudiation of the contract by a state buyer

III. CONTACTS

Trade Department
6 Andrea Araouzou Str.
1421 Nicosia
Tel: ++357 2 867100
Fax: ++357 2 375120
Internet: www.mcit.gov.cy/mcit/trade/trade.nsf
        /Main?OpenFrameSet
Email: mintrade@spidernet.com.cy

ECUADOR
CORPORACION FINANCIERA
NACIONAL (CFN)
ENGLISH: NATIONAL FINANCE CORPORATION

I. INTRODUCTION

CFN is a public and autonomous financial institution that provides funding for the development and growth of all sectors of Ecuador's economy. For the period 1999 to 2004, CFN expects to fund nearly USD 3 billion, of which 50 percent is to be targeted at the exporting industry. In 2001, CFN's assets totaled more than USD 574 million.

II. PRODUCTS

Short Term (up to 180 days)

FOPEX
This credit finances the pre-shipment, pre- and post-shipment, or post-shipment phases of exporting. It can finance packaging, insurance, freight, and local expenses as well.

Specifications

The loan can be for up to USD 250,000 FOB and must be in U.S. dollars. Larger amounts are available subject to CFN approval, but the exposure to any single economic group cannot exceed USD 1 million. The length of the term for pre-shipment and pre- and post-shipment is up to 180 days, while post-shipment is only up to 90 days. The repayment of the loan and interests is done on maturity in a single payment. Only legal entities or individuals legally established in Ecuador that export their goods or that participate in exports are eligible.

III. CONTACTS

Head Office:
Av. Carlos J. Arosemena KM $1^1/_2$
Guayaquil, Equador
Tel: 593 (4) 220-4080
     593 (4) 220-3896
Fax: 593 (4) 220-4030
Internet: www.cfn.fin.ec
Email: cae1@q.cfn.fin.ec

HONG KONG, CHINA
HONG KONG EXPORT CREDIT INSURANCE CORPORATION (HKECIC)

I. INTRODUCTION

The Hong Kong Export Credit Insurance Corporation (HKECIC) began its operations in 1966 and is currently not an OECD member. The current contingent liability of HKECIC is HKD 10 billion (USD 1.28 billion). Its capital is wholly-owned by the government.

II. PRODUCTS

HKECIC provides a wide range of insurance facilities covering exports on credit terms of up to 180 days. The services offered range from credit insurance to asset management to discounting of export bills and advice on solving payment problems. Some of HKECIC's products are comprehensive cover policy, small and medium enterprises policy, cover on export of services, cover on sales to overseas buying offices in Hong Kong, cover on sales to local exporter, cover on country risks, and various tailor-made policies.

Short Term

As the bulk of Hong Kong exports are consumer goods involving credit not exceeding 180 days, HKECIC's most important credit facilities include various tailor-made policies to cover manufacturers and exporters in Hong Kong against both commercial and political risks.

Comprehensive Contracts Policy

Designed for general consumer exports such as garments, toys, electrical appliances, electronics, clocks, watches, and shoes, the comprehensive contracts policy caters to the specific needs of Hong Kong exporters. HKECIC has other tailored programs with similar structure to the comprehensive policy, but their purposes are different. Examples include the comprehensive confirming house extended terms policy, the specific shipments policy, and the specific contracts policy. Cover can be provided by endorsement to comprehensive policies for components or raw materials sent for processing abroad against risks of confiscation or expropriation, war, civil disturbances, and natural disasters. Cover is also available by endorsement to comprehensive policies for sale of goods to buying offices domiciled in Hong Kong but owned by overseas buyers, provided such goods are intended for export. Risks of insolvency and payment default of the Hong Kong buying office are covered.

Specifications

The ECIC does business with everyone except for the countries that the United Nations has sanctioned. In addition, it considers mainland China a separate country so it provides insurance to mainland China without repercussions. Ninety percent of ECIC's underwriting is short term (up to 180 days).

Comprehensive Cover Policy

This policy was designed for Hong Kong exporters and manufacturers. It provides cover not only for all export business on credit terms (documents against payment, documents against acceptance and open account) for goods shipped from Hong Kong, but also for those transported directly from suppliers' countries to their destination without passing through Hong Kong. HKECIC provides cover for such transactions as long as the exporters are the principals in the contracts of sale. Cover commences from the date of shipment.

Specifications

The regions that HKECIC covers are China, Indonesia, South Korea, Macau, Malyasia, the Philippines, Singapore, Sri Lanka, Taiwan, and Thailand. They cover buyer and country risks for up to 90 percent, but HKECIC does not specify terms of payment limitations. HKECIC calculates premium rates on the basis of the amount insured, how well disbursed the risks are, the destination, and length of payment. The riskier the country, or the longer the arrangement for length of payment, the higher the premium rates are. HKECIC holds information provided confidential under its own oath of confidentiality.

The Small and Medium Enterprises Policy (SMEP)

The SMEP was designed to save SMEs paperwork and yet offer them comprehensive protection for their accounts receivable. Comprehensive cover is available to protect businesses for services rendered to their overseas clients. Services covered may include freight forwarding and transport, computer software development, advertising and market research, engineering, construction and architectural services, media and publishing services, management consultancy, etc.

Specifications

HKECIC will indemnify its clients 90 percent and will share 90 percent of the expenses for pursuing debts, collateral for discounting export bills, and access to credit management services. SMEP supports the domestic exports from Hong Kong and re-exports from Hong-Kong to many countries in the Asian region. Any transaction involving the export of goods and services may be insured provided that HKECIC is satisfied with the risks involved. All companies doing business in Hong Kong are eligible for cover. Premiums are charged on the gross invoice value of goods or the contract value. They are based on several factors, including the buyer's country, the length of credit, the nature of goods, and the volume and quality of an insured's business and claims experience. The average premium is 0.54 percent. Generally, claims will be paid four months after the event that caused the loss occurred. ECIC will not disperse payment until after disputes, resale, or bankruptcy issues are settled.

Cover on Export of Services

This program promotes and supports Hong Kong's exports with comprehensive protection and offers tailor-made coverage to suit the particular service industry.

Cover on Sales to Overseas Buying Offices in Hong Kong

This program was designed for the many buying offices in Hong Kong that act as principals in transactions with local manufacturers or suppliers and expose the local manufacturers to nonpayment risks that it cannot legally pursue. This product protects local exporters from the credit risks that arise in a sale to a client with a buying office set-up in Hong Kong.

Medium- and Long-Term Credit

HKECIC can provide a specific policy to cover suppliers' credit for the export of capital goods and projects on medium- and long-term credit (two years and more). The specific policy can be tailor-made to meet the individual needs of exporters.

Extended Terms Export Credit Policy

This program was designed for heavier equipment with longer payment terms. It covers the nonpayment risk for exports and re-exports of consumer durables and semi-capital goods.

Specifications

Terms become effective from the date of shipment. The extended terms credit period will typically be from 181 days to 2 years. The goods for which this program is most suitable are plastic injection machinery, other light machinery, agricultural equipment, consumer durables, yachts, trucks, etc.

Services

Aside from short-, medium-, and long-term products, HKECIC provides financial services such as credit management, advice on solving payment problems, credit insurance, and collateral for discounting bills. A convenience service called e-link allows Internet users to submit a shipment declaration.

Credit Management

ECIC has 55,000 buyers and has numerous on-line connections with a number of credit agencies worldwide. ECIC can approve a credit limit within one to two business days if the application information is complete and if the other parties involved prove efficient and capable.

III. CONTACTS

Informational: ECIC will normally reply to queries within ten days. If the query involves complex matters, then the reply may take longer.

2/F, Tower 1, South Seas Centre, 75 Mody Road
Tsimshatsui East, Kowloon
Tel: 852 2723 3883
Fax: 852 2722 6277
Internet: www.hkecic.com
Email: info@hkecic.com

Joyce Yan
Deputy General Manager
Tel: 852-2732-9983

Cynthia Chin
Deputy General Manager
Tel: 852-2732-9030

Walter Tse
Deputy General Manager
Tel: 852-2732-9008

INDIA
EXPORT CREDIT GUARANTEE
CORPORATION (ECGC)

I. INTRODUCTION

Created in 1957 by the Indian government, ECGC today is the fifth largest credit insurer in the world in terms of coverage. The Export Credit Guarantee Corporation was established to strengthen exports from India by covering the risks involved in export credit. Administratively, the ECGC functions under the Ministry of Commerce, and it is managed by a Board of Directors comprised of members of the government; Reserve Bank; and the banking, insurance, and export community. The expected paid-up capital of ECGC for 2002 is Rs 500 crores (USD 103 million).

II. PRODUCTS

Standard Policy
Also known as the shipments policy, this is ideally suited to cover the risks involved in short-term export credit (not exceeding 180 days). The policy covers both commercial and political risks from the date of shipment. Political risks include government restrictions that delay or block transfer of payment, war, import

restrictions, cancellation of importing license, interruption or diversion of the shipment, or any other cause of loss occurring outside of India that is outside of the control of the exporter and buyer. Commercial risks are buyer insolvency, failure by the buyer to repay within a certain time frame, and a buyer's failure to accept goods. There is a minimum premium of Rs 10,000 (USD 207), which will be adjusted against the actual premium payable on shipments declared. ECGC will normally cover up to 90 percent of the cost of the loss. This policy is intended to cover all shipments made by the exporter within a 24-month period.

Specific Shipment Policy
Similar to the standard policy, this program of insurance is intended to cover one or more shipments only under a particular contract. The exporter can choose between coverage for both commercial and political risks or just political risks.

Financial Guarantees
These are issued to banks to protect them from the risks involved in extending pre- and post-shipment credit to exporters.

Overseas Investment Insurance
This scheme protects Indian investments abroad, especially those involving equity capital or untied loans for greenfield projects or expansions. The insurance period covered should not exceed 15 years, but can be extended to 20 years.

III. CONTACTS

Express Towers, 10th Floor
Nariman Point, P.O.B. No. 11677
MUMBAI-400 021
Tel: 91(22) 284-5452 / 284-5463
Fax: 91(22) 204-5253 / 202-3267
Internet: www.ecgcindia.com
Email: ecgcedp@bom2.vsnl.net.in

NATIONAL MARKETING DIVISION
Cambatta Bldg., 2nd Floor
42, Maharshi Karve Marg
Churchgate, Mumbai - 400 020
Tel: (022) 2837462/2044519
Fax: (022) 282 9968
Internet: www.ecgcindia.com
        www.indianexportregister.com
Email : ecgcmktg@bom5.vsnl.net.in

BRANCH OFFICES

Western Region:

Bandra Branch
The Metropolitan, 7th Floor
Plot No. C-26/27, "E" Block
Bandra-Kurla Complex
Bandra (E), Mumbai - 400 051
Tel: (022) 6571600/2353
          6572775-77
Fax: (022) 6572779/6572046
Email: ecgcmumb@bom5.vsnl.net.in

Churchgate Branch
Cambatta Bldg., 2nd Floor
42, Maharshi Karve Marg
Churchgate, Mumbai - 400 020
Tel: (022) 2822214/65
Fax: (022) 281 8859
Email: chb@ecgcindia.com

Thane Branch
Kusumanjali, 1st floor
Gokhale Road,
Thane (West)
Tel: (022) 534 7807
Fax: (022) 534 7815
Email: ecgctnb@vsnl.net

Project Export Branch
The Metropolitan, 7th Floor
Plot No. C-26/27, "E" Block
Bandra-Kurla Complex
Bandra (E), Mumbai - 400 051
Tel: (022) 6572775/76/77/2303
          6572775-77
Fax: (022) 6572302
Email: ecgcped@bom4.vsnl.net.in

Large Exporters Branch
Dalamal House, 3rd Floor
Plot No. 206, J.B.Marg
Nariman Point, Mumbai - 400 020
Tel: (022) 2828261/68,
          2040749
Fax: (022) 2040704
Email: ecgclbbm@ecgcindia.com

Bank Business Branch
Dalamal House, 3rd Floor
Plot No. 206, J.B.Marg
Nariman Point, Mumbai - 400 020
Tel : (022) 2040720,
        2040749/5831
        2828261/68
Fax: (022) 2040704
Email: mmmondal@ecgcindia.com

Ahmedabad
Nagindas Chambers, 1st Floor
Opp. NTC Showroom, Usmanpura
Ashram Road, Ahmedabad - 380 014
Tel: (079) 7544499/7544932
Fax: (079) 7542094
Email: bmahmedabad@ecgcindia.com

Pune
Vastu Chambers, 1st Floor
1202/39, Shivaji Nagar, PB. No. 880
Shirole Road, Pune - 411 004
Tel: (020) 5331998
Fax: (020) 5331388
Email:ecgcpune@giaspn01.vsnl.net.in

Indore
419-C, 4th Floor, City Centre
570, M.G.Road, Indore - 452 001
Tel: (0731) 544215
Fax: (0731) 544431
Email: ecgcindo@bom4.vsnl.net.in

Eastern Region:

Kolkata
AC Market Complex, 9th Floor
1, Shakespeare Sarani, Kolkata - 700 071
Tel: (033) 2820963 to 66
Fax: (033) 2820939/2820967
Email: ecgccal@cal.vsnl.net.in

Varanasi
PCF Plaza, Commerical Complex, 3rd Floor
Unit No.1, Mint House, Nadesar
Varanasi - 221 002

Tel: (0542) 340180/340243
Fax: (0542) 348492
Email: ecgcvrbo@nde.vsnl.net.in

Bhubaneshwar
A-77, Saheed Nagar, Bhubaneshwar - 751 007
Tel: (0674) 521772
Fax: (0674) 545837
Email: ecgc@satyam.net.in

Guwahati Sub-office
H.P. Brahmachari Rd.
P.O. Rehabari, Guwahati - 781 008
Tel: (0361) 635983

Southern Region - I

Chennai
Spencer Towers, 7th Floor
770-A, Anna Salai, Chennai - 600 002
Tel: (044) 8522998/3146/2616/4550
Fax: (044) 8522537/5715/8514550
Email: ecgcchen@md3.vsnl.net.in

Coimbatore
Charan Plaza, 2nd Floor
1619, Thirchy Rd., Opp.Shripathy Theatre
Coimbatore - 641018
Tel: (0422) 304775/76/78
Fax: (0422) 304777
Email: ecgc_cbe@kovai.tn.nic.in

Madurai
Rajah Muthaiah Mandaram, 2nd Floor
Dr. Ambedkar Road, Madurai - 625 020
Tel: (0452) 651221
Fax: (0452) 651220
Email: ecgcmdu@giasmd01.vsnl.net.in

Salem
Opal Ratna Complex, 1st Floor
315/C-34, Brindavan Rd., A.V.K. Nagar,
Salem - 636 004
Tel: (0427) 442275/330265
Fax: (0427) 330274
Email: slm_ecgcslm@sancharnet.in

Tirupur
137/2, C.G.Complex, 2nd Floor
Kumaran Rd., Tirupur - 641 602
Tel: (0421) 232998/234354/232997
Fax: (0421) 248359
Email: ecgctpr@sancharnet.in

Southern Region - II

Bangalore
Raheja Towers, 11th Floor
West Wing, 26, M.G.Rd.
Bangalore - 560 001
Tel: (080) 5589775/5591729/5585375
Fax: (080) 5589779
Email: ecgcbang@blr.vsnl.net.in

Kochi
HDFC House, 2nd Floor
Ravi Puram Junction, M.G.Rd., Ernakulam
Kochi - 682 015
Tel: (0484) 382124/354447/374273/361437
Fax: (0484) 374016
Email: ecgckoch@giasmd01.vsnl.net.in

Hyderabad
HACA Bhawan, 2nd Floor
Opp. Public Gardens, Hyderabad - 500 004
Tel: (040) 3234334, 3240833, 3296383
Fax: (040) 3231346
Email: ecgchyd@hd1.vsnl.net.in

Northern Region:

Large Business Branch
Prakash Deep, 8th Floor
7, Tolstoy Marg, New Delhi - 110001
Tel: (011) 3712640/ 3317505/ 3319125
Fax: (011) 3317708
Email: ecgclbb@vsnl.com

New Delhi Metro Branch
NBCC Place, South Tower, 4th Floor
Pragati Vihar, Bishma Pitamah Marg
New Delhi - 110 003
Tel: (011) 4365465/53/93/95
Fax: (011) 4369734/ 4365694
Email: ecgcdel@del2.vsnl.net.in

Ludhiana
Suryakiran Complex, 2nd Floor, 92, The Mall
P.O. Box No. 281, Ludhiana - 141 001
Tel: (0161) 441082/403349/445174
Fax: (0161) 441339
Email: ecgcldh@jla.vsnl.net.in

Kanpur
147/17, Sky Lark, 3rd Floor, Chunniganj
P.O. Box No. 116, Kanpur - 208 001
Tel: (0512) 210024
Fax: (0512) 214855
Email: ecgckan@giasde01.vsnl.net.in

Moradabad
Pt. Shankar Dutt Sharma Marg, Civil Lines,
Moradabad - 244 001
Tel: (0591) 415476
Fax: (0591) 410244
Email: ecgcmbd1@up.nic.in

Jaipur
B-17/B, Chomu House, Sardar Patel Marg
"C" Scheme, Jaipur - 302 001
Tel: (0141) 361172/367292
Fax: (0141) 363044
Email: ecgcjpr@jp1.net.in

Agra
Deepak Wasan Plaza
17/2/4, Sanjay Place, 2nd Floor
Agra - 282 002
Tel: (0562) 354948/521676
Fax: (0562) 350136
Email: ecgcagra@nde.vsnl.net.in

Panipat
Malik Plaza, 1st Floor, G.T. Road
Panipat - 132 103
Tel: (01742) 34933
Fax: (01742) 34937
Email: ecgc@pnp.nic.in

SALES PROMOTION AGENTS

Shah Trading Corporation
Jayshree Vyapar Bhavan
Opp. Saurashtra Cold Storage
Malaviya Rd., Rajkot - 380 002, Gujarat
Tel: (91-281) 368811 to 368817
Fax: (91-281) 368819
Email: spaecgc@hotmail.com

Fund Point Finance Ltd.
G-9, First Floor, Yenopoya Shopper's Gallery
V.T.Rd., Kodialbail, Mangalore - 575 003
Tel: (0824) 496901

INDIA
EXPORT-IMPORT BANK OF INDIA (EX-IM INDIA)

I. INTRODUCTION

India created the Export-Import Bank of India in 1982 for the purpose of financing, facilitating, and promoting foreign trade. Ex-Im India received the 2002 Association of Development Financing Institutions in Asia and Pacific's Trade Development Award for its efforts to support and expand export capabilities. With Rs 74 billion (USD 1.5 billion) in resources, Ex-Im India supports Indian trade with many different programs.

II. PRODUCTS

Ex-Im India offers multiple programs to encourage and expand exports, including working capital, project financing, guarantees, loans, and credits. Most are available for short, medium and long terms.

Short Term

Ex-Im India defines short term as a period of 180 days to two years.

Foreign Currency Pre-Shipment Credit Program
The foreign currency pre-shipment credit program (PCPC) is a loan to exporters or commercial banks with exporting clients. The loan is issued in any foreign currency.

This program offers loans for terms of up to 180 days. The loan is repayable in the currency in which it is issued in order to eliminate two-way exchange fees. This loan is intended to finance inputs for goods to be exported. Interest rates usually do not exceed two percent more than the London Inter Bank Offer Rate.

Working Capital Term Loan Programme for Export Oriented Units

This program provides working capital for export-oriented products, the importation of capital goods under the export promotion capital goods scheme, or the expansion or modernization of existing capacity with an export orientation. These loans have a term of two years, and are available in rupees or a foreign currency. A program also exists for medium- to long-term loans with similar eligibility requirements.

Andean Development Corporation

Ex-Im India extended lines of credit under this program worth USD 10 million each to the Andean Development Corporation and the Banco Industrial de Venezuela to promote Indian exports to Latin America. In addition, Ex-Im India signed an in-principle agreement with Banco Mercantil, the largest commercial bank in Venezuela, for another USD 10 million line of credit.

Medium and Long Term

The Export-Import Bank of India generally does not offer programs with terms greater than ten years.

Program For Export Facilitation

This program is available for minor port expansion, software training institutes, and infrastructure facilities that promote trade. The programs offer seven- to ten-year terms for port programs or up to five years for software training institutes in rupees or a foreign currency. Interest rates are tied to Ex-Im India's minimum lending rate, or in the case of a foreign currency, to floating or fixed interest rates based on Ex-Im India's cost of funds.

Export Product Development Program

This program is designed to support export product development focusing on industrialized markets. Established enterprises with a product development program dedicated to export are eligible for these loans. They are intended to be used for research and development, pre-production, process development, and product launch costs. Loans are available for terms of seven to ten years and can be denominated in rupees. Interest rates are set on a case-by-case basis.

III. CONTACTS

Centre One Building, Floor 21
World Trade Centre Complex
Cuffe Parade, Mumbai 400 005
Tel: 91 (22) 2185272
Fax: 91 (22) 2182572
Internet: www.eximbankindia.com
Email: eximindi@vsnl.com

1750 Pennsylvania Avenue N.W.
Suite 1202, 12th Floor
Washington, D.C. 20006 U.S.A.
Tel: (202) 223-3238/ 3239
Fax: (202) 785-8487
Email: indexim@worldnet.att.net

Tower 1, Floor 8
Jeevan Bharati Building
124, Connaught Circus
New Delhi 110 001
Tel: 3326375/ 3326625
Fax: 3322758/ 3321719
Email: eximnd@del2.vsnl.net.in

Golden Edifice Building, 2nd Floor
6-3-639/640, Rajbhavan Road
Khairatabad
Hyderabad - 500 004
Tel: (040) 330 7816
Fax: (040) 3317843

Ramanashree Arcade, Floor 4
18, M.G. Road, Bangalore 560 001
Tel: (080) 5585755/ 5589101-04
Fax: (080) 5589107
Email: eximbro@blr.vsnl.net.in

Via Disciplini, 7
20123 Milan, Italy
Tel: 39 (02) 584 30 546
Fax: 39 (02) 583 02 124
Email: exim.india@tin.it

158, Jan Smuts, Ground Floor
9, Walters Avenue
Rosebank
Johannesburg 2196
P.O. Box 2018, Saxonwold 2132
Johannesburg, South Africa
Tel: 27 (11) 4428010, 4422053
Fax: 27 (11) 4428022
Email: eximindia@icon.co.za

INDONESIA
ASURANSI EKSPOR INDONESIA (ASEI)
ENGLISH: INDONESIA EXPORT CREDIT AGENCY

I. INTRODUCTION

ASEI is a state-owned enterprise established in 1985 as Indonesia's export credit agency. Its primary commitment is to support the export of Indonesia's goods and services, and to improve Indonesian small- and medium-sized exporters' competitiveness in international markets. Through export credit insurance, bank guarantees, and bond insurances, ASEI is geared towards enhancing the development of exports and foreign exchange earnings.

II. PRODUCTS

All of ASEI policies are short-term programs with payment terms of up to one year.

Export Credit Insurance

ASEI provides comprehensive export credit insurance for both commercial and political risks. Commercial risks considered under ASEI credit insurance include buyer's insolvency, buyer's payment failure after six months of the payment due date, and failure or refusal by the importer to accept goods exported. Political, or noncommercial, risks covered by ASEI include the cancellation of import license, war, social disturbance, or any other exogenous factor occurring outside the control of the Indonesian exporter.

Eligibility: ASEI has no nationality requirements or limits on foreign content for an insurance policyholder as long as the person/company is a resident and doing business in Indonesia. ASEI covers a wide range of goods and services; however, ASEI is particularly interested in stimulating non-oil and gas exports.

Term: The bank provides short-term credit insurance policies for up to one year.

Coverage: ASEI indemnifies the exporter for as much as 85 percent of losses incurred. Credit limits are fixed by ASEI on a case-by-case basis after assessing both the creditworthiness of the parties involved and the situation prevailing in the country of destination.

Fees: Interest rates are determined by country risk, presence of payment securities, and period of credit. Generally, an interest rate for short-term comprehensive insurance plans ranges between 0.2 percent (for shipments to the United States, Australia, Europe, and Japan) to 4 percent (for shipments to high-risk countries).

Export Guarantee
ASEI offers two kinds of credit guarantees. One offers guarantees to insure lenders of Indonesian exports against the nonrepayment of short-term credit contracts up to 360 days. The other provides a guarantee for credit beyond the maximum legal lending limit. Export guarantee programs are generally limited to those institutions lending to small- and medium-sized exporters.

Specifications
ASEI's export guarantee programs do not have nationality or foreign content requirements for lending institutions as long as they are doing business in Indonesia. Export guarantee programs provide coverage for short-term contracts of up to 360 days for both commercial and political risks. ASEI has a premium ranging between 0.2 and 2.2 percent of the amount guaranteed depending on export destination, exporters' terms of payment, and the nature of the transaction.

Bond Insurance
ASEI offers up to 85 percent short-term bond indemnity coverage for custom and surety bonds.

Specifications

ASEI bond insurance is issued on a short-term basis for periods of up to one year and covers both commercial and political risks. The interest payment period of the bonds begins on the first day of the term of the bond and ends on the day before the redemption date. The interest payment is effected via the bank's holding accounts and is redeemed on the redemption date.

III. CONTACTS

Main Office
ASEI
Sarinah Building 13th Floor, Jl. MH. Thamrin No. 11
10350 Jakarta, Indonesia
Tel: (62 21) 390-3535
Fax: (62 21) 390-3575
Internet: www.asei.co.id
Email: asei01@asei.c.id

IRELAND
EXPORT CREDIT DIVISION

I. INTRODUCTION

The Export Credit Division (ECD) of Ireland's Department of Tourism and Trade was founded based upon the Insurance Act of 1953, which promotes the extension of state guarantees in order to increase exports of Irish goods and services. The ECD's resources for credit insurance claims are monies paid by the Minister for Industry and Commerce voted by the Oireachtas (Parliament). The Minister's liability limit is currently set at Ir£ 500 million, yet is designed such that there is no net loss of public funds.

II. PRODUCTS

The ECD provides a variety of insurance and guarantees, as well as export finance. However, eligibility is limited to goods and services of "reasonable Irish content," and the political and economical situation of the buyer's country is a determining factor. Also, the buyer's creditworthiness, provision of state, bank, or parent company guarantees are factors in certain situations.

Insurance

ECD operates five insurance policies for exporters. Both the short- and medium-term policies cover political risks. However, the medium-term policies also cover commercial risks. All policies offer a maximum 90 percent coverage. The available policies are:

- Political risks shipments
- Political risks services
- Political risks contracts
- Specific contracts
- Specific services

Short Term

The political risks services policy covers the supply of services over the short term from political risks. Cover begins at the date of contract or invoice.

Medium Term

The terms of the specific contracts policy cover pre- and post-shipment risks for sales of capital on extended credit terms. Typically the maximum cover is up to 5 years, but up to 8.5 years may be arranged.

The specific services policy covers larger service contracts.

Generally speaking, all policies are based on the following terms:

1. Down payments of 15 to 20 percent for credits of one or more years
2. Repayment in consecutive, equal semiannual amounts, beginning six months from the date of shipment (no grace period)
3. Interest is payable on outstanding declining balances
4. Credit duration allowed is directly linked to the contract's value

Guarantees

Guarantees are given through the ECD to funding banks for particular policies. These guarantees provide 100 percent cover to the banks and become active on presentation of shipping documents.

Export Finance Programs

ECD offers interest subsidies to those who qualify. Monies are voted out by Oireachtas (Parliament), and are not available for intra-EC exports.

III. CONTACTS

Department of Tourism and Trade
Setanta Centre
South Frederick Street
Dublin 2
Tel: (353 1) 66 21 444
Fax: (353 1) 67 76 696
    (353 1) 67 76 694
Telex: 93478 TRDC EI

ISRAEL
THE ISRAEL FOREIGN TRADE RISKS INSURANCE CORPORATION (IFTRIC)

I. INTRODUCTION

The Israel Foreign Trade Risks Insurance Corporation (IFTRIC) was established in 1957 as a government-owned and supported agency that provides Israeli exporters with a range of risk-neutralizing services to promote Israeli businesses in domestic and foreign markets. In 2000, USD $6.3 billion in transactions were insured through IFTRIC.

II. PRODUCTS

Short, Medium, and Long Term

Export Credit Insurance
IFTRIC offers a series of insurance policies that provide coverage for those institutions involved in Israeli exports. IFTRIC insurance policies are implemented on a short-term basis (up to 360 days) and a medium- and long-term basis (1–15 years). Short-term foreign trade risk insurance is usually issued in the form of a comprehensive policy covering both political and commercial risks. The insurance services covered by IFTRIC cover a range of industries including agriculture, engineering, pharmaceuticals, telecommunications, and high-tech. Specific polices include:

- Specific shipment (supplier's credit): In this policy, IFTRIC insures the exporter of Israeli goods or services against the possible risks that may occur during the shipment.
- Pre-shipment insurance: Designed for export transactions of non-standard products produced for a specific buyer's specifications,

169

which, if cancelled before the shipment, can cause the exporter financial damage.

- Buyer's credit: Exporters often require immediate payment for their goods or services; however, buyers generally do not have the liquidity. In this case, a foreign buyer may take a loan from an Israeli bank. IFTRIC's buyer credit program insures the loaning bank that the buyer's loan will be repaid. This creates the liquidity needed to generate Israeli exports and insure payment and/or delivery to all parties involved.

Eligibility: The main criterion for IFTRIC coverage is the benefits to the Israeli economy that may accrue from the transaction. Coverage is given to those transactions that will further the region's economy by creating jobs, expanding capital ownership, generating net foreign income, facilitating the transfer of resources and technology, or utilizing local resources. Transactions must involve goods and/or services that are wholly or partially manufactured in Israel, with a minimum Israeli content requirement of 80 percent.

Term: Export credit can be obtained on a short-term (up to 360 days) and medium/long-term (1–15 years) basis, with possibility of renewal.

Coverage: In all cases, IFTRIC export insurance polices cover up to 90 percent of the transaction value. The specific percentage of cover for each transaction depends on the nature of the buyer and the designated country. Short-term transactions are covered by a comprehensive policy covering both the political and commercial risks involved. Commercial risks include bankruptcy, cash-flow difficulties, and similar nonpayment situations. Political risks involve macro circumstances that are not under the control of the exporter such as war, rebellion, disasters, and other similar situations. For medium- and long-term credit, IFTRIC insures transaction over a year against political risks. Medium- and long-term contracts are considered on a case-by-case basis involving specific policies that are tailored to the transaction.

Fees: Rates are also tailored to the specific transaction and nature of goods exported. All IFTRIC contracts require a down payment from the buyer of 15 percent of the value of the transaction.

Bank Guarantees

IFTRIC works with the Israeli government in issuing short-, medium-, and long-term guarantees for loans given by Israeli banks to Israeli exporters. Bank guarantees (working capital, factoring, shipments, and performance guarantees) are offered to those Israeli institutions looking to fund exports and/or services in foreign markets. Guarantees are given to insure the Israeli lender (bank) that it will be paid back the amount specified in its contract for up to 100 percent of the loan.

Eligibility: Coverage is given to those transactions that will further the region's economy by creating jobs, expanding capital ownership, generating net foreign income, facilitating the transfer of resources and technology, or utilizing local resources.

Transactions must involve goods and/or services that are wholly or partially manufactured in Israel, with goods containing an Israeli 80 percent minimum content value. Guarantees are given only to Israeli-owned or controlled banks.

Terms: The maturity for short-term guarantees is generally up to half a year, but can be extended. For medium- and long-term guarantees the maturity is generally up to five years for capital goods and construction projects.

Coverage: The government and IFTRIC share the risk in issuing guarantees through a joint program. In most cases the government will provide coverage up to 95 percent, while IFTRIC covers the remaining 5 percent. Both political and commercial risks can be included with IFTRIC guarantees, but polices are determined on a case-by-case basis.

Fees: Interest rates are also determined on a case-by-case basis and are tailored to the specific nature of the transaction. IFTRIC generally issues an administration fee and other fees may apply depending on the nature of the transaction.

Bateman Middle East

In December 2001, an Israeli-based gas and oil company called Bateman Projects Ltd., a subsidiary of Bateman Middle East, signed a USD 158.5 million contract with IFTRIC for the design, supply, and management of a booster compressor station for natural gas in Uzbekistan. The project was financed on guarantees from IFTRIC and the U.S. Ex-Im Bank, with the initiative completed within two years. The Israeli company has general control over the project, operating the supply of parts while advising Uzbeki workers on-site.

Investment Insurance

IFTRIC offers investment insurance to those projects that will further Israel's economic development by expanding capital ownership, generating net foreign currency income, facilitating the transfer of resources and technology, or utilizing local resources.

Eligibility: To qualify for IFTRIC investment insurance a company must be domiciled and registered in Israel, or an overseas subsidiary controlled by an Israeli company. The investment must obtain the necessary approval of the host country and the required approval of the investment by the Bank of Israel. The main criterion for providing cover for any investment is the benefit that could accrue to the Israeli economy and to the business development of the investing Israeli company. The following types of investment are eligible to be included in IFTRIC investment insurance:

- Industrial or agricultural enterprises that increase the production ability of the host country, whose products are designed for export or import substitution and that are based on the regular supply of raw materials, semi-finished products, or knowledge from Israel
- Subsidiaries of Israeli exporting firms that function as a marketing pipeline for Israeli products in the host country
- Infrastructure enterprises in the fields of energy, communications, or medicine, based on the export of equipment from Israel
- Industrial or agricultural enterprises based on the export of equipment and knowledge from Israel
- Tourism enterprises, such as hotels, that are designed to increase incoming tourism to the host country
- Banks that are likely to intensify commercial contact between Israel and the host country or a third country in the region

Terms: IFTRIC will provide coverage for up to six years with a possibility of renewal if necessary.

Coverage: Coverage is decided on a case-by-case basis, but IFTRIC provides coverage for up to 90 percent of the value of the investment. IFTRIC's policy covers most political risks including nationalization, confiscation, war, hostile acts, uprising, revolution, riots, or other events that may occur outside the policyholders' influence.

Fees: Premiums are determined on a case-by-case basis depending on the nature of the investment, but are generally levied at up to 1.2 percent per annum of the amount of the investment covered. The size of the premium will be determined according to the economic situation of the host country and the extent of the proposed cover.

III. CONTACTS

IFTRIC
Main Office
65 Petach Tikva Rd., P.O. Box 20208
Tel Aviv 61201, Israel
Tel: 972-3-5631700
Fax: 972-3-5631708
Internet: www.iftric.co.il
Email: iftric@iftric.co.il

Uri Bernstein
Managing Director
Tel: 03-5631-1782
Email: uri_b@iftric.co.il

Bene-Zion Yaffe
Deputy Managing Director
Tel: 03-5631-1746
Email: benzi_y@iftric.co.il

JAMAICA
NATIONAL EXPORT-IMPORT BANK OF JAMAICA LIMITED (EXIM BANK)

I. INTRODUCTION

Established in 1986, EXIM Jamaica continues the functions previously administered by the Jamaica Export Credit Insurance Corporation. EXIM Jamaica is fully owned by the government of Jamaica and mainly focuses on trade financing and export credit. In 2001 EXIM Jamaica held over USD 51 million, a 13 percent growth from the previous year.

II. PRODUCTS

Short Term

Local Currency Short-Term Working Capital Loans
Available for exporters only, these short-term revolving discounting facilities are available on a pre-shipment and post-shipment basis. The export credit facility can finance up to 80 percent of the C.I.F. value of a shipment already made for a maximum

period of 120 days. Similar is the banker's export credit facility, which allows EXIM Jamaica to act as a mezzanine institution. Pre-shipment loans can cover up to 65 percent of the F.O.B. value of an order, and are for a maximum of 90 days. Post-shipment financing is limited to 80 percent of the C.I.F. value of a shipment already made and are granted for a maximum period of 120 days on a revolving basis.

Export Factoring Program

This facility is operated in conjunction with Sun Trust Bank (U.S. and Canadian markets) and Hong Kong Shanghai Bank (European markets). Through this facility, EXIM Jamaica purchases a company's export receivables on a recourse and nonrecourse basis. Eligible companies are those that export to the United States, Canada, and the United Kingdom. Advances are provided for up to 80 percent of the invoice value, and are granted for a maximum period of 120 days at an interest of 10- to 12 percent per annum. Factoring does not require a commercial bank guarantee, but exporters are required to demonstrate creditworthiness.

Long Term

Modernization Fund for Exporters

This fund was created to respond to the needs of the exporting sector to modernize their businesses. Loans are to be used for acquisition of capital equipment needed for retooling, refurbishing, and efficiency improvement. The maximum loan amount is J$25 million (USD 500,000), with an interest rate of 12 percent per annum on the reducing balance. These loans can be made in either local or foreign currency.

Export Credit Insurance

This insurance covers the exporter from the risk of nonpayment by a foreign buyer. There are two types of policies available: the shipments policy (that relates to the export of goods only) and the services policy (that covers services rendered overseas). The insurance covers up to 85 percent for commercial risks, and up to 90 percent for political risks.

EXIM Jamaica Supports Agro-Processors

EXIM Jamaica launched a special $20 million loan scheme to help agro-processors who supply goods to exporters. Under the scheme, to be operated in conjunction with export trading houses, agro-processors benefit directly from working capital loans from EXIM Jamaica. The loan scheme is beneficial to small- and medium-sized producers who supply goods for export, but who are not direct exporters.

This scheme gives the export's supplier access to funding at concessionary rates of interest, and also helps to ensure consistency and reliability of Jamaican export products. The agricultural sector and small farmers are expected to benefit significantly.

III. CONTACTS

National Export-Import Bank of Jamaica Limited (EXIM Bank)
P.O. Box 3
48 Duke Street
Kingston, Jamaica, West Indies

Mrs. Pamella McLean
Managing Director
Tel: (876) 922-9690-9
Fax: (876) 922-9180-3, 1 (800) 225-5288
Email: pmclean@eximbankja.com
Internet: www.eximbankja.com

LUXEMBOURG
SOCIETE NATIONALE DE CREDIT ET D'INVESTISSEMENT (SNCI)

I. INTRODUCTION

There are two organizations that offer export credits, insurance, and guarantees. The Societe Nationale de Credit et d'Investissement (SNCI) provides medium-term loans and the Office du Ducroire (ODL) provides insurance. SNCI is a public banking institution created in 1997. SNCI's financing operations are designed to promote economic development. As of December 21, 2000, the SNCI's own resources (paid-up capital, reserves, and provisions for general banking risks) stood at EUR 401 million (USD 391 million). The ODL was created in 1961 under the authority of the Ministry of Finance. Its objective is to improve Luxembourg's economic and financial relations by supporting exports, imports, and international investments. In 2001, ODL insured 3,000 operations, amounting to EUR 300 million (USD 292.8 million), an increase of 6.8 percent from the previous year. ODL's current capital is EUR 40 million (USD 39 million).

II. PRODUCTS

Short Term

ODL's main activity in this area is to insure commercial and political risks except for transactions in the following countries: EU countries, Australia, Canada, Iceland, Japan, New Zealand, Norway, Switzerland, and the United States. ODL offers the following policies: global policy, SME policy, and multinational policy.

Global Policy

This policy is designed for all Luxembourg enterprises or those that have a connection with a Luxembourg enterprise. This policy covers commercial operations with repayment terms of up to 180 or 360 days, depending on the products.

Specifications
The political risks covered are losses due to moratorium on payments, nontransfer, war, revolution, prolonged mass strikes, natural disasters, protracted default of a public buyer, and decisions of Luxembourg authorities that prevent the carrying out of an established export contract. The commercial risks covered are bankruptcy, insolvency, and protracted default. Commercial risk coverage is up to 95 percent if it is a public debtor, 90 percent if it is private debtor, and 95 percent if the guarantor is a bank. Political risk coverage is 95 percent.

Contract Insurance

This policy is designed to insure transactions of machines or production goods used by companies in Luxembourg. This insurance is for enterprises located and operating in foreign countries that provide "ready to use" products to Luxembourg companies.

Specifications
The policy covers the risk of infringement on the right of ownership: the exporter legally remains owner of the raw materials or the semifinished products it dispatches and/or of the hardware that it lends to companies located abroad. The political coverage is up to 95 percent, and commercial coverage is up to 90 percent.

Medium and Long Term

The SNCI does not provide the complete financing for investment projects or export transactions but—with risk-sharing in mind—seeks instead to ensure an appropriate balance between the various sources of finance available. Its approach is therefore one of co-financing with the private banking sector. As a rule, SNCI loans cover on average 25 percent of the cost of industrial projects, and up to 75 percent of the eligible investment incurred by young craftsmen, traders, hoteliers, or restaurant owners starting out in business for the first time. SNCI is responsible for granting equipment loans, innovation loans, medium- and long-term loans, and export credit. The latter is granted at a preferential rate based on the special refinancing costs enjoyed by the SNCI.

Export Credit Loans

For export credit to be granted, the seller and the buyer must have concluded a contract that sets out all the financial terms of the transaction. Export credit may, in particular, take the form of supplier's credit or buyer's credit. The products that these loans cover are capital goods or services manufactured or provided by enterprises established in Luxembourg. Where such products and/or services are part of a composite package of which one component is of foreign origin, SNCI financing is, in principle, restricted to that part of the package that is of Luxembourg origin.

Terms: The currency of the loan may be in euros or foreign currencies. The duration of the loan is a minimum six months and a maximum of five years. The maximum duration may be extended to ten years.

Cover: The loan may cover the value of the order, less the minimum advance laid down by international standards. SNCI financing may cover between 25 and 75 percent of the eligible value of the transaction to be financed. In practice, SNCI refinances 50 percent of the export credit granted by the intermediary bank. Credit insurance from the Office du Ducroire is required in order to cover export credit. A special SNCI guarantee fund covers possible losses on the share of credit not covered by the Office du Ducroire.

III. CONTACTS

Societe Nationale de Credit et d'Investissement (SNCI)
7, rue du Saint Esprit
L-1475 Luxembourg
Postal Adress: B.P. 1207 L-1012 Luxembourg
Tel: (352) 461971
Fax: (352) 461979
Email: snci@snci.lu
Internet: www.snci.lu

Office du Ducroire (ODL) L-2981 Luxembourg
Tel: (352) 423939 -320
Fax: (352) 438326
Email: odl@cc.lu
Internet: www.ducroire.lu

SNCI:
Georges Schmit
Chairman
Tel: 352 46 19 71-21

Georges Bollig
General Manager
Tel: 352 46 19 71-23

Industrial Department:
Marco Goeler
Tel: 352 46 19 71-26

Marc Weber
Tel: 352 46 19 71-27

SME Department:
Jean Schroeder
Tel: 352 46 19 71-31

Marc Steyer
Tel: 352 46 19 71-25

Secretariat:
Marie-Anne Schetgen
Tel: 352 46 19 71-22

Pascale Theis
Tel: 461971-31

MALAYSIA
MALAYSIA EXPORT CREDIT INSURANCE BERHAD (MECIB)

I. INTRODUCTION

Created in 1977 as a joint venture with the Malaysian government, MECIB is the official export agency of Malaysia. MECIB supports the exports of goods and services, investments overseas, and the opening of nontraditional markets to Malaysian companies through providing export and domestic credit insurance and guarantees. MECIB is supported by over USD 482 million in assets and covered RM 825.3 million (USD 217.3 million) in exports last year.

II. PRODUCTS

Short Term

MECIB offers a short-term (up to one year) export/trade credit insurance policy including a comprehensive plan that covers both the commercial and political risks associated with Malaysian foreign trade.

Export/Trade Credit Insurance (Comprehensive Policy)

Under its short-term comprehensive policy, MECIB covers risks associated with nonpayment by the buyer for goods and/or services wholly or partly manufactured in Malaysia (30 percent Malaysian content requirement), such as raw materials, consumer goods, and consumer durables, being traded on credit terms not exceeding 180 days. Within the comprehensive coverage, MECIB provides two types of policies:

- Comprehensive policy (sshipments): Provides full coverage to the exporter from the date of the shipment.
- Comprehensive policy (contracts): Provides full coverage from the date of the contract.

Risks covered under the MECIB short-term comprehensive insurance policies include the commercial risks of buyer insolvency, payment default, and buyer failure to accept goods, along with the economic/political risks of blockage, delay, imposition or cancellation of import license, war, and any other cause of loss beyond the exporter's control.

Specifications
Eligibility for MECIB comprehensive policy requires creditworthiness of both the exporter and country of destination. The supplier must be a Malaysian-controlled company, and the goods/services must satisfy the minimum 30 percent Malaysian content requirement. MECIB provides up to 90 percent coverage for commercial-related loss, and up to 95 percent for loss resulting from economic/political risks. The MECIB comprehensive policy carries an average interest rate of 5.5 percent, and Malaysian exporters are only eligible once an irrevocable letter of credit

(ILC), documents against payment (DP), documents against acceptance (DA), and an open account (OA) have been issued.

Medium and Long Term

MECIB provides medium- and long-term coverage for Malaysian exporters/investors involved in the transfer of high-value capital goods and services. The medium-term coverage that MECIB provides ranges from one to four years, and long-term coverage policies range between two and ten years.

Guarantees for Banks

MECIB offers bank guarantees to insure the Malaysian lenders against the nonrepayment of medium- and long-term credit contracts involving high-value capital goods and services. Guarantee programs cover the commercial and political risks for up to 100 percent of the principal amount including interest. Bank guarantee agreements are made with the lending institution and MECIB. If the foreign buyer defaults on its loan repayments, then MECIB will make direct payments to the owed lending institution.

Specifications

To be eligible for a bank guarantee, MECIB requires that the loan be in support of a cash contract with minimum value of RM 2 million (USD 527,000), and that the contract should be for at least two years but not exceed ten years. The goods and services transferred must have a minimum Malaysian content of 30 percent and the supplier/contractor must be a Malaysian-controlled and incorporated company. The cost of coverage is generally between 0.15 and 0.5 percent of sales depending on the nature of the transaction.

Bond Insurance

MECIB offers up to 100 percent coverage for medium/long-term bond indemnity support for contracts involving projects of high-value capital goods and services. Bid/tender bonds carry a 1.25 percent interest rate, while all others (advance payment bonds, performance bonds, retention bonds, progress payment bonds, and warranty bonds) carry a 1.5 percent interest rate.

Specifications

To qualify for the MECIB bond indemnity support guarantee, the contract must be valued at RM 1,000 (USD 264,000) or more, have cash or near cash payment terms, be accepted by MECIB for credit insurance, and have a risk coverage period specified by MECIB.

Overseas Project Insurance/Finance

MECIB offers Malaysian companies the ability to be involved in long-term joint and independent overseas investments in manufacturing, infrastructure, port development, telecommunications, and other sectors that promote the utilization of Malaysian goods and services. Projects that involve strategic exports are given priority, though each contract is dealt with on a case-by-case basis. Strategic industries include the exports of capital goods, Malaysian-made vessels, power generation projects, telecommunications, and information technology. MECIB will finance projects up to 85 percent of project costs or contract value depending on the contract's nature. MECIB will insure projects up to 90 percent against both commercial and political risks.

Specifications

MECIB requires a contract value minimum of RM 2 million (USD 527,000), with a length of between three and ten years. To be eligible for project finance, the supplier/contractor must be a Malaysian-controlled and incorporated company. The capital goods, intermediate goods, manufactured goods, and services to be exported must satisfy the minimum 30 percent Malaysian content requirement.

MECIB-Malaysia

In August 1997, MECIB signed an indemnity agreement with Compagnie Bancaire De L'Afrique Occidentale of Senegal to provide indemnity to Malaysian exporters. "Before this, Malaysian exporters were not very confident of exporting to non traditional countries in Africa and they have to be extra careful with corresponding banks there," said MECIB general manager Mohd Noordin Abbas. The agreement encouraged Malaysian exporters to export their goods to Senegal on irrevocable letters of credit.

The irrevocable letters of credit was a deferred payment issued for up to 180 days for USD 5 million. MECIB's agreement encouraged the export of Malaysian-manufactured products and palm oil to the nontraditional market in West Africa.

III. CONTACTS

Head Office:
Malaysia Export Credit Insurance Berhad
(32522-U) Level 17, Bangunan Bank Industri, Bandar Wawasan,
    No 1016, Jalan Sultan Ismail, P.O. Box 11048, 50734 Kuala
    Lumpur, Malaysia
Tel: (603) 2691 0677
Fax: (603) 2691 0353
Internet: www.mecib.com.my
Email: mecib@mecib.com.my

Regional Office (North)
Tel: 604-332-1862
Email: ron@mecib.com.my

Regional Office (South)
Tel: 607-223-1191
Email: ros@mecib.com.my

MEXICO
BANCOMEXT
BANCO DE COMERCIO EXTERIOR, S.N.C.
ENGLISH: MEXICAN BANK FOR FOREIGN TRADE

I. INTRODUCTION

BANCOMEXT was founded in 1937 to promote and finance foreign trade and foreign direct investment, excluding oil products.
BANCOMEXT is wholly-owned by the Mexican government. Its
principal activities are granting export- and import-related credits, as well as issuing guarantees, to assist Mexican companies
engaged in foreign trade. In 2001 BANCOMEXT's assets
amounted to USD 10 billion with a net worth USD 711 million.
BANCOMEXT has 34 regional and state offices, and a network of
42 representative offices located in 30 countries.

II. PRODUCTS

Short Term

Working Capital Credit
This credit is for the purchase or payment of production materials and services that are part of final production cost. The financing can be used for raw materials, wages, and other production

expenses, etc. There is also a working capital credit for small exporters (up to USD 50,000).

Terms: Up to 70 percent of the cost of the invoices, orders, and/or contracts, or up to 100 percent of the production cost, can be financed. The term of the credit is set according to the production cycle of each business. On a case-by-case basis longer terms can be accepted. The loans could be denominated either in dollars or Mexican pesos.

Export Sales Financing

This program allows exporters to extend credits to the buyers of their goods and services.

Terms: The maximum amount that can be financed is 90 percent of the cost of the invoices, orders, and/or contracts of short-term sales. In the case of long-term sales, 85 percent of the cost of the invoice or 100 percent of the national content produced, whichever is less, can be financed.

Eligibility: Direct and indirect exporters.

Basic Product Import Financing

This credit is designed to finance the payment of basic products or livestock coming from the United States. This is done through the lines of credit that BANCOMEXT has with U.S. banks or foreign banks with offices in the United States, with the guarantee of the Commodity Credit Corporation.

Terms: The term of the loan can be up to 180 days from the date of the negotiation of the irrevocable letter of credit. Terms 360 days can be granted depending on the operation. If the credit is in dollars the repayment is made in one payment at the maturity of the loan. In Mexican pesos the repayment is made each semester.

Eligibility: Importers of U.S. agricultural products.

Post-Shipment Guarantee

This guarantee protects exporters from the risk of nonpayment by the buyer for their products and services. The guarantee covers nonpayment due to political risks like the cancellation of the authorization to import, changes in the legislation on imports of the buying country, impossibility of import due to war, inconvertibility of the currency of the importing country, or nontransferability of the buyer's funds.

Terms: For political risks, up to 90 percent of the total net loss. The guarantee is good for one year.

Eligibility: Direct or indirect exporters.

Export Credit Insurance

This insurance protects exporters against the risks of nonpayment by the buyer for their products, as a consequence of certain commercial risks. These can include insolvency and extended nonpayment.

Terms: The insurance covers up to 90 percent of the net total loss and is good for one year.

Eligibility: Direct and indirect exporters.

Export Receivables Automatic Discounting

Through this service, BANCOMEXT provides automatic financing based on export receivables, discounting the documents that have nonpayment insurance.

Terms: The term of each individual discounting operation cannot exceed 360 days. The total amount that can be contracted is based upon projected sales, while the total amount per operation depends on the risk coverage on each letter of credit.

Eligibility: Direct or indirect exporters that have an insurance policy, or with risk coverage given by a financial institution accepted by BANCOMEXT.

Long-Term

Imported Equipment Financing

This credit is designed to help Mexican exporters to purchase imported equipment or machinery to improve their productivity, taking advantage of the lines of credit established by the ECAs of many countries.

Terms: The term of the loan can be up to five years and is established based on the projected cash flow from the project. The repayment is made each semester and is also based upon the cash flow. The financing can cover up to 85 percent of the cost of the machinery to be purchased.

Eligibility: Direct and indirect exporters or firms that import the equipment to increase their production capabilities.

Buyer Credit

This credit allows Mexican exporters to sell products and services abroad with financing for the buyer. The exporter eliminates the payment risk and the need to fund the operation by receiving the payment up front.

Terms: For immediate consumption products the term is up to 360 days. For durables the term is up to two years. For capital goods and services, the term is up to five years.

The amortization schedule, principal and interests, can be on a quarterly, semiannual, or annual basis according to the requirements of the operation.

Percentage of financing: Up to 100 percent of invoice value within a one-year term; up to 100 percent of Mexican content for more than a one-year term; up to 85 percent if the Mexican content is greater than 70 percent.

Eligibility: Importers of Mexican goods and services. There must be a minimum of 30 percent Mexican content.

BANCOMEXT has opened up lines of credit with several banks in Bolivia, Costa Rica, Guatemala, Republica Dominicana, BCIE, Colombia, Peru, Uruguay, and Venezuela that are available for the Mexican exporters as well as Latin American buyers.

Project Finance

Through this credit, BANCOMEXT finances the creation of new projects, or the modernization or enlargement of existing ones.

Terms: The credit can cover up to 50 percent of the total amount to be invested in a new project, or up to 85 percent for the modernization or enlargement of one that already exists. The term of the loan can be up to 10 years based upon the projected cash flows of the project. Longer terms of up to 20 years are also possible but are decided on a case-by-case basis. The repayment of the loan is made each month, quarter, semester, or year, depending upon the cash flows.

Eligibility: Projects in Mexico or abroad that will be executed by Mexican companies.

Equipment Financing

This credit helps Mexican companies to acquire the machinery and equipment they need to improve their production capacity and competitiveness in the international marketplace. This may include production process-related machinery, packaging tools, and transportation equipment.

Terms: The term can be up to seven years long without a grace period. The credit can cover up to 85 percent of the total cost of the machinery or equipment, and repayment can be made each month, quarter, or semester.

Eligibility: Producers of goods for direct or indirect export, or that substitute imports.

BANCOMEXT Success Story

BANCOMEXT provided financial support for the acquisition of Mexican urban buses by the government of the city of Guatemala through the line of credit established with the Central America Bank of Economic Integration.

III. CONTACTS

In the United States:
Trade Commission of México
375 Park Avenue, 19th floor
New York, NY 10152
Tel: (212) 826-2916

In Mexico:
Camino a Santa Teresa # 1679
Jardines del Pedregal
Delegacion Alvaro Obregon, Mexico 01900 DF
Tel: 52 5 481 6042
Fax: 52 5 481 6157
Internet: www.bancomext.gob.mx
Email: guarantee@bancomext.gob.mex
           ctapia@segbxt.com.mx

Abel Jacinto I.
Deputy President of Business Promotion
BANCOMEXT
Tel: (52 55) 54-81-60-23
Fax: (52 55) 5481-66-36
Email: ajacinto@bancomext.gob.mx

Ramón García Torres
General Director / Insurance Division
Seguros BANCOMEXT
Tel: (52-55) 52-88-28-28
Email: rtorres@bancomext.gob.mx

Enrique Escalante Lazúrtegui
Internacional Credit Promotion Director
BANCOMEXT
Tel: (52 55) 54-81-62-32
Fax: (52 55) 5481-6036
Email: eescalan@bancomext.gob.mx

Edmundo Gonzalez Herrera
Trade Commissioner and Financial Representative of
    BANCOMEXT in New York
Tel: (212) 826-29-16
Fax: (212) 826-29-79
Email: egonzalh@bancomext.gob.mx

NEW ZEALAND
GERLING NCM EXGO

I. INTRODUCTION

EXGO is a New Zealand government agency under the administration of the State Insurance Office providing guarantee and insurance protection for New Zealand exporters and investors. EXGO programs offer coverage to contracts involved with the sale of goods and/or services wholly or partially produced or manufactured in New Zealand and provide protection against both the political and commercial risks of foreign and domestic defaults.

II. PRODUCTS

EXGO financing programs include short-, medium-, and long-term programs, including credit insurance for exporters, guarantees for banks, and bond insurance.

Short Term

EXGO offers short-term export/trade credit insurance with policies ranging between 180 days to 12 months depending on the type of goods and contract arrangements. Insurance plans provide full insurance coverage for the commercial, political, and economic risks associated with New Zealand foreign trade.

Trade Credit Insurance

EXGO provides trade credit insurance protection to both exporters and buyers for the risks associated with transactions in New Zealand and overseas. Insurance policies on specific transactions are available to cover political risks alone or commercial and political risks combined.

Eligibility: EXGO requires adequate creditworthiness of both the buyer and country of destination.

Coverage: Up to 90 percent coverage is provided on contracts for the sale of goods or services wholly or partially produced in New Zealand. Terms of payment are consistent with those normal for the product in international trade.

Fees: Cost of coverage depends upon the type of business, risks involved, payment terms, the period of credit, and the creditworthiness of the parties involved. Costs are typically between 0.10 and 0.75 percent of sales. General contracts collect an average of

0.42 percent, while transactions covering export of capital goods and services are considered on a case-by-case basis. Also, an administration cost and premium for political coverage (when applicable) is levied.

Medium and Long Term

EXGO provides medium- and long-term coverage plans for New Zealand exporters/investors. EXGO provides medium-term coverage ranging from one to five years, and long-term policies for up to ten years.

Guarantees for Banks

EXGO offers bank guarantees to insure New Zealand lenders against the nonrepayment of medium- and long-term credit contracts involving high-value capital goods and services. Guarantee programs cover up to 100 percent of the principal amount including interest, and are often comprehensive, including commercial and political risks. Bank guarantees are made directly to the lending institution by EXGO, and guarantee payment if the foreign buyer defaults in its loan repayments.

Specifications
To be eligible for a bank guarantee, EXGO requires that the contract should befor at least two years with a maximum of ten years, the goods and services transferred must be wholly or partially manufactured/produced in New Zealand, and the supplier/contractor must be a New Zealand-controlled company. The cost of coverage for comprehensive guarantees is 0.15 percent, and for specific guarantees the cost is 0.5 percent.

Bond Insurance

EXGO offers up to 100 percent coverage from political and commercial risks on advanced payment performance, progress payment, and maintenance bonds. Coverage is calculated at 0.5 percent of the bond's face value. Advance payment bonds, performance bonds, and progress payment bonds collect a face value interest rate of 1.5 percent.

Specifications
To qualify for EXGO bond support guarantees, EXGO requires that the contract be for at least two years with a maximum of ten years, the goods and services transferred must be wholly or partially manufactured/produced in New Zealand, and the supplier/contractor must be a New Zealand-controlled company.

III. CONTACTS

Gerling NCM EXGO
P.O. Box 3933
Wellington 6015
New Zealand
Tel: (64 4) 472-4142
Fax: (64 4) 472-6966
Internet: www.exgo.co.nz
Email: info@gerlingEXGO.co.nz

Mr. Arthur Davis
Email: arthur.davis@gerlingEXGO.co.nz

OMAN
EXPORT CREDIT GUARANTEE AGENCY (S.A.O.C.)

I. INTRODUCTION

The Export Credit Guarantee Agency S.A.O.C. (ECGA) began in November 1991 and was charged with the role of providing export credit insurance and financing to Omani exporters. Operating as an export credit agency of the Sultanate of Oman, the agency is funded by the government of the Sultanate, allowing it to cover its financial needs and build up the necessary reserves. Among the Gulf Cooperation Council (GCC) States, the Sultanate of Oman was a pioneer in setting up its own national export guarantee and financing scheme.

The function of the ECGA is to provide insurance coverage to Omani exporters against commercial and political risks, assist exporters in commercial bank borrowings for export financing at concessional interest rates, and issue guarantees to commercial banks to grant pre-shipment financing facilities to exporters.

II. PRODUCTS

Short Term

The primary product of the ECGA is an export credit insurance policy. This policy covers export sales made on credit terms of 180 days or less. The export credit insurance policy provides the standard 80 to 85 percent protection against commercial and political risks.

Exporters may choose between two types of options. The first is a shipments policy for general consumer goods, with the credit insurance taking effect from the date of shipment. The second is a contracts policy for goods of a special design or catering for a specific market, with cover commencing from the date the contract is signed. These services are open to any Omani exporter regardless of whether they are in the industrial, commodity, or service sector.

III. CONTACTS

Export Credit Guarantee Agency (S.A.O.C.)
P.O. Box 3077
Muscat
Postal Code 112
Sultanate of Oman
Tel: (968) 771 3979/80
Fax: (968) 771 2380
Internet: www.ecgaoman.com
Email: info@ecgaoman.com

ROMANIA
EXIMBANK ROMANIA

I. INTRODUCTION

The main objective of Eximbank Romania since its beginning in 1992 has been to provide financial support to Romanian exporters and increase their competitiveness by covering commercial and political risks at levels comparable to those provided by more developed countries' export credit agencies. Eximbank's share capital is ROL 317 billion (USD 9.8 million). It is 75 percent state owned and 25 percent private owned. Romania hopes that the percent owned by private investment companies will increase in the future.

II. PRODUCTS

Export credit insurance is provided to cover both commercial and political risks. Eximbank provides cover for short-, medium-, and long-term risks. They do not provide aid finance. The policies offered for the account of Eximbank can be expressed in Romanian lei or in foreign currencies. The former may have additional cover for depreciation of the lei, provided a supplementary premium is paid. Eximbank's insurance policies are accepted as collateral by commercial banks involved in export finance.

Short Term

Export Credit Insurance

Eximbank Romania covers the commercial, political, and force majeur risks that are associated with the export of goods and services. This coverage includes the risk of nonpayment in connection with government buyers, difficulties from the debtor, protracted default, political events, ineffective legal action, delays (exceeding 180 days) in transferring foreign currency, and natural disasters.

Eximbank covers short-term commercial export credit risks for its own account, but is reinsured by a foreign export credit agency. For short-term political risks, Romania Eximbank underwrites policies for the state account. Export credit insurance is granted under a whole turnover insurance policy designed with the Globalliance contract by the Credit Alliance (of which Eximbank Romania has been a member since 1998).

Specifications
All exporters registered and established in Romania are eligible for cover under Eximbank's insurance scheme. Eximbank Romania does not specify a foreign content restriction for short-term export credit insurance, but the medium- and long-term export credit insurance restriction is 50 percent. Coverage is usually 85 percent of commercial, political, and force majeur risks. The premium rates depend on the risks covered, payment conditions, the buyer's country risk category, the buyer's legal status, and other pertinent factors. The premiums are paid in advance as a rule, but in certain cases the premium may be paid in installments. Payment can be in either a foreign currency or in the Romanian lei. If an additional premium is paid, the depreciation of the lei will be covered. Additional fees are charged for the insurance application and the issuance of credit limits.

Export-Import Credits

This program facilitates pre- and post-shipment financial responsibilities for Romanian exporters who have foreign purchase orders. For importers, export credits can be used to purchase or facilitate imports related to exporting, such as raw materials, spare parts, and equipment. Exporters have access to credit lines that are based on a pre-agreed budget.

Direct Credits

Direct credits are loans to exporters. The Eximbank has a direct liability when it decides to extend this type of support. It is for this reason that Eximbank provides short-term direct export credits on a limited basis. The Romanian Eximbank can finance up to 85 percent of the contract value to help meet pre- and post-shipment financial requirements for export contracts in execution.

Medium and Long Term

Supplier Credit and Buyer Credit

These programs were designed for the payment needs of the exporter and importer. With a supplier credit, an exporter can take out a line of credit with a bank and also make payments toward that line of credit as the foreign buyer repays the exporter for the goods or services that it provided. There are two types of policies for supplier credit, one for capital goods and another for construction work. With the buyer credit, the supplier will receive immediate payment from the bank and the buyer will repay the bank according to the payment terms agreed to with the bank.

Specifications

Terms are two to five years. The procedures for medium- and long-term cover are subject to the Arrangement and the Berne Union Understandings. Any Romanian exporter domiciled in the country is eligible for Eximbank's assistance. The medium- and long-term export credit foreign content restriction is 50 percent. Eximbank Romania will finance 85 percent of the export credit value. The interest rate will be based on the local market rate and should be paid monthly unless some other payment arrangement has been made. Eximbank Romania assesses the transaction upon the risks involved, payment terms, buyer's country risk category and credit rating, supplier's credit rating, and other pertinent factors. Payment can be in either a foreign currency or in the Romanian lei. Additional fees are charged for the application and the issuance of credit limits.

Export Credit Insurance

This program insures the exporter that the foreign buyer will pay for the exports received. The percentage of cover is usually 85 percent. There are specific medium- to long-term programs tailored for capital goods. Eximbank Romania covers the commercial, political, and force majeur risks that are associated with the export of goods and services. This coverage includes the risk of nonpayment in connection to government buyers, financial difficulties of the debtor, protracted default, political events, ineffective legal action, delays in transferring foreign currency (exceeding 180 days), and natural disasters.

Specifications

Medium- to long-term export credit insurance periods exceed one year, but are generally not longer than seven years. The structure is similar to supplier and buyer credits.

Export Financing and Refinancing for Small- to Medium-Size Enterprises (SMEs)

Eximbank has a special program devoted to aiding small- to medium-size enterprises (with up to 250 employees). With this program, Eximbank hopes to give a helping hand to Romanian companies that could not obtain financial support on the commercial market.

Specifications

Any Romanian exporter with 250 employees or less is eligible for financing or refinancing with the Eximbank. The terms are for up to five years with a one-year grace period and up to EUR 1 million. Certain commercial Romanian banks are prepared and ready to participate in this program with the Eximbank, specifically, Kreditanstalt fur Wiederaufbau-Germany.

Technical Analysis of Projects for State Guarantees

Eximbank studies the technological and economic aspects of investment projects using equipment and technology from Romania. If after the analysis the Eximbank finds the project positive, it will issue either a letter of intent or a preliminary commitment. The Eximbank will then present their findings to the Interministerial Committee for Foreign Trade Credits and Guarantees that makes the final decision. The Ministry of Finance can then issue the state guarantee.

Specifications

Any exporter or importer domiciled in Romania is eligible for cover under Eximbank. A guarantee issued for the account of the state has a maximum guarantee limit set by the Ministry of Finance. The guarantee fee is determined on the basis of the risk rating of the supplier, buyer, and the recipient country. The terms of payment and the amount of the contracts also factor into the total cost of cover. State guarantees can be issued in foreign currency in the form of a bid bond, advance payment reimbursement, and a performance bond.

Bank Guarantee Program

This program covers guarantees for imports of technology intended to develop export capacities, for nonpayment of foreign loans, as well as bid bonds, advanced payment reimbursement, and performance bonds. The guarantee for import of technology gives access to credits from commercial banks. Eximbank issues the guarantee on its behalf and on behalf of its account.

Specifications

Any financial institution domiciled in Romania and lending support to a Romanian export or export-related company is eligible for a guarantee. For its account, Eximbank will set the maximum guarantee for each transaction. A guarantee issued for the account of the state, however, has a maximum guarantee limit set by the Ministry of Finance. The guarantee fee is determined on the basis of the creditworthiness of the bank and its history of lending to exporters. The terms of payment and the amount of the contracts also factor into the total cost of cover.

Refinancing for Banks

This program was designed for investment projects in Romania. Eximbank refinances pre-qualified commercial banks with funds from external sources that the state has arranged. The banks will then be able to offer their customers more favorable terms under which to invest in Romania and build infrastructure. Refinancing is offered for export-related investment projects and for short-term export finance.

Specifications

A financially viable company from any industrial sector that is planning on investing in Romania is eligible and encouraged to apply for bank refinancing. The costs include a refinancing interest rate, an agent spread, and a commitment fee.

Interest Subsidies

This is a credit facility designed to reduce the cost of using export credits. Any Romanian export or export-related company is eligible for interest subsidies under which the company can retrieve up to 50 to 60 percent of the export credit interest paid. The export credits must be denominated in ROL in order to be covered with this budgetary fund, devoted to export output and/or complex projects abroad, and funded until payment of goods and services has been received.

The OECD Arrangement is always applied as a benchmark at Eximbank Romania and the interest subsidies product is no exception.

Project Finance for Romanian Development
Eximbank will finance up to 40 percent of the total project cost for development ventures involving purchasing buildings, land, equipment, vehicles, installations, licenses, patents, trademarks, construction, and working capital financing.

Specifications
Project finance approval depends on the ability of the project to produce revenues that can repay the loan. The Eximbank will evaluate the project in depth and this will cost the project sponsors more time and money. The assessment of the project will be more important than assessing the risks covered, payment conditions, country risk category, and sponsor's creditworthiness, but these traditional variables will also be taken into consideration. Additional fees are charged for the outside consultants used to study the project. Repayment can be in either a foreign currency or in the Romanian lei.

III. CONTACTS

Victoria Clem - Director
Insurance and Guarantee Monitoring
Tel: 336.41.80
Fax: 336.61.87
Email: vclem@eximbank.ro

Splaiul Independentei 15, sector 5
Bucharest 761042
Tel: 40 (1) 336 6162; 40 (1) 336 4186
Fax: 40 (1) 336 6380
Internet: www.eximbank.ro
Email: stragcom@eximbank.ro

Ms. Mariana Diaconescu
President and CEO
Tel: 40 (1) 336-1134
     40 (1) 336-6129
Fax: 40 (1) 336-6176
Email: mdiaconescu@eximbank.ro

Mr. Iulian Velicu
Vice-President
Tel: 40 (1) 336-1139
Fax: 40 (1) 336-6165
Email: cpvelicu@eximbank.ro

Mr. Vasile Dedu
Vice-President
Tel: 40 (1) 336-1137
Fax: 40 (1) 336-6178
Email: vdedu@eximbank.ro

Mr. Vasile Pop
Vice-President
Tel: 40 (1) 336-1881
Fax: 40 (1) 336-6166
Email: sgvpop@eximbank.ro

RUSSIA
ROSEXIMBANK

I. INTRODUCTION

The Russian EximBank is owned nearly in its entirety by the Russian government, and is the agent of the Russian Federation for realization of the state policy of support and stimulation of export.

II. PRODUCTS

The bank works primarily in export and import financing, although they are developing credit and guarantee operations.

RosEximBank's largest current financing project is a USD 150 million (EUR 158 million) contract to modernize a power plant in Bulgaria.

III. CONTACTS

RosEximBank
г. Москв 119121
3-й Неопаимовский пер.
дом 13/5, строение 1
Tel: 246-89-89
Fax: 246-37-88
Internet: www.rosexim.com
Email: reib@rosexim.com

SINGAPORE
EXPORT INSURANCE CORPORATION OF
SINGAPORE LTD. (ECICS)

I. INTRODUCTION

Incorporated in 1975, ECICS assumed the credit insurance functions of its parent company, ECICS Holding Ltd., which in turn is a subsidiary of the Singapore government holding company, Temasek Holding (Pte) Ltd. ECICS covers a range of credit insurance risks and can also provide bonds and guarantees.

II. PRODUCTS

ECICS can issue performance bonds and a host of other contract and payment guarantees. ECICS does not provide any form of direct export credit, although financing options such as factoring, leasing, and purchase facilities are available from a sister company, International Factors (Singapore) Ltd. ECIS does not offer aid finance. The coverage that ECIS offers is comprehensive. The programs include:

- Comprehensive policies (contracts covering pre-shipment and post-shipment risks)
- Comprehensive policies (shipments)
- Specific policies (covering transactions and projects on credit terms of two years or more)
- Bonds and guarantees

ECICS can provide cover on a wide range of credit risks, whether for short-term or for medium- and long-term transactions. To date, however, its business has focused largely on short-term trade (usually on credit terms not exceeding 180 days). Domestic and export credit insurance is available. Risks insured include commercial and political risks, such as insolvency of the buyer, nonpayment, transfer delay, nonacceptance (for government buyers only), and war and civil disturbances in the buyer's country.

Eligibility: ECICS credit insurance is available to any company registered in Singapore. Cover can be granted on Singapore exports and, to a lesser extent and on a selective basis, to third-country trade. Insurance cover can be given to an exporter or to a bank financing a transaction for which a guarantee has been issued by ECICS. Basic criteria taken into account in considering applications for cover include creditworthiness of the buyer, creditworthiness of the buyer's country and any conditions and limits set by ECICS on the country concerned, nature of transactions, terms of credit involved, and spread of business offered for cover.

Cost of cover: For short-term policies, a matrix of premium rates applies, depending on the assessment of country, buyer risks, terms of payment, volume of business to be declared, etc. The average premium rate at present is 0.56 percent. A minimum premium is levied at the commencement of the policy and can be refunded under normal circumstances. A claims discount is also possible at the end of each annual review of the policy if there has been good experience on claims. Credit limit applications are also charged a premium, depending on the number of applications involved, and the cost varies according to whether inquiries are on Singapore-based or overseas buyers.

Guarantees for Banks

Commercial banks financing an exporter's transactions insured with ECICS can request guarantees. Types of guarantees include unconditional guarantees and letters of assignment. Guarantees are available for buyer as well as supplier credits.

III. CONTACTS

141 Market Street
10-00 International Factors Building
Singapore 0104
Tel: (65) 272-8866
Fax: (65) 323-5093; (65) 224-0939
Telex: RS 21524
Internet: www.ecics.com.sg
Email: buecics@ecics.com.sg

SLOVAKIA
EXPORT-IMPORT BANK OF SLOVAKIA

I. INTRODUCTION

The Export-Import Bank of Slovakia (Slovak Ex-Im) was established in 1997 to support Slovak trade. By 1999, its operating capital was SKK 2.37 billion (USD 55 million). Results for 2001 show that the Slovak Ex-Im supported Slovak exports worth SKK 33.1 billion (USD 770 million), which was a 40 percent increase from 2000.

II. PRODUCTS

Short Term

Short-term coverage is extended on supplier credit insurance, individual contract insurance, commercial and political risk insurance, refinancing for commercial banks, and the bill of exchange program.

Supplier Credit Insurance

Designed for exporters who agree to a deferred payment plan with a foreign buyer, supplier credit insurance mitigates the exporter's risk and allows it to provide terms.

Specifications

Short-term supplier credit insurance covers for up to one year 75 to 90 percent of political risks and 65 to 85 percent of commercial risks. Either the lender or supplier may apply for a letter of interest, preliminary commitment, or final commitment. The average application takes six days to process.

Individual Contract Insurance

Slovak Ex-Im provides commercial and political risk insurance for the short term to individual transactions or individual cases. Most of the coverage is for either capital goods or projects.

Specifications

Similar to the supplier credit insurance program.

Preliminary Offers

These offers are designed to enable exporters to participate in public bids for contracts.

Specifications

Eximbank will cover 75 to 90 percent of the political risks and 65 to 85 percent of the commercial risks. This product will cover commercial and political risks for up to six months, but the preliminary offer insurance premium must be paid in the Slovak koruny. The premiums are set at 0.2 percent.

Refinancing of Export Credits with Commercial Banks

Refinancing a customer's credit enables the exporter's bank to obtain funds that it can use to lend to the foreign customer. Foreign buyers can consolidate debt, get more credit, and make payments on more favorable terms if the Slovak Ex-Im bank underwrites the exporter's bank for refinancing. Refinancing of import credits differs in that the bank is refinancing the credit of the exporter rather than the foreign buyer. Co-financing and direct financing export/import credit programs are also available for the short-term.

Bills of Exchange

The bills of exchange program provides financing using bills of exchange (a check is an example of a bill of exchange). The bills eligible for discounting are by a commercial bank and accepted by the exporter. Slovak Ex-Im purchases the bill for a short term, usually 90–180 days, then sells it back to the drawer prior to maturity.

Medium- and Long-Term

Medium- and long-term financing agreements are extended on supplier credit, buyer credit, and commercial and political risk insurance. The Slovak Ex-Im Bank charges a premium, but the premium can be capitalized into the loan value. Slovak Ex-Im can insure up to 95 percent of 85 percent of the eligible contract value. During construction, up to 85 percent of commercial and political risks can be covered, but the interest accrued during construction cannot be capitalized. Local content can be insured as long as half the content originated in the Slovak Republic. Medium term means anywhere from one to five years and long-term means nothing less than a five-year term.

Individual Contract Insurance

This product was designed for capital goods and construction projects that have a term of longer than 12 months.

Direct Financing, Co-Financing, or Re-Financing of Export Credit

This program lends credit to the supplier for the purchase of machinery, equipment, and investment assets that will support the manufacturing of exports.

Financing for Investments Abroad

This program provides medium- to long-term credits to support exporters' investments abroad.

Direct Financing, Co-Financing, or Re-Financing of Import Credit

This program lends credit to the supplier for the purchase from foreign exporters of machinery, equipment, and investment assets that will support the manufacturing of exports.

Direct Supplier Credit
This program was designed for the supplier so that it could receive payment immediately from the bank while the foreign buyer postpones payment. A direct loan can also be arranged in place of the supplier credit.

III. CONTACTS

Grösslingová 1
P.O. Box 56
813 50 Bratislava
Tel: (421 2) 59 39 81 11
Fax: (421 2) 52 93 1624
Internet: www.eximbanka.sk

Cooperating Banks:
Istrobanka
Polnobanka
Komercini Banka
Banka Slovakia
Prya komunalna Banka
VUB
Slovenska Sporitelna
ING Bank Bank Austria
Creditanstalt
Citibank, Ludova Banka (before assignment)

Subsidiaries of U.S. banks in Slovakia:
American Express Ltd.
C/o Tatra banka
Vajanskeho nabrezie 5
810 06 Bratislava, Slovak republic
Tel: (42/7) 2104133
          2104163
Fax: (42/7) 2103907

Citibank (Slovakia) a.s.
Viedenska cesta 5 (Incheba bldg.)
852 51 Bratislava, Slovak Republic
Tel: (42/7) 894111
Fax: (42/7) 894200

Contacts at Slovak Eximbank:
Seitzová Mária
Governor
Tel: 02-59-39-85-11
Fax: 02-52-96-55-95
Email: maria@eximbanka.sk

Libuša Kulíšková
Vice-Governor for Banking
Tel: 0-2-59-39-82-05
Fax: 0-2-52-96-56-24
Email: kuliskova@eximbanka.sk

Mgr. Alena Adamíková
Vice-Governor for Insurance
Tel: 421-2-59-39-85-14
Fax: 421-2-52-96-56-21
Email: adamikova@eximbanka.sk

Renáta Majovská
Vice-Governor for Finance and Economics
Tel: 02-59-39-82-04
Fax: 02-52-96-55-98
Email: Borgula@eximbanka.sk

SLOVENIA
SLOVENE EXPORT CORPORATION (SEC)

I. INTRODUCTION

SEC is a joint-stock company established in 1992. The Slovene government owns 91 percent of its shares, but SEC has a privatization plan that it hopes will decrease the government's share. As of December 1999, its share capital was 9.3 million Slovenian tolars (USD 40,000), and its guarantee capital was 16 billion SIT (USD 69 million). SEC is the only credit insurer in Slovenia that provides comprehensive export credit insurance and the only organization that provides whole turnover cover for domestic and export credit transactions.

II. PRODUCTS

SEC offers guarantees, financing, and insurance. Operations for its own account are short-term export credit insurance, project finance, trade finance, guarantees, and various client services. Operations for the state of Slovenia are export credit insurance for noncommercial risks, investment insurance against noncommercial risks, medium-term export credit commercial insurance, short-term noncommercial export credit insurance, and protection against exchange rate risks. SEC has concluded risk-sharing agreements with commercial creditors when it is considered desirable to limit its exposure. It may also coinsure or reinsure risks with private credit insurers. SEC's insurance business for its own account (insurance of short-term export and domestic credits against commercial risks) is operated on the basis of market principles.

Short Term

Most SEC short-term products have a limit of six months/180 days, but can be up to one year.

Insurance of Export Credits

This program was designed for companies that export on open account. SEC can insure these export companies' short-term export credit risks by agreeing to pay the exporter if a foreign buyer defaults. If a buyer defaults, then SEC will disburse the due payment to the exporter within 30 days. Normally, SEC's payment will be 85 percent of the contract value, but if the contract was made with a high-risk country, the SEC payment may be less than 85 percent. The uninsured percentage is designed to distribute the risk so that all parties have incentive to prevent a default. SEC has revolving insurance agreements with exporters on their open account sales so that each transaction does not need separate approval.

SEC offers a number of special export credit insurance programs: (1) for small- to medium-sized companies, (2) for pre-shipment only export credit insurance, and (3) for domestic credits for Slovenian importers. The export credit program for small- to medium-sized businesses has the same basic specifications as for regular export credit insurance except that SEC cooperates with a commercial bank to reduce the paperwork and cost. Pre-shipment insurance and importer's domestic credit have similar structure and specifications to the export credit insurance.

Specifications

Cover is customarily 85 percent of loss, 90 percent for commercial risks and 90 percent for noncommercial risks. Regular export credit insurance coverage is comprehensive and includes pre-shipment and post-shipment coverage. Pre-shipment, commercial, or noncommercial risk insurance is also available. The terms are up to 180 days, but consumer durables may be covered for up to one year. With revolving export credits, premiums are paid on a monthly basis for actual shipments made. The premium rates depend on volume of sale, average payment terms, payment history, the buyer's credit, the beneficiary country risk rating, and the percent uninsured. All exports are eligible. Selective cover can be provided for sales on the domestic market, one or a limited number of foreign countries, a special business sector, or individual transactions. The SEC does not specify a foreign content limit nor a domestic content minimum.

Supplier Credit

With this program, SEC finances or co-finances with a commercial bank the supplier or investor. If the foreign buyer defaults on payment, then SEC pays the claim to the exporter or the exporter's bank. This program is also available for medium- and long-term products.

Specifications

The credit can be distributed and repaid with domestic or foreign currency. In short-term cases, financing can be up to 90 percent. For co-financing, the maximum ratio for financing from SEC is 80 percent. Short-term is 180 days to one year, but this program is also offered for medium- and long-term products.

Buyer Credit

This program finances the buyer to order goods or services from a Slovenian supplier. SEC has an agreement with the exporter's bank. They agree that if the foreign buyer or foreign bank does not repay the loan, then SEC will repay the exporter's bank. Buyer credits are available for the short, medium, and long term.

Specifications

SEC will pay 95 percent if a commercial or noncommercial risk occurs. SEC will not insure against an import ban imposed by a foreign government, a one-sided breach of contract, or a confiscation of goods by the foreign state. All other noncommercial risks mentioned above will be covered.

Medium and Long Term

Insurance against Exchange Rate Risks

This insurance is offered to Slovenian exporters who already have their exports insured (i.e., this program provides supplementary insurance). For these exporters, SEC will further reduce their risk and encourage a foreign trade transaction by providing insurance against the depreciation of foreign currency. This is a flexible program in which the exporter can choose the percent coverage.

Specifications
Only offered for medium-term products. Coverage ranges from 25 to 100 percent.

Bonds and Guarantees
Bond insurance indemnifies bank guarantors and/or exporters against losses due to unfair calling of on-demand guarantees or bonds (bid bonds, performance bonds, advance payment bonds, etc.) and for fair calling of bonds owing to noncommercial risks as well. This is usually supplementary cover, an extension of normal pre-shipment and credit risk cover.

Specifications
Coverage is up to 100 percent. SEC charges a 0.1 percent processing fee [minimum of SIT 50,000 (USD 218), maximum of SIT 300,000 (USD 1,300)], and a quarterly fee, which ranges from 0.1 to 0.6 percent. All fees paid up-front are considered part of the premium if the guarantee or bond is approved. Premiums are based on the risk assessment of the buyer, supplier, and receiving country. It also depends on the type and depth of cover, the volume of the transaction, and the agreed terms of repayment. Guarantees and bonds can cover the risks of nonsigning, nonpayment of advanced payments, nonperformance of contract, failed warranty, post-shipment nonpayment, and nonpayment of customs duties. In principle, SEC insures regardless of export foreign content, but if there are many risks involved in the transaction the SEC may enforce a 40 percent maximum foreign content of the total contract value.

Guarantees for Banks
For banks giving loans to foreign buyers or banks, SEC will guarantee the banks for the loans and indemnify them by 95 percent if the buyer or foreign bank defaults on payment. The bank must bear at least 5 percent of the loss, for which it may not have recourse to the exporter or foreign financial institution. For project, nonrecourse, or limited recourse loans, SEC will provide cover for the banks on a case-by-case basis and only for defined political risks.

Specifications
Percentage of cover is up to 95 percent. The beneficiary can be either the exporter or guarantor. Terms are flexible.

Medium-Term Export Credit Insurance

Insurance cover may either be on a lease, or a supplier or buyer credit basis. In the case of a supplier credit, the insurance policy covers the risk of nonpayment of credits extended by an exporter to a buyer and is therefore issued to the exporter, who may assign the rights from the insurance policy. The buyer credit insurance policy is issued to a bank. Medium-term export transactions are generally covered through specific insurance policies covering both commercial and noncommercial risks, while whole turnover policies may be issued in exceptional cases. During the pre-contractual negotiation period, an exporter or lender may apply for a binding or nonbinding offer, which is usually valid for three months but may be extended.

Specifications
Insurance will cover exports of capital and quasi-capital goods, construction work, and certain services. Credit insurance terms may be for 5, 8.5, or 10 years, depending on the type of goods and/or services exported, the size of the contract, and the importing country. Percentage of cover is up to 95 percent. A minimum down payment of 15 percent is required.

Investment Insurance

Investment insurance (INVEST) insures Slovenian residents investing in foreign countries. Their investment can be direct or indirect, through various forms of equity, shareholder or non-shareholder loans, and loan guarantees. Banks can also be insured under SEC's INVEST programs. The investor's insurance will cover equity, shareholder and nonshareholder loans, or cash against documents.

Specifications
Standard cover is against the risks of war and civil disturbance, expropriation, and lack of convertibility/transfer restrictions, but breach of cover, denial of justice, and natural disaster can be supplemented. The investor is free to choose the percentage (90 percent maximum) and/or amount of cover for each risk. The insurance period lasts from 3 (5 in case of loans) to 15 years. Cover is given preferentially to new direct outward investments. Premiums are charged annually for the current amount of insurance.

Premiums are based on indicative premium rates established for individual risks and industries, on a case-by-case basis, taking into account the host country's risk rating and the individual investment. The premiums for a stand-by amount of insurance reserved for additional investments are lower approximately by half.

The Slovene aid program is currently limited to Southeastern Europe and is administered by the Ministry for Economic Relations and Development. The program is allocated a rather small amount of budgetary resources annually to be given as grants for eligible projects and countries.

III. CONTACTS

Financing and Guarantees Contacts
Mr. Marko Plahuta
Deputy Chairman & Executive Director
Tel: 386 1 20 07 530
Fax: 386 1 20 07 575
Email: marko.plahuta@sid.si

Insurance Contacts
Ladislav Artnik
Deputy Chairman & Executive Director
Tel: 386 1 20 07 510
Fax: 386 1 20 07 575
Email: ladislav.artnik@sid.si

Ulica Josipine Turnograjske 6
SI 1000 Ljubljana, Slovenia
Tel: 386 (61) 200-7500
Fax: 386 (61) 200-7575
Internet: www.sid.si
Email: info@sid.si

Aid finance
Ministry of Economic Relations and Development
(Economic Bilateral Department)
Kotnikova 5
SI – 1000 Ljubljana
Slovenia
Tel: (386 1) 478 35 94
Fax: (386 1) 478 35 77
Internet: www.sigov.si/meor/slo/odnosi/3bil.html
Email: info@gov.si

SRI LANKA
SRI LANKA EXPORT CREDIT INSURANCE
CORPORATION (SLECIC)

I. INTRODUCTION

The Sri Lanka Export Credit Insurance Corporation, established in 1979, operates under the Ministry of Internal & International Commerce & Food. Its purpose is to provide export credit insurance and guarantee support services for the exports of Sri Lanka using innovative and attractive methods. SLECIC provides insurance policies to exporters of goods and services against both delayed and nonreceipt of payments due to both commercial and noncommercial risks. The organization issues guarantees to banks and financial institutions in order to aid in the granting of pre- and post-shipment finance. It issues guarantees to persons and institutions abroad for goods and services from Sri Lanka. Currently, SLECIC is secured by two guarantees: one government guarantee of LKR 500 million (USD 5.2 million) and an additional guarantee of LKR 100 million (USD 1.04 million).

II. PRODUCTS

SLECIC offers several types of insurance policies and bank guarantees.

Insurance Policies
Risks Covered: The first type of risk covered is commercial risk: 64 to 80 percent coverage for repudiation of contract, 80 to 90 percent for insolvency and 80 to 90 percent for protracted defaults. The second type of risk covered is noncommercial, or political risk, which is 85 to 95 percent covered.

Bank Guarantees
SLECIC provides coverage to financial institutions against nonpayment by direct as well as indirect exporters due to insolvency or protracted default.

Export Production Credit Guarantee
This guarantee provides for manufacturers, producers, and suppliers looking to obtain finance on "liberal terms" against domestic letters of credit opened on an international export contract. The guarantee provides 75 percent coverage.

Pre-Shipment Credit Guarantee

This guarantee is available on two scales, standard and small, and is used for purchasing, packing, and processing goods for export. The standard scale guarantee has 66 2/3 percent coverage while the small scale has 75 percent coverage.

Post-Shipment Credit Guarantee

Similar to the pre-shipment guarantee, the post-shipment guarantee also comes on two scales, standard and small. It is used to assist exporters in obtaining a bill-paying facility and in the replenishment of working capital. The coverage under the standard scale is 75 percent, and under the small scale is 85 percent. However, for L/C shipments only, coverage is 75 percent.

Export Performance Guarantee

Under this guarantee, exporters are able to provide "counter-guarantees" on liberal terms. There are three provisions under this guarantee:

1. Due to director-general of customs, which helps to postpone import duty until the proceeds from exports are realized. This helps to import raw materials and export accessories.
2. Bid/performance bonds.
3. Direct guarantee, which covers ATA Carnet system for exporters participating in fairs and exhibitions abroad.

Bank Guarantee Scheme to Assist Sri Lanka Going Abroad for Employment

This is used for Sri Lankans traveling abroad, specifically for employment so that financial institutions are encouraged to provide financing for airfare. Coverage is 66 2/3 percent.

Whole Turnover Bank Guarantee Scheme Covering Cost of Passage

The purpose of this guarantee is to reduce cost of passage problems for Sri Lankans going abroad for employment. It benefits the export of services by reducing unemployment and increasing foreign exchange earnings. Coverage is 70 percent, but the coverage for commercial banks is set at 66 2/3 percent of the guaranteed loss.

III. CONTACTS

Sri Lanka Export Credit Insurance Corporation (SLECIC)
Level 4
Export Guarantee House
Nawam Mawatha, Colombo 2
Sri Lanka
Tel: 94-74-719410 - 13
Fax: 94-74-719400
Internet: www.tradenetsl.lk/slecic/#WAS
Email: slecic@tradenetsl.lk

CHINESE TAIPEI
TAIWAN
TAIPEI EXPORT-IMPORT BANK OF
CHINA (EXIMBANK)

I. INTRODUCTION

The Taiwan Export-Import Bank of China (Eximbank) was established in 1979 with the aim of facilitating export and import trade
by offering export credit insurance, the re-lending facility, and
other various kinds of financing facilities and products. It is
wholly owned by the government with a fully paid-in capital of NT
10 billion (USD 286 million) and assets of NT 119 billion (USD
3.56 billion).

II. PRODUCTS

Short Term

Short-Term Export Credit Insurance
Export insurance provides protection against political and commercial risks associated with exports or other international transactions. Political risks covered by Eximbank's insurance schemes
include war, revolution, insurrection, and expropriation; commercial risks include buyers' insolvency or protracted default.
Exporters or commercial banks lending to exporters can utilize
this product.

Specifications
Short-term export credits generally last for 180 days, but can be for
up to 360 days. Its coverage is comprehensive. Eximbank will cover
up to 90 percent of the export value. Exporters with a risky credit
whose buyers also have a marginal credit rating might have a less

favorable percent insured. Eximbank does allow for the rights of a policy to be assigned to a commercial bank for export financing.

Short-Term Safety Export Credit Insurance

Safety export credit insurance is for small- and medium-sized enterprises to cover the commercial and political risks of short-term credit sales based on document against payment and document against acceptance, as well as letter of credit (L/C) payment terms.

Specifications

For political risk, the amount insured can be up to 100 percent of the insurable amount; for commercial risk, 80 to 90 percent of the insurable amount. The insurable amount equals the export bill amount or gross value of exported goods or L/C amount. The insurance period is from the date of shipment to the date of payment received or the maturity date of the draft under the L/C.

Comprehensive General Export Credit Insurance

This guarantee covers export sales on an L/C basis against political and commercial risk that occurs either before shipment and prevents cargo from being delivered or after shipment and prevents payment from being remitted.

Specifications

For political risk, the amount insured is limited to 90 percent of the insured amount; for commercial risk, 60 percent of the insured amount; and for additional commercial risk, 50 percent of the insured amount. The insurance period is limited to one year from the date of the insurance contract.

Medium and Long Term

Export insurance covers sales of machinery, equipment, other capital goods or turnkey industrial plants on deferred payment terms ranging from one year to a maximum of ten years, up to 90 percent of invoice value after deducting 20 percent of the down payment on or before delivery.

L/C Export Credit Insurance

This product covers the political and commercial risks of the irrevocable sight L/C and usance L/C.

Specifications

For political risks, the amount insured can be covered up to 100 percent of the L/C amount, for commercial risk, 85 to 90 percent of the L/C amount. The insurance period is from the shipping date to the maturity date of the draft under the L/C.

To be eligible, risks must be manageable for Eximbank and the participants. Insurance premiums are determined by the nature of risks, such as the payment terms, insurance period requested, and an appraisal of importing countries' political and economic conditions, together with the credit standing of the importers or guarantors involved. Premiums for medium- and long-term export insurance are charged on a case-by-case basis.

Comprehensive Open Account Export Credit Insurance

This guarantee covers the political and commercial risks based on O/A (open account) payment terms.

Specifications

For political risk, the amount is up to 90 percent of the insurable amount, for commercial risk, 70 to 85 percent of the insurable amount. The insurance period is from the shipping date to the expected date of payment received.

Long-Term Overseas Investment Insurance

Overseas investment insurance covers overseas investors against losses of investment due to specific political risks. This insurance policy does not cover any loss on investment due to commercial risks.

Specifications

The percentage of coverage is up to 85 percent of the insured amount. Insurable dividends and bonuses will be limited to 10 percent of the insured share of the investment. The insurance period runs up to seven years; if approved by Eximbank, it may be extended to ten years. Premiums are charged annually on the basis of the amount insured and conditions in the investment area.

Overseas Construction Works Insurance

Overseas construction works insurance covers against foreign political or commercial risk during the period of construction up to 90 percent of the insured amount.

Specifications

For payment and costs incurred, the insurance period runs from the date when construction and engineering or technical service begins to the date of final reimbursement. For equipment delivered to the workplace, cover runs in periods of one year, starting from delivery. Premiums consist of prime fees and deviance fees. For payment and costs incurred, prime fees are 0.46 percent for the first three months, and 0.195 percent for every additional three months. For equipment, prime fees are 0.45 percent a year. Deviance fees are charged in accordance with country risk.

Guarantees

Eximbank offers protection against risks on debt obligations acquired by Republic of China (ROC) exporters, importers, and overseas investors. Guarantees provided are mostly for medium- and long-term transactions. Cover is 100 percent of the guarantee amount stipulated in a contract.

Overseas construction guarantees are offered to ROC contractors engaged in overseas construction projects. Import guarantees are provided to foreign suppliers to insure repayment purchases by firms in ROC.

Vessel export guarantees are offered to help ROC shipbuilders export ships, by certifying repayment if shipbuilding contracts are not fulfilled. Turnkey plant export guarantees are provided to foreign buyers to assure them that the turnkey plants will be punctually delivered, installed, or tested.

Overseas investment guarantees are provided to ROC enterprises to assist in raising working capital for investments abroad through loans from banks located abroad.

Specifications

Risks must be acceptable. Fees normally are up to 0.5 percent of the guarantee amount, depending on the nature of each case.

Re-lending Facility

Taipei's re-lending facility creates bank-to-bank arrangements between Eximbank and commercial banks. Under these arrangements, Eximbank provides lines of credit to foreign financial institutions for re-lending to their eligible clients to purchase Taiwanese manufactured goods on a fixed or floating interest rate.

Specifications

Intermediaries are selected on a case-by-case basis. Credit lines do not usually exceed USD 2 million. Financing covers up to 85 percent of the gross purchase price of each eligible transaction for a period ranging from six months to five years. Repayment of interest is on a semiannual basis, beginning six months from the date of disbursement. Repayment of principal is scheduled in approximately equal semiannual installments, starting 12 months from the date of disbursement. Prior commitment is required for a total Eximbank financing that exceeds USD 250,000, but no commitment fee is charged. Interest rates applicable to Eximbank's financing programs depend on the denomination of currency (either Taiwanese dollars or U.S. dollars), the type of program, and repayment terms. For medium- and long-term export credits on a U.S. dollar basis, Eximbank generally applies the minimum Arrangement interest rates for export credit uniformly to Category III countries.

III. CONTACTS

8th Floor, No 3 Nan Hai Road
Taipei, Taiwan
Tel: 886 (2) 2321-0511
Fax: 866 (2) 2394-0630
Telex: 26044 EXIMBANK TAIPEI
Internet: www.eximbank.com.tw/english/default.html
Email: eximbank@eximbank.com.tw

Head Office
Tel: 886 (2) 2321-0511
Fax: 886 (2) 2394-0630

Taipei Branch
Tel: 886 (2) 8780-0181
Fax: 886 (2) 2723-5131

Kaohsiung Branch
Tel: 886 (7) 224-1921
Fax: 886 (7) 244-1928

Taichung Branch
Tel: 886 (4) 2322-5756
Fax: 886 (4) 2322-5755

Offshore Banking Branch
Tel: 886 (2) 2321-0511
Fax: 886 (2) 2394-0630

Thailand
Export-Import Bank of Thailand

I. INTRODUCTION

The Export-Import Bank of Thailand (Ex-Im Thailand), owned entirely by the Royal Thai Government under the Ministry of Finance, offers extensive services to Thai exporters and their overseas clients. These services include insurance, direct loans, and project financing. With resources of 58 billion baht (USD 1.3 billion), Ex-Im Thailand has promoted and supported the exports of Thailand for the past six years. In 2000, the bank approved 13 projects with a total value of 1.3 billion baht (USD 29 million). It is a growing bank that has seven branches and as of March 2002 had a total of 571 employees.

II. PRODUCTS

Ex-Im Thailand adapts its programs to fit the market and meet its exporter's needs. In 2001, it announced four concentration areas for projects: (1) financial facilities for overseas investment, (2) financial facilities for Thai restaurants overseas, (3) financial facilities for overseas contract (which includes, among other things, building, renovation, decoration, machinery maintenance, machinery upgrade, and technical consultancy), and (4) long-term credit for the export of Thai capital goods. Ex-Im Thailand also offers its customers extensive services along with its financing, insurance, and guarantees programs.

Short Term

Pre-Shipment Financing
Pre-shipment financing provides working capital to Thai exporters in baht, yen, or U.S. dollars. This program provides a revolving line of credit to exporters of all kinds. Once the exporter has the line of credit agreement signed, he can find financing using a letter of credit or a purchase order. After each drawdown, the exporter must issue a promissory note to Ex-Im Thailand in the currency agreed upon. The promissory note must be in an amount that is proportionate to the L/C contract or purchase order (P/O). After the shipment of goods has been made, Ex-Im Thailand and the exporter will negotiate the export bills and use the agreed-upon currency to repay the credit. This

revolving credit line facility is convenient and advantageous for the exporter because the repayments act as a drawdown against other purchasing documents.

Specifications
It allows an exporter to produce its goods on a credit line for a term that usually does not exceed 120 days. Thailand requires a number of documents in order to qualify for pre-shipment financing. They are records of exportation and business performances, L/C, contract or P/O, company registration certificate, bank and company financial statements, and collateral documents.

Packing Credit and Direct Packing Credit
This product is funded by Ex-Im Thailand and provided by commercial banks to Thai exporters or export-related manufacturers for financing both pre-shipment and post-shipment. It provides low-cost financing to exporters in the local currency by partially funding the commercial banks.

Specifications
Exporters must apply for credit line approval from the commercial bank. The creditworthiness of the exporter is left to the discretion of the commercial bank. Exporters must also apply for eligible exporter or exporter-manufacturer oriented status with Ex-Im Thailand. This involves submitting the required, records of exportation and business performances, L/C, contract or P/O, company registration certificate, bank and company financial statements, and collateral documents.

Export Credit Insurance
This program provides exporters with payment risk coverage for all types of exports to any market. Ex-Im Thailand agrees to indemnify an exporter that fulfills its part of a supply contract but due to commercial and noncommercial risks does not receive payment for the supplies. Export credit insurance allows exporters to be more aggressive and confident in seeking out new markets and new buyers, plus it allows exporters to offer its customers more favorable terms of payment.

There are four export credit insurance programs:

- Export credit insurance for irrevocable letter of credit
- Export credit insurance for D/P and D/A
- Export credit insurance for D/P, D/A, and O/A
- Small export bill insurance (SEBI)

Specifications

Upon approval, an export credit policy, maximum liabilities, and buyer's credit limits will be assigned. The same documents previously mentioned will be required for an application.

There are differences in the coverage and terms between the four different programs. The specifics of each program is as follows:

- Export credit insurance for irrevocable letter of credit
  - The payment term does not exceed 180 days, 85 percent of commercial risks and 90 percent of political risks will be indemnified, and indemnification will arrive 120 days after the claim request.
- Export Credit Insurance for D/P and D/A, or D/P, D/A, and O/A
  - The payment term can not exceed 180 days, and 85 percent of commercial risks and 90 percent of political risks will be indemnified. If the buyer claims bankruptcy, then Ex-Im Thailand will indemnify the exporter immediately. If buyers refuse to pay, then Ex-Im will pay within 120 days of the request.
- Small export bill insurance (SEBI)
  - The terms will last for 90 days after shipment date. Seventy percent of commercial risks and 90 percent of political risks will be indemnified within 90 days after a claim request has been made.

Medium and Long Term

Term Loan for Business Expansion

This program offers working capital on a medium- to long-term basis and allows exporters to expand their production capacity. The loans can be used for factory expansion, to purchase additional equipment, invest in fixed assets, or invest in new domestic manufacturing plants. As long as the loans further exports or attract foreign capital, the projects or purchases will be eligible under the business expansion facility.

Term Loan For Machinery Upgrading

This program offers medium- to long-term loans for the purposes of upgrading, replacing or modifying used machinery. The appropriate purposes for the machinery upgrades are for environmental conservation or relocation of factories into industrialized areas.

Specifications

A business expansion loan has terms of no less than two years, but no longer than five years. The term loan for machinery upgrading has longer terms, from five to seven years. In both cases, the term agreed to depends on the financial viability of the customers and their ability to generate income. An export or export-oriented manufacturing company is eligible for both the business expansion program and the machinery upgrading program. Both programs also make their loans available in either baht or U.S. dollars.

Merchant Marine Financing

This program was designed for merchant marine businesses to finance the purchase of old and/or new ships. Ex-Im Thailand's ultimate aim was to reduce Thailand's current account deficit by promoting Thai ownership of ships. The merchant marine financing program will make Thai's export and trade business more independent and more profitable for Thailand.

Specifications

The loan is for a term of up to seven years for as much as 75 percent of the value of the ship. The loan is divided into two portions, the first half denominated in baht with an interest rate of up to 7 percent, to be paid in no more than five years, and half denominated in U.S. dollars at a market rate. Eligible businesses must show proof of registration in Thailand and have over 50 percent of capital contributed by Thai shareholders. The merchant marines must be the primary business, and the loans must be used to finance a ship that will be registered in Thailand and sailed under the Thai flag. The ships' operating period must not exceed 20 years. Other documents such as records of exportation and business performances, L/C, contract or P/O, company registration certificate, bank and company financial statements, and collateral documents may be required.

Long-Term Credit of Thai Capital Goods

This long-term direct credit program was designed to facilitate the import process for overseas business that want to purchase new or used capital goods from Thailand. Ex-Im Thailand offers two ways of extending its credit to foreign buyers, either a direct credit to the buyer or an indirect credit through the buyer's foreign bank. The buyer and bank credits are both extended in U.S. dollars.

Specifications
Loans are granted in U.S. dollars for terms of three to seven years for 85 percent of the export value of the goods.

Cambodia Air Traffic Service Company

In May 2001, Ex-Im Thailand made a USD 15,000,000 loan to Cambodia Air Traffic Service Co., Ltd. (CATS), which is 100 percent owned and operated by Samart Corporation Public Company Limited. The loan will provide the financing to build a modern air traffic control system in three Cambodian airports: Phnom Penh, Siem Rap, and Stung Treng. The financing will cover the payment for the equipment, installation, interest during construction, and pre-construction expenses.

III. CONTACTS

1193 Exim Building
Phaholyothin Rd.
Bangkok 10400
Tel: 66 (2) 271-3700
Fax: 66(2) 271-3204
Telex: 20893 EXIMBK TH
Internet: www.exim.go.th
Email: info@exim.go.th

Rama IV Branch
Mr. Vichai Harnsutivarin
Manager
Green Tower 3656/2 Rama 4 Rd., Klongton,
Klongtoey, Bangkok 10110
Tel: 0-2367-3300-6
Fax: 0-2367-3308
Map: Rama IV Branch

Sathorn Branch
Mr. Vitavas Punyalam
Manager
Empire Tower, Ground Floor
195 South Sathorn Road, Yannawa
Sathorn, Bangkok 10120
Tel: 0-2670-0300-8
Fax: 0-2670-0309
Map: Sathon Branch

Hat Yai Branch
Mr. Somchai Piyajariyakul
Manager
Sinbenjapol Building, 24 Soi P. Nataphol 2
Sripuwanart Rd., Hat Yai, Songkhla 90110
Tel: 0-7442-8722-6, 0-7422-1131-2
Fax: 0-7422-1133-4
Map: Hat Yai Branch

Pratunam Pra-in Branch
Miss Sasipa Kajitsri
Manager
125 Moo 7, Phaholyothin Rd., Chiangraknoi, Bang Pa-in,
    Ayudhaya 13180
Tel: 0-3521-9793-8
Fax: 0-3521-9802
        0-3521-9799
Map: Pratunam Pra-in Branch

Leam Chabang Branch
Mr. Somboon Wongpakdee
Manager
53/71-74 Moo 9 Sukumvit Road, Thungsukhla, Sri Racha,
    Chonburi 20230
Tel: 0-3833-0121-7
Fax: 0-3833-0128
Map: Laem Chabang Branch

TRINIDAD
TRINIDAD AND TOBAGO EXPORT CREDIT
INSURANCE CO. (EXCICO)

I. INTRODUCTION

EXCICO, established in 1980, is an agency developed by the government to provide credit insurance and financing to exporters of Trinidad and Tobago. Services are available to all qualified manufacturing and agricultural exporters. It primarily serves the areas of Trinidad and Tobago, but has begun to expand its services to the wider Caribbean and Latin American areas. EXCICO's aims are to expand export trade, aggressively enter new markets, and provide credit on liberal terms.

II. PRODUCTS

Export Credit Insurance

This product is used to protect exporters against a series of political and commercial risks. Specifically, the risks covered are insolvency of the buyer, nonpayment by the overseas buyer, import control risks, transfer and inconvertibility risks, war (within the buyer's country, civil, or with the buyer's country), diversion, and any others outside the country and out of the exporter's control.

Export Financing

EXCICO offers two types of export financing: pre-shipment guarantee and post-shipment financing.

Pre-Shipment Guarantee

This provides an advance for the purpose of raw materials, packaging, and input costs. The maximum advance available is 180 days, and liability is released upon export of the goods in question.

Post-Shipment Financing

This product aids the exporter by increasing the cash flow after shipment. It is available through EXCICO or through joint financing with commercial banks. The exporter may receive 85, 95, or 100 percent of the shipment value.

III. CONTACTS

Trinidad and Tobago Export Credit Insurance Co. (EXCICO)
Fifth Floor Victoria Park Suites (Penthouse)
14-17 Victoria Square
Port-of-Spain, Trinidad, West Indies
Tel: 868 624 0047
Fax: 868 624 0028

UZBEKISTAN
UZBEKINVEST NATIONAL EXPORT-IMPORT INSURANCE COMPANY

I. INTRODUCTION

The Uzbekinvest National Insurance Company was established by the Government of the Republic in 1994. Later in 1997, the company was reorganized and renamed the Uzbekinvest National Export-Import Insurance Company with backing from the National

Bank for Foreign Economic Activities of the Republic of Uzbekistan and the Ministry of Finance of the Republic of Uzbekistan. Today, Uzbekinvest is one of the leading insurance companies in the Republic with a wide variety of coverage and services.

II. PRODUCTS

Comprehensive Export Contract Insurance
The policy protects an exporter from failure by a foreign buyer to fulfill its payment obligations as a result of commercial or political risk. This policy is applicable to a single export contract as well as all export contracts included in the portfolio of an Uzbek exporter.

Insurance against Export Contracts Repudiation by the Foreign Buyer
This policy covers failure by a foreign buyer to fulfill its contractual obligations before shipment of goods as a result of political risks

Non-honoring of a Guarantee/Irrevocable Letter of Credit by the Guarantor of the Foreign Buyer
This policy provides insurance protection against failure by a foreign guarantor or bank issuing a guarantee/irrevocable LC to fulfill their financial obligations where the guarantor/bank has no right or basis in accordance with the terms and conditions of the guarantee or irrevocable LC to refuse payment of the sum due to an Uzbek exporter.

Buyer Export Credit Insurance for Uzbek Commercial Banks
This policy covers failure by a foreign partner, as a result of commercial and political risks, to fulfill its financial obligations for credits extended by the commercial banks of the Republic of Uzbekistan to a foreign bank or foreign buyer for payment under export contract.

Lease Insurance
This insurance protects against failure by lessee to fulfill its financial obligations caused by commercial risk.

Unfair Calling of Guarantee Insurance
This insurance policy provides insurance coverage against fair calling of payment due to political risks and unfair calling of payment under the guarantee for the performance of contract conditions, provided by Uzbek contractors to foreign customers.

Provision of Performance Bond for National Exporters (Contractors)

This is a bond for foreign partners for the performance of the contract terms and conditions on behalf of national exporters (contractor).

Investment Insurance

This insurance policy provides insurance cover against confiscation, expropriation, and nationalization of the property in a host country or inability of an Uzbek investor to send home its investments from the host country.

III. CONTACTS

Suyun Khalilov
General Manager
Export Risks Insurance Department
Tel: (99871) 133 21 74
Fax: (99871) 133 07 04
133 21 74
Internet: www.unic.gov.uz
Email: export@unic.gov.uz

ZIMBABWE
EXPORT CREDIT GUARANTEE CORPORATION (ECGC)

I. INTRODUCTION

ECGC began its operations in April 2000 as a subsidiary of the Reserve Bank of Zimbabwe. ECGC is the national export credit insurance agency, and exhibits strong ties to industry and commerce in domestic and international business sectors. It is managed by a board of directors and its main functions are to provide export credit insurance and export finance guarantees.

II. PRODUCTS

Export Payment Insurance Policy

This policy is designed to protect Zimbabwe's exporters from losses that may arise from a variety of commercial and political risks inherent in all export transactions. This protection will also enhance their capacity to compete in the international markets and enable them to break into new markets, introduce new products, and take up new buyers.

Specifications
Commercial risks, including insolvency of the buyer, protracted default of the buyer, and non-acceptance of exported goods are covered up to 90 percent. Note: Where shipments are made against letters of credit (L/C), the policy provides cover against the risks of insolvency and protracted default of the L/C issuing bank.

Political Risks are also covered up to 90 percent and include war, civil disturbances, moratorium, imposition of new import or exchange control regulations, and transfer delay.

Certain risks are not covered under this policy. These risks are insolvency or failure of any agent of the exporter, failure of the exporter or the buyer to obtain necessary authority to execute the export contract, exchange rate fluctuations, general and marine insurance risks, and trade dispute between the exporter and the buyer.

Pre-Shipment Export Finance Guarantee
This product guarantees up to 80 percent of the loss by banks due to nonrepayment by the exporter. Banks, for loans to small and medium exporters, may be granted an "enhanced cover" of up to 90 percent of the loss. Any institution that is granted the right to deal in foreign exchange by the Reserve Bank of Zimbabwe and grants pre-shipment loans to exporters is eligible to apply for this guarantee.

Specifications
Both insolvency of the buyer and protracted default of the exporter are covered under this policy.

III. CONTACTS

Export Credit Guarantee Corporation of Zimbabwe (Pvt) Ltd
15th Floor, CABS Centre, Jason Moyo Avenue
P.O. Box CY2995
Causeway, Harare
Tel: (263-4) 252800-11
Fax: (263-) 252814 / 252815 / 252819
Internet: www.ecgc.co.zw/body_products.html
Email: ecgc@telco.co.zw

Regional Export Credit Agencies

I. INTRODUCTION

AFREXIM Bank was established in 1993 to facilitate, promote, and expand trade within Africa and globally. It is able to do this by extending credit to African exporters, providing credit to exporters and importers of African goods, and providing pre- and post-shipment finance.

II. PRODUCTS

Short Term (up to 360 days)

Direct Financing Program

This program provides pre- and post-export financing. Firms must have an annual turnover of at least USD 10 million and a balance sheet of at least USD 2 million to be eligible.

Forfeiting Program

Through this program, AFREXIM purchases essential imports on a short-term basis. However this program may also be used on a medium-term basis when used to purchase export-generating or other essential equipment. The benefit of this program is that importers may receive "fixed rate tenured credits" because risk has been transferred to AFREXIM.

Long Term

Line of Credit Program

This program is for SMEs that are unable to qualify for direct lending. This provides funded and unfunded credit lines to eligible banks that act as trade finance intermediaries (TFIs) for continued lending to sub-borrowers.

Project Financing Program
This program provides support to African exporters by encouraging the importing of manufacturing equipment for essential projects. Projects that increase demand for African exports may also be covered.

Syndications Program
This program is designed as a risk-sharing program. It promotes the influx of trade and project finance to Africa. With a shared risk, international banks are more likely to fund projects in Africa.

Special Risk Program
By transferring part of the risk to AFREXIM credit risk, there is less risk on the part of banks' extended facilities. Country risk guarantees and export insurance are covered under this program.

Factoring/Invoice Discounting Program
Under this program AFREXIM buys and sells debt receivables. Typically, a local bank must guarantee payment. AFREXIM, however, does not provide collection services to the original beneficiary of the items. Also, the receivables are considered individual self-liquidating transactions.

Note Purchase/Discounting Program
Through this program, banks are issued promissory notes in international format that are guaranteed by at least one local bank.

Financial Future-Flow Pre-Financing Program
This program provides an opportunity for financing for projects that generally have a difficult time finding proper financing. "Financial future-flow" transactions are future-flow debt offerings reliant on receivables that do not come from the exporting of physical goods. This could include credit card, checks, migrant remittances, etc.

Infrastructural Services Financing Program
This program aids exporters and importers of infrastructure services by providing financing. However, financing under this pro-

gram is conditional on payment receipt from project promoters/users in Africa.

III. CONTACTS

Head Office:
World Trade Center Building
1191 Corniche El Nil
Cairo 11221
Egypt

Postal Address:
P.O. Box 404 Gezira
Cairo 11568
Egypt
Tel: + 202 5780281-6
Fax: + 202 5780276-9
Telex: 20003 AFRXM UN
Internet: www.Afreximbank.com
Email: info@afreximbank.com

Harare Branch:
Eastgate Building
3rd Floor Gold Bridge (North Wing)
2nd Street, Harare
Zimbabwe
Tel: + 263 4 729 751-5
Fax: + 263 4 729 756
Telex: 26770 AFXYBK ZW

EASTERN AND SOUTHERN AFRICAN TRADE AND DEVELOPMENT BANK (PTA BANK)

I. INTRODUCTION

The PTA Bank was formed in 1985 following the treaty that established the Preferential Trade Area (PTA), which is now the Common Market for Eastern and Southern African States (COMESA). The purpose of PTA Bank "is to act as a tool or a vehicle for contributing towards the socio-economic development of its Member States through promoting intra-COMESA trade and the economic integration of the COMESA sub-region."

II. PRODUCTS

Trade Finance Loans

PTA finances public/private sector export-related projects or "self-liquidating" transactions that generate foreign currency. Also, it provides financing for imports of raw materials into the COMESA region. The loans are given at a minimum amount of USD 250,000.

Project Finance

PTA also provides project financing through direct loans, co-financing, lines of credit to financial intermediaries, equity participation, and loan guarantees.

Direct Loans

Medium- to long-term loans are provided to projects within the member states.

Co-financing

Co-financing is provided in conjunction with local/foreign agencies. This includes other developmental institutions as well as commercial banks.

Lines of Credit

This financing provides funding to national development agencies to promote small- to medium-sized enterprises, as well as other projects considered too small for direct financing.

Equity Participation

The bank will provide an equity investment of a maximum of 15 percent of the project's share of capital of one enterprise. In this method, the bank also requires its involvement in the decision-making process of the project.

Loan Guarantees

Guarantees are accepted from certain public agencies of member states. The guarantee requires a guarantee fee, as well as a 1 percent front-end fee, and a 1 percent commitment fee per annum.

III. CONTACT

P.O. Box 48596
Nairobi
Kenya
Tel: 254 2 2712250 (8 lines)
Fax: 254 2 2711510
Telex: 22826 PTA BANK
Email: official@ptabank.org

ARAB TRADE FINANCING PROGRAM (ATFP)

I. INTRODUCTION

The Arab Trade Financing Program (ATFP) is dedicated to the development of Arab trade through supporting Arab producers and exporters. Arab countries include Algeria, Bahrain, Djibouti, Egypt, Iraq, Jordan, Kuwait, Lebanon, Libya, Mauritania, Morocco, Oman, Palestine, Qatar, Saudi Arabia, Somalia, Sudan, Syria, Tunisia, United Arab Emirates, and Yemen. The program was established in 1989 with an initial capital investment of USD 500 million. Arab financial organizations, central banks, Arab producers and exporters, and regional monetary funds all contribute to the program's capital. In addition to its financial facilities, the ATFP also offers a wide variety of information on Arab trade to all parties involved through the Intra Arab Trade Network (IATIN).

II. PRODUCTS

ATFP is focused on promoting exports of Arab goods and services through the bank's facilities. To be covered under the following ATFP facilities, goods must contain at least 40 percent Arab value added. ATFP offers its financial services through national agencies that spread throughout the Arab world and coordinate arrangements with the local banking authorities.

Lines of Credit
ATFP can refinance up to 100 percent of the lines of credit of a national agency, provided that it is confined to imports from Arab countries.

Types of Credits

Under the contract of a national agency, the ATFP may choose to refinance credits that include pre-export credits, post-shipment credits, buyers' credits, and import credits. Financing without recourse may also be arranged in case of the availability of credit insurance or a guarantee acceptable to ATFP.

Pricing & Tenors

ATFP's refinancing programs provides prices that are competitive over convenient terms. The maximum term for transactions involving consumer goods is 12 months. Other transaction terms are as follows: 18 months for raw materials, 24 months for intermediary goods, and 60 months for capital goods.

Applying for ATFP Credit

Those eligible for ATFP refinancing may contact any of the national agencies of the program, which would then apply for refinancing of the credit provided to the customer.

III. CONTACTS

P.O. Box 26799
Abu Dhabi, United Arab Emirates
Tel: (+9712) 316999
Fax: (+9712) 316793
316299
Telex: 24166 ATFP
Internet: www.atfp.org.ae
Email: atfphq@atfp.org.ae

BANCO LATINOAMERICANO DE EXPORTACIONES, S.A. (EXPORT BANK OF LATIN AMERICA) BLADEX

I. INTRODUCTION

BLADEX began under the mission of channeling funds for the development of Latin America and the Caribbean regions by providing integrated solutions for the exports in those regions. The bank receives its funding through the deposits of the region's central and local banks, credit facilities from international banks, and capital markets.

II. PRODUCTS

Country Risk Guarantees

BLADEX's financial products allow clients to guarantee up to 100 percent of their schedule of payments against country or financial risk. Country risk guarantees appeal to direct investors, exporters, and importers who want to insure their schedule of payments against government actions that may threaten payment in 23 Latin American and Caribbean countries.

Financial Risk Guarantees

Financial risk guarantees protect against currency inconvertibility and transferability as well as moratorium, confiscation, expropriation, nationalization, war, and civil disturbance. The benefits to these two guarantees include mitigation of cross-border exposure, protecting balance sheets against unpredictable events, facilitating access to financing, more competitive pricing, and increasing sales.

International Factoring

International factoring is an alternative to traditional sources of trade finance for companies that export on an open account basis, offer their clients payment terms of up to 120 days, and wish to increase their cash flow and sure payment of their export receivables. For the exporter, international factoring allows for a commitment by its local bank ensuring the payment of invoices prior to shipment, allows possible advances of up to 80 percent of the face value of the assigned invoices, and assigns the administration and collection of international invoices to a financial institution.

Trade Finance

BLADEX offers multiple types of trade finance in the short and medium term covering the import of raw materials and capital goods and pre- and post-export finance. Additionally, BLADEX offers services in working capital financing, structured finance, and capital expenditure (CAPEX) finance. Commercial letters of credit include banker's acceptances, discount of bills of exchange, and bank-to-bank reimbursements. Other BLADEX services include stand-by letters of credit, bank guarantees, documentary collections, syndicated loans, and commercial risk guarantees.

III. CONTACTS

BLADEX
Banco Latinoamericano de Exportaciones, S.A.
Apdo. 6-1497, El Dorado
Panamá, República de Panamá
Tel: +(507) 210 8500
Fax: +(507) 269 6333
Telex: 2240, 2356
Internet: www.blx.com/eng.html
Email: webmaster@blx.com

CENTRAL AMERICAN BANK FOR
ECONOMIC INTEGRATION (CABEI)

I. INTRODUCTION

The mission of the Central American Bank for Economic Integration (CABEI) is, "To promote the progress and integration of the isthmus in order to form a bloc of highly productive nations that can position itself competitively in the ever more demanding new international arena of the twenty-first century." To do this, CABEI is committed to improving social and economic development by providing credit resources and technical assistance to Central America.

II. PRODUCTS

CABEI was established in 1961 but has weathered poorly, suffering severe financial problems during the 1980s. It was not until the 1990s that CABEI finally instituted trade finance facilities. These facilities are limited to short-term rediscounting of trade paper.

Central American Program for Promotion of Non-traditional Exports

To help facilitate the export of non-traditional goods, CABEI provides financing for work and fixed investment capital for the acquisition of goods and services to support export production. The program also allocates financial resources to business involved in the export process.

III. CONTACTS

Head Office:
Apartado Postal 772
Tegucigalpa, MDC
Honduras
Tel: (504) 228-2243
Fax: (504) 228-2185
     (504) 228-2186/7
Internet: www.bcie.org/
Email: relex@bcie.org

Guatemala
16 Calle 7-44, Zona 9
Ciudad de Guatemala, Guatemala
Tel: +(502) 331-1260,65,66
Fax: +(502) 331-1457
Email: WebMail-gt@bcie.org

El Salvador
Edificio Torre Roble, 8 nivel
Metrocentro
San Salvador, El Salvador
Tel: +(503) 260-2244 al 47
Fax: + (503) 260-3276
Email: WebMail-sv@bcie.org

Honduras
Edificio Sede BCIE
Boulevard Suyapa
Tegucigalpa, Honduras
Tel: (504) 228-2182
Fax: (504) 228-2183
Email: WebMail-hn@bcie.org

Nicaragua
Plaza España
Managua, Nicaragua
Tel: + (505) 266-4120 al 23
     +(505) 266-7088 al 92
Fax: +(505) 266-4143
Email: WebMail-ni@bcie.org

Costa Rica
25 Metros al este de la Fuente de la Hispanidad
San Pedro Montes de Oca
San José, Costa Rica
Tel: (506) 253-9394
Fax: +(506) 253-216
Email: WebMail-cr@bcie.org

CORPORACION ANDINA DE FOMENTO (CAF)

I. INTRODUCTION

CAF is a financial institution composed of twelve countries in Latin America and the Caribbean, of which its principal shareholders are the five Andean Countries: Bolivia, Colombia, Ecuador, Peru, and Venezuela. Its wide customer base is comprised of public and private sector organizations, governments of shareholder countries, and financial institutions. Primarily, it acts as a liaison between industrialized countries and the international market, while financing the development of productive infrastructure, "specifically where it facilitates physical and border region integration." CAF was established in June 1970, in Caracas, Venezuela. This establishment was based upon the *Declaration of Bogota* of 1966, which outlined a program of action to implement "economic integration measures and for policy coordination among participating countries in the areas of trade, industry, finance and technical cooperation services."

II. PRODUCTS

Loans

CAF offers short-, medium-, and long-term loans to be used in any stage of project development.

Limited Recourse Lending
This type of loan is used primarily for the infrastructure sector, usually arising from government-awarded concession contracts, mining, oil, or gas projects. Typically, it is used for "build operate and transfer (BOT)" or "build operate and own (BOO)" projects.

A/B Loans and Co-financing
The purpose of this type of lending is to attract external resources to the shareholder countries by providing the "A" portion from its own funds and distributing the "B" portion to international banks

or institutional investors. This loan becomes mutually beneficial to the shareholder countries and the borrower.

Trade Finance
CAF also offers trade finance loans, primarily to support exporting operations. These are typically offered under special circumstances and as part of a "comprehensive credit relationship."

Equity Investments

CAF's equity investments developed in participation with companies and investment funds in strategic sectors, usually based on several core characteristics. These include the amount by which resources are "mobilized," the development impact on the particular region, CAF's decision-making rights, profitability, and exit mechanisms.

Investment Alternatives

CAF participates in deposit and regional bond issues, in addition to investment products. These options are obtained at interest rates comparably favorable to the international market, and are denominated in U.S. dollars. The client base consists of institutional depositors and investors in shareholder countries.

Deposits
Deposits are made in the short term (one day to one year) and consist of a minimum amount of $1 million.

Regional Bond Issues
Bond terms are three years in duration with semiannual interest payments and principal payable upon maturity. Minimum deposit is $50,000 and investments may be redeemed every six months on interest payment dates.

Investment Banking

CAF provides seven investment-banking products. They provide underwriting services, special purpose trusts, partial guarantees, corporate finance, interest-rate swaps and derivatives, financial advisory services, and political risk insurance.

Special Funds

Technical Cooperation
CAF offers, as part of its special funds, technical cooperation. Although this is primarily used for reforms in the public sector

(privatization, decentralization, etc.), it is also used as a means to promote exports. In general, this assistance comes in reimbursable, nonreimbursable, and contingently reimbursable forms.

III. CONTACTS

Head Office:
Corporacion Andina de Fomento (CAF)
P.O. Box Carmelitas 5086
Ave. Luis Roche, Torre CAF
Altamira, Caracas
Venezuela
Tel: (58212) 209-2111 (master)
Fax: (58212) 284-5754
    (58212) 284-2553
Télex: 27418, 23504
Internet: www.caf.com
Email: infocaf@caf.com

Bolivia:
Edf. Multicentro - Torre "B", Piso 9
P.O. Box No. 550
Calle Rosendo Gutiérrez, Esq. Ave. Arce
La Paz - Bolivia
Tel: (5912) 443333 (master)
Fax: (5912) 443049
Telex: 2287CAFBV

Colombia:
Edf. Corporación Financiera de Caldas
P.O. Box 17826
Carrera 7ª. Nº 74-56, Piso 13
Bogotá - Colombia
Tel: (571) 3132311 (master)
Fax: (571) 3132787
Telex: 41207CAFCO

Ecuador:
Edf. World Trade Center
P.O. Box 17-01-259
Torre A, Piso 13
Ave. 12 de Octubre Nº 1942 y Cordero
Quito - Ecuador
Tel: (5932) 224080 (master)
Fax: (5932) 222107
Telex: 22402 CAF-ED

Peru:
Ave. Enrique Canaval Moreyra No. 380
P.O. Box 18-1020, Lima 18
Edf. Torre Siglo XXI, Piso 10, Oficina 1002
San Isidro - Lima 27 - Perú
Tel: (511) 2213566
Fax: (511) 2210968
Telex: 21074 PE CAF PERU

CARIBBEAN
ORGANIZATION OF EASTERN CARIBBEAN STATES (OECS)

I. INTRODUCTION

The Organization of Eastern Caribbean States' Export Development Unit (EDU) was established in 1997. Its purpose is to develop, promote, and expand exports through financial support, specifically for manufacturing and agriculture. It has assumed the services previously provided by the Eastern Caribbean States Export Development Agency (ECSEDA) and the Agricultural Diversification Coordinating Unit (ADCU).

II. PRODUCTS

OECS provides financing in the form of pre-shipment guarantees.

III. CONTACTS

Morne Fortune
P.O. Box 179
Castries
Saint Lucia
Tel: (758) 452 2537
Fax: (758) 453 1628
Internet: www.oecs.org
Email: oesec@oecs.org

THE EUROPEAN BANK FOR RECONSTRUCTION AND DEVELOPMENT (EBRD)
EBRD

I. INTRODUCTION

The EBRD was created in 1991 when communism was crumbling in Central and Eastern Europe and ex-Soviet countries needed support to nurture a new economic environment. The EBRD uses tools of investment to help build market economies in 27 countries in Central and Eastern Europe and Asia. Through providing financing for the region's banks, businesses, industries, and investments, the EBRD helps restructure, bolster, and protect these new market economies. The EBRD is owned by 60 shareholders (58 countries, the European Investment Bank, and the European Community), and operates with EUR 20 billion (USD 19.5 billion) in capital. While it is thought of primarily as a developmental financial institution, it also is a source of export financing.

EBRD countries of operation include Albania, Armenia, Azerbaijan, Belarus, Bosnia and Herzegovina, Bulgaria, Croatia, Czech Republic, Estonia, FYR Macedonia, Georgia, Hungary, Kazakhstan, Kyrgyzstan, Latvia, Lithuania, Moldova, Poland, Romania, Russian Federation, Slovak Republic, Slovenia, Tajikistan, Turkmenistan, Ukraine, and Uzbekistan.

II. PRODUCTS

Short, Medium, and Long Term

Direct Financing

The EBRD provides direct financing for private sector activities, restructuring, and privatization as well as funding for the infrastructure that supports these activities. EBRD provides financing for both export and project investments. The main forms of EBRD financing are loans and guarantees, with an investment range generally between USD 500,000 and USD 2.5 million.

Parker Drilling Company

The EBRD made a USD 12.5 million loan to a company to be formed as a wholly-owned subsidiary of Parker Drilling Company to finance the construction and operation of three drilling rigs in Western Siberia. The loan helped to transfer modern and winterized drilling technology that was critical in reversing the decline in Russian oil production. Before the loan the company was producing around 25,000 barrels of oil per day, but after purchasing three drilling rigs and other modern oilfield technology production increased to 150,000 barrels a day.

Loans

The EBRD provides loans to selected banks in its countries of operation. These loans are structured to fund trade-related advances to local companies exclusively for the purpose of pre-shipment finance, post-shipment finance, and other financing of working capital necessary for the performance of foreign trade contracts.

Specifications

Loans are given to those projects that will further the EBRD region's social and economic development by creating jobs, expanding capital ownership, generating net foreign currency income, facilitating the transfer of resources and technology, or utilizing local resources. Loan contracts' tenor, interest rates, and fees are determined on a case-by-case basis, with creditworthiness and countries involved as determining factors. An administration fee of USD 100 is levied for consideration of all loans.

Bank Guarantees

EBRD provides guarantees to international confirming banks. EBRD guarantees cover the commercial and political risk of non-payment by issuing banks in the countries where EBRD operates. EBRD guarantees can cover up to 100 percent of the face value of the underlying trade finance.

Specifications

All international commercial banks with an established record of trade finance operations in EBRD's region of operation are eligible for guarantees. There are over 65 issuing banks in 21 EBRD countries and about 200 confirming banks throughout the world. Interest rates and contract tenors are all determined on a case-by-case basis depending on the nature of the goods and services. For example, the maximum tenor for guarantee contracts involving Albania is 180 days, while the maximum tenor for contracts in Latvia is three or more years. EBRD issues have a USD 100 administration fee for all contracts considered, but more fees apply depending upon the nature of the contract.

Kazakhstan Wheat

A guarantee program issued by EBRD supported the export of wheat from Kazakhstan to Madeira for USD 1 million. A regional bank took 50 percent of a USD 2 million transaction risk and EBRD provided its guarantee for USD 1 million. The transaction promoted the transition process by supporting a Kazakh export to a destination that had little experience of foreign trade, thereby helping to establish an export market.

Special Funds

The EBRD administers some special regional investment funds provided by public institutions and government bodies. These provide both debt and equity financing under the same approval procedures as regular EBRD investment programs. These are:

- The Baltic Investment Special Fund, promoting private sector development through SME's in Estonia, Latvia, and Lithuania.
- The Financial Intermediary Investment Special Fund, supporting SMEs through financial intermediaries in the EBRD's countries of operation.
- The Balkan Regional Special Fund, supporting SMEs and micro-businesses operations in southeastern Europe.

III. CONTACTS

Head Office:
One Exchange Square
London EC2A 2JN
United Kingdom
Tel: (44 207) 338-6372
Fax: (44 207) 338-6690
Internet: www.ebrd.com
Email: generalenquiries@ebrd.com

Holger Muent
SME Specialist
Tel: 44 20 7338 7413
Email: Muenth@ebrd.com

Ms. Yelena Tonna
TFP Administrator
Tel: 44 20 7338 6813
Email: TonnaY@ebrd.com

Rogers LeBaron
Bank Lending Department
Tel: 44 20 7338-6554
Email: generalenquiries@ebrd.com

INTER-AMERICAN DEVELOPMENT BANK (IADB)

I. INTRODUCTION

IADB is a multi-lateral institution established in 1959 for the purpose of furthering economic development in Latin America and the Caribbean. The bank has 28 member countries in the Western Hemisphere, including 18 nonregional countries. IADB policies promote the social and economic development of Latin America and the Caribbean through extended loans, guarantees, grants, and finance for the public and private capital investments of the region's businesses. In 2000, IADB financed 79 new projects (63 investment projects, 5 policy-based loans, and 11 private sector operations) for a total of $5.2 billion, resulting in a total active portfolio of 538 projects with $44.7 billion in commitments (as of December 31, 2000). Although IADB is primarily a project lender, it does offer certain programs to exporters.

II. PRODUCTS

Short, Medium, and Long Term

Latin American exporters and lenders can obtain short-, medium-, and long-term financing depending on the nature of the transaction.

Trade Credit Insurance

The purpose of IADB trade credit insurance is to facilitate the export of manufactured and semi-manufactured goods and services that will directly contribute to the economic and social improvement of the countries involved. IADB offers credit insurance coverage with policies for all terms up to 15 years. The bank's credit insurance covers both the political and commercial risks involved with Latin American foreign transactions. Short-term policies cover all raw materials, semi-manufactured, and consumer goods up to six months; medium-term polices cover all consumer durables and quasi-capital goods up to 5 years; and long-term policies cover all capital goods up to 15 years.

Eligibility: Requirements for short-term credit insurance are primarily dependent upon social and economic benefits expected from the transaction and the creditworthiness of the parties involved. The exporting company must be controlled by an IADB member country and all goods and services must be wholly or partially produced in an IADB member country.

Term: Though medium- and long-term guarantees are encouraged, coverage is provided to all term periods up to 15 years (20-year policies are available for exceptional cases).

Coverage: IADB provides coverage up to 85 percent (or 100 percent for exceptional cases) of the transaction's costs.

Credit and Political Risk Guarantees

IADB provides credit and political risk guarantees to private lenders seeking coverage for their loans to projects in Latin America and the Caribbean. Though medium- and long-term guarantees are encouraged, coverage is provided to all term periods up to 20 years.

Bank guarantees (working capital, factoring, shipments, and performance guarantees) are offered to institutions looking to fund the IADB region's exports and/or services. Guarantees are given to insure the lender (bank) that it will be paid back the amount specified its contract.

Credit Guarantees

Several types of comprehensive (umbrella) guarantees are offered to those Latin America lenders looking to fund the region's exports and/or services in foreign markets. All-risk guarantees provide coverage for the commercial risks involved in the region's foreign trade and are tailored on a case-by-case basis according to the specifications of the contract.

Eligibility: To be eligible for IADB support lenders should be funding private infrastructure projects, expanding an existing enterprise that provides infrastructure services, opening a new export market, financing debt, or developing a capital market within Latin America or the Caribbean. IADB does not have any nationality requirements for lenders, but transactions must be supporting the IADB region's economic and/or social development.

Term: Coverage is applied to all maturities of a selected loan up to 20 years, but tenors typically range between 4 and 15 years.

Coverage: IADB limits its participation in the private sector to loans with 25 percent of a project's total cost, with a per project cap of USD 75 million. For projects located in pre-specified regions, typically smaller or least developed economies, IADB offers support up to 40 percent of a project's total cost (the USD 75 million cap still applies).

Interest Rates: Loans are made at fixed or floating interest rates and are priced at market conditions. Interest rates are set considering loan term, sponsor and project financial strength, and market conditions.

Fees: Additional fees are applied depending on the nature of the loan, but generally include an analysis fee, commitment fee, one-time front-end fee, structuring fee, and administration fee.

Political Risk Guarantees

IADB offers several types of political risk guarantees covering specific risks and other noncommercial factors. Guarantees are tailored on a case-by-case basis depending on the nature of the contract.

Eligibility: Coverage is given to those transactions that will further the region's economy by creating jobs, expanding capital ownership, generating net foreign income, facilitating the transfer of resources and technology, or utilizing local resources. Transactions must involve goods and/or services that are wholly or partially manufactured in IADB countries of operation.

Term: Political risk guarantees typically range between 4 and 15 years, though 20-year policies are available.

Coverage: IADB political risk coverage extends up to 50 percent of project costs or USD 150 million, whichever is less.

Interest Rates: Loans are made at fixed or floating interest rates and are priced at market conditions. Interest rates are set considering loan term, sponsor and project financial strength, and market conditions.

Fees: Additional fees are applied depending on the nature of the loan, but generally include an analysis fee, commitment fee, one-time front-end fee, structuring fee, and administration fee.

III. CONTACTS

Inter-American Development Bank
1300 New York Avenue, NW
Washington. DC 20577
Tel: (202) 623-2277
Internet: www.IADB.org
Email: pic@iadb.org
        webmaster@iadb.org

Esteban Molfino
Funding Department
Tel: (202) 623-2369
Email: estebanm@iadb.org

Souheil Hajjar
Investment Department
Tel: (202) 623-2320
Email: souheilh@iadb.org

Private Sector Department
Tel: (202) 623-1000

All Sectors (Caribbean Region, Uruguay, Paraguay, Argentina,
   Brazil, Mexico, Venezuela)
Tel: (202) 623-2159

All Sectors (Andean Region)
Tel: (202) 623-2159

INTER-ARAB INVESTMENT GUARANTEE CORPORATION (IAIGC)

I. INTRODUCTION

Beginning in Kuwait in 1975, the Inter-Arab Investment Guarantee Corporation was established with the mission of improving trade and investment between Arab nations. The two objectives of the corporation are first to insure inter-Arab investments against noncommercial risks and export credits against commercial risks, and second to improve inter-Arab investment flows by keeping potential investors aware of investment opportunities, conditions of institutional support, and development of human capital.

II. PRODUCTS

Investment Guarantee
The investment guarantee protects against noncommercial risks that include expropriation, nationalization, inconvertibility, wars, and civil disturbances. Both direct investments and loans are eligible for coverage under this program. Only Arab nationals are eligible provided that their nationality is different from the host country, or financial institutions operating outside of the Middle East if 50 percent or more of the capital is Arab owned. Guarantees

come in various types that include direct investment guarantee, equity participation guarantee, loan guarantee, and contract equipment guarantee.

Export Credit Guarantee

Export credit guarantees cover both political and commercial risks. To be eligible, goods must be of Arab origin, goods need to be shipped from one Arab country to another, and the exporter must be an Arab national. Export credit guarantees come in many varieties depending on the needs of the client. Comprehensive guarantee contracts cover commercial and political risk for several importers in one or more Arab countries. The specific guarantee contract covers commercial and political risks for an importer in the private sector regardless of the length of the credit period. The specific noncommercial risk guarantee covers both commercial and political risk for a single importer for any length of credit period. A buyer credit guarantee is signed with Arab and joint Arab-foreign banks who extend credit facilities for Arab importers to finance their purchase of Arab goods. The consignment guarantee annex covers political risks for goods or materials exported by an Arab national to a country other than his own for the purpose of storing, re-export, or sale The corporation involved will sign an annex with an exporter who has signed a comprehensive guarantee. A letter of credit guarantee covers commercial and political risk for export transactions against a letter of credit opened by any Arab or joint Arab-foreign bank eligible for the guarantee.

III. CONTACTS

Head Office:
The Arab Organization Building
Al Matar Road
Jamal Abdelnasser St.
Al-Shuwaikh
Kuwait

Postal Address:
P.O. Box 23568
Al-Safat 13096
Kuwait
Tel: (965) 484-4500
Fax: (965) 481-5741
Telex: 22562 KAFEEL KT
Internet: www.iaigc.org/
Email: info@iai.org.kw

ISLAMIC CORPORATION FOR INSURANCE OF INVESTMENTS AND EXPORT CREDITS (ICIEC)

I. INTRODUCTION

The Islamic Corporation for Insurance of Investments and Export Credits (ICIEC), an affiliate of the Islamic Development Bank (IDB), was established in August 1994 to offer Islamic-compatible insurance for investments and export credit. The objective of ICIEC (the Corporation) is to enlarge the scope of trade transactions and the flow of investments among member states of the Organization of the Islamic Conference (OIC). To fulfill this objective, the Corporation provides export credit insurance to cover the nonpayment of export receivables resulting from commercial (buyer) or noncommercial (country) risks; and also provides investment insurance against country risks, mainly the risks of exchange transfer restrictions, expropriation, war and civil disturbance, and breach of contract by the host government.

The authorized share capital of the Corporation is ID 100 million (USD 126.9 million). IDB has subscribed to half of the authorized capital, while the other half was left for the subscription of the member countries of OIC. The member countries are Algeria, Bahrain, Bangladesh, Brunei, Cameroon, Chad, Egypt, Gambia, Guinea, Indonesia, Iran, Jordan, Kuwait, Lebanon, Malaysia, Mali, Mauritania, Morocco, Pakistan, Qatar, Saudi Arabia, Senegal, Sudan, Syria, Tunisia, Turkey, Uganda, United Arab Emirates, and Yemen.

II. PRODUCTS

There are two major types of insurance policies offered: export credit insurance and investment insurance. Export credit insurance covers the risks of non-payment that result from exporting operations. This insurance scheme has three policies: the comprehensive short-term credit insurance, the supplemental medium-term policy, and the bank master policy. The investment insurance policy covers member countries against the risks that arise from investing in foreign markets.

Short-Term

ICIEC considers short-term policies those that are under one year. Short-term products include comprehensive short-term credit insurance and bank master policy. Export credit insurance covers exporters against both political and commercial risks. The commercial risks that may be insured by the Corporation are the insolvency of the buyer, repudiation or termination by the buyer of the purchase contract or his refusal or failure to take delivery of the goods despite the seller's fulfillment of all his obligations towards the buyer, and refusal of the buyer to pay the purchase price to the seller or his failure to do so despite the seller's fulfillment of all his obligations towards the buyer. The noncommercial risks covered are transfer restrictions, expropriation and similar measures, breach of contract, and war and civil disturbance.

Comprehensive Short-Term Policy
The comprehensive short-term policy is available only to eligible exporters and covers all contracts or shipments made during the period of insurance. The period of insurance runs up to 12 months, in accordance with the Hijra year or the Gregorian year, as selected by the policyholder, and may be renewed every 12 months. Under this policy, cover for each contract begins when the goods are shipped. The amount covered is the amount of the credit limit approved in relation to each buyer.

Bank Master Policy
The bank master policy is available to any bank that is eligible as a policyholder. This policy applies to all contracts financed by a bank in accordance with the principles of Islamic Shariah and declared by that bank and accepted by the Corporation during the period of insurance irrespective of the period of credit granted under the contract.

Specifications
The period of insurance is up to 12 months and may be renewed at each anniversary for an additional 12 months, subject to mutual agreement. Cover begins on the date when such contract becomes effective or on the date when the Corporation approves cover, whichever is later. ICIEC covers up to 90 percent of commercial and political risks.

Application Process: Exporters and banks are invited to contact ICIEC and discuss how export credit insurance could promote their business. ICIEC will provide any interested exporter with a specimen policy for him to read and a proposal form to be completed and returned for ICIEC's consideration. If the proposal is acceptable, ICIEC will issue an offer letter, which includes a quotation of premium rates. There is no obligation on the part of the exporter to accept the offer. Upon acceptance of the offer and payment of policy fees the policy will be issued.

Medium and Long Term

ICIBC considers medium- and long-term insurance policies those with terms over 1 and up to 15 years, and in some cases 20 years. The medium-term policies offered are the supplemental medium term-policy and the investment insurance system.

Supplemental Medium-Term Policy

The supplemental medium-term policy is only available to eligible exporters who also hold a comprehensive short-term policy. However, in the case that the underwriters are satisfied, and the interest of the Corporation will not be prejudiced by waiving the requirement for a comprehensive short-term policy, a supplemental medium-term policy alone may be issued.

Specifications

Cover for each contract begins on either the date when the contract becomes effective or the date when the contract is approved for cover by the Corporation, whichever is latest.

ICIEC covers up to 90 percent of commercial and political risks.

Investment Insurance System

Investment insurance could make a difference to the investment decision by substantially mitigating an investor's exposure to political risks in the host country. Investments may be made in monetary form or in assets such as machinery, patents, or technical services. Investments must be seen to contribute to the overall developmental objectives and strategies of the host country and must not be in contravention of the principles of Shariah. The currency may be the Islamic dinar, the U.S. dollar, or the French franc, depending entirely on the investor's choice or any other currency subject to the approval of ICIEC's board of directors.

Terms: Each investment is underwritten individually and a separate policy is issued for each investment. Policies apply for a minimum of 1 year and normally a maximum of 15 years, although up to 20 years may be allowed in special circumstances.

Eligibility: ICIEC covers investments made by members or nationals of member countries living in other member countries. The types of eligible investments are direct investments in enterprises (including their branches and agencies) either public or private, or investments in the share capital of enterprises, as well as principal amounts of loans made or guaranteed by holders of equity in the enterprises, as well as principal amounts of loans made or guaranteed by other lenders. Both equity and non-equity direct investments (such as production-sharing arrangements, licensing agreements, and operating leases) are eligible.

Coverage: ICIEC's investment insurance policy covers 90 percent of the investor's loss arising from the political risks of transfer restrictions, expropriation, and war. Cover against the breach of contract by the host country (in cases where the investment is substantially dependent on such a contract) may be offered under an endorsement to the investment insurance policy.

Fees: The investor is required to pay a nonrefundable application fee of USD 500, together with the preliminary application. In addition, the investor must pay a processing fee of USD 5,000, which is subject to a refund or additional payment depending on actual cost incurred by ICIEC to process the application. However, the full processing fee paid will be credited to the first year's premium in the event that a policy is issued.

III. CONTACTS

P.O. Box 5925
Jeddah 21432 Saudi Arabia
Tel: 966 (2) 644 5666
Fax: 966 (2) 637 9504
Email: iciec@isdb.org.sa

Manager
Tel: 966 (2) 637 4061
Fax: 966 (2) 637 9504
Email: Ataha@isdb.org.sa

Marketing Officer
Tel: 6463307
Fax: 966 (2) 644 3447
Email: Ksalemal@isdb.org.sa

Ahmad Zubir Hashim
Senior Underwriter
Tel: 966 (2) 6463305
Fax: 966 (2) 644 3447
Email: Ahashim@isdb.org.sa

Underwriting Officer
Tel: 966 (2) 6463308
Fax: 966 (2) 644 3447
Email: Iabdulka@isdb.org.sa

ISLAMIC DEVELOPMENT BANK (ISDB)

I. INTRODUCTION

The Islamic Development Bank was established in 1975 with the purpose of developing member countries economically and socially in accordance with Islamic law. The functions of the bank include participating in equity capital and grant loans, and operating special funds for assistance to Muslim communities in nonmember countries. Additionally, the bank is responsible for promoting foreign trade, providing technical assistance, and aiding personnel engaged in development activities in Muslim countries to conform to the Shari'ah.

II. PRODUCTS

ISDB has several financing options:

Import Trade Financing

This financing typically provides 100 percent cover for developmental goods. The term generally spans 9 to 24 months for raw materials/intermediary goods and up to 30 months for capital goods. This service is intended to promote import trade for the IDB member countries.

Export Financing

This financing provides 100 percent cover for consumer, intermediate, and capital goods. The various terms range from 6 to 120 months depending on the type of good. This service aids export trade by member countries but also covers goods being exported to nonmember countries.

Arab Export to African Countries

This financing is known as "Arab Export to African Countries—Non member of the Arab League." It covers 100 percent of the total transaction value over a maximum term of 36 months. Also, unlike the other financing options, this service is denominated in U.S. dollars.

Trade Cooperation & Promotion Program

This service is designed to promote trade between member countries of ISDB through two activities, trade promotion, and capacity building. The objective of this program is to match "trade opportunities among member countries" and to build "capacity of member countries on issues related to trade."

III. CONTACTS

Head Office:
Islamic Development Bank
P.O. Box 5925, Jeddah 21432
Kingdom of Saudi Arabia
Tel: (+9662) 6361400
Fax: (+9662) 6366871
Telex: 601 137 ISDB SJ
Internet: www.isdb.org
Email: idbarchives@isdb.org.sa

Berne Union: An international union of 51 members in 42 countries that works for international acceptance of sound principles of export credit insurance and foreign investment insurance. Berne Union also provides a vital forum for exchange of information, experience, and expertise between members. With extensive international contacts, Berne Union is able to wield its leverage and speak with international financial institutions and individual buying countries on behalf of its members.

Bid Bond: A guarantee issued by a financial institution of a supplier when bidding on a major project. It normally covers 5 percent of the contract price. A bid bond will compensate the buyer if the supplier fails to fulfill the terms of the bid after having been declared the successful bidder.

Buyer Credit: A financial agreement in which a bank or export credit agency makes a loan directly to an overseas purchaser to import goods and services. Disbursements may be made either directly to the exporter or to reimburse the buyer for previous payments already made.

Case Reserves: Funds set aside by an export credit agency to meet anticipated payments to exporters based on claims for specific transactions.

Cash Payment: The portion of the contract price (for medium- and long-term credits only) that a foreign buyer must pay the exporter on or before the delivery of the goods or services. The minimum cash payment is generally 15 percent of the contract price, and can be financed by another institution.

Category I, II, and III Countries: After the OECD agreement, it was established that Category I countries would be those with a 1979 income per capita of $4,000 per annum and higher. Category II countries do not meet the criteria of categories I or III. Category III are those countries that are eligible for international development agency (IDA) credits or those where per capita GNP falls below IDA eligibility requirements.

Claim: An application filed with an export credit agency for payment under an export credit insurance police or guarantee to an insured/guaranteed bank or exporter resulting from nonpayment by a foreign buyer.

Co-financing: The ECAs and lenders agree to a common legal structure that presents the buyer with one financial package rather than a series of separate deals (e.g., there is only one loan agreement which is backed proportionately by each ECA's guarantee or insurance cover according to each country's national share of the export).

Coinsurance: Export credit risk assumed jointly by two or more export credit insurers on an export transaction.

Commercial Interest Reference Rates (CIRRS): The official lending rates of export credit agencies. They are calculated monthly and are based on government bonds issued in the country's domestic market for the country's currency.

Commercial Risk: Risk of nonpayment on export credit by a buyer or borrower due to bankruptcy, insolvency, protracted default, and/or failure to accept goods shipped by the terms of the supply contract. Typically, export credit agencies do not cover commercial risks on sales to affiliated firms and nonpayment arising from disputes between the parties about product quality, supplier performance, and so on.

Commitment Fee: The fee charged by a lender, often an export credit agency, to compensate for committing funds, based on undisbursed balances.

Comprehensive Coverage: Insurance or guarantee cover that combines both commercial risk coverage and political risk coverage.

Concessionality Level: The total percentage value of a subsidy provided in combination with export financing. Example: In addition to export credit, an exporter receives a grant of 25 percent of the export value. The percent of the grant is the concessionality level.

Consensus: Commonly called the Organization for Economic Cooperation and Development (OECD) Consensus or Arrangement on Export Credits, it is an agreement concluded in February 1976 among major industrial countries that established guidelines for maximum repayment terms and minimum interest rates, and procedures for the notification of non-adherence to these guidelines. The consensus was superceded in April 1978 by the Arrangement on Guidelines for Officially Supported Export Credits and accepted by twenty members of the OECD Export Credit Group.

Country Categories: Classification of levels of political risks (usually four or five levels) in different buyer countries. Risks are usually rated by letter grades. Example: A= low political risk.

Delegated Authority: Authority granted to commercial banks or exporters to approve insurance/guarantees without specific approval from the ECA. Typically, the ECA gives this approval based on previous experience with the bank/exporter.

Direct Loan: Loan from an export-financing agency to a foreign buyer for the purchase of specific goods or services on credit terms. The loan is usually secured by a bank guarantee in the buyer's country or by an export credit insurance policy.

Discretionary Credit Limit (DCL): The maximum amount of credit per buyer on which an insured exporter may ship and receive insurance coverage under an export credit insurance policy without prior approval of the specific buyer by the export credit insurance agency.

Export Contracts: Transactions involving the sale or lease of equipment/services across borders. The value of these contracts may include the full value of imported goods/services contracted between the buyer and seller.

Export Credit Agency (ECA): A financial agency directed to offering loans, guarantees, credit insurance, or financial technical assistance to support exporters.

Export Credits: Financing provided to an exporter or foreign buyer from a commercial bank or export credit agency during pre- or post-shipment operations. Financing arising from particular export contracts is said to be directly "tied" to such contracts. However, financing for general purchases are defined as "untied."

Exposure: The amount of liability in the event of nonpayment by a foreign buyer or buyers.

Financial Guarantee: A commitment or assurance that in the event of nonpayment of an export credit by a foreign borrower, the export credit agency will indemnify the financing bank if the terms and conditions of its guarantees are fulfilled.

First Loss: An amount normally borne by the insured, which is absorbed before any claim payment is calculated.

Foreign Content: Any portion or value added to an exported good or service that is manufactured, assembled, or supplied by another country.

Global Policy: An export credit insurance policy that covers the short-term credits extended to all of an exporter's foreign buyers during a specified time period. A global policy can be comprehensive or cover only political or commercial risks.

Grace Period: An interval of time allowed to the borrower by the lender after loan proceeds are disbursed and before repayment begins.

Guarantee: Used generally to denote any assurance of payment or compensation given to the entity financing an export credit, which is to be honored in the event of default or nonpayment by the primary obligor.

Hold Harmless Agreement: A guarantee that assumes payment to the financing commercial bank irrespective of the violations of export credit insurance policies and sales contracts by the exporter. This results in the assumption of the "exporter risk" by the credit-insuring agency.

Insurance: Cover that indemnifies the insured (often both exporters and banks) from loss due to a specified type of contingency or peril.

Letter of Interest (LI): A pre-export tool that helps to obtain financing. For example, the LI is an indication of U.S. Ex-Im Bank's willingness to consider financing for a given export transaction and locks in the exposure fee for six months.

Levels Of Payment: Amortization pattern in which the sum of principal and interest on each installment are the same. This implies increasing amounts of principal and decreasing amounts of interest as the date of final payment approaches.

Local Costs: Expenses incurred for goods and services purchased from suppliers in the buyer's country. Export credit agencies may finance or guarantee up to a maximum of 15 percent of the export value.

London Club: Forum in which committees from commercial banks negotiate the restructuring of debt owed to them by lenders in countries that are either incapable or unwilling to repay foreign debt.

Medium Term: Repayment terms usually ranging from 181 days, 365 days, or up to 5 years. Based on the OECD Arrangement, the range for medium term is 2 to 5 years.

Mixed Credit: Financial arrangement that includes a combination of export credit agency credit and concessional financing. Under the OECD Arrangement, if the subsidy element is greater than 25 percent, then the whole credit is considered aid or tied aid.

Non-Acceptance Risk: Risk that a foreign buyer does not accept goods shipped due to failure or refusal, provided that this failure is not the fault of the insured exporter. Insurance against non-acceptance risk is typically found as a part of an export credit insurance policy covering commercial risk.

Non-Recourse Financing: Financing that removes the exporter from all risks of nonpayment through an agreement by the financing bank to not seek recourse on the exporter in the event of nonpayment by the buyer.

OECD Arrangement: Agreement adopted in 1978 by members of the Paris-based Organization for Economic Cooperation and Development (OECD) to limit credit competition among member governments in officially supported export credits. The OECD arrangement superseded the OECD consensus.

Official Fixed Rate Support: Offer of protection against interest rates during the cover period of an export credit. This support varies with each specific ECA involved. For example, support through U.S. Ex-Im Bank is provided by direct fixed rate loans.

Officially Supported Export Credits: Credits that benefit from the financial support of export credit agencies.

Organization for Economic Co-Operation and Development (OECD): A group of thirty member countries sharing a commitment to democratic government and the market economy. With a global reach of over seventy countries, NGOs, and civil societies, OECD is best known for its publications and statistics on various economic, education, technology, and development issues. OCED also produces internationally agreed instruments, decisions, and recommendations to promote the rules of the game in areas where multilateral agreement is necessary for individual countries to make progress in a global economy.

Parallel Financing: Each ECA provides finance for its exporter's portion with no significant attempt made to coordinate or harmonize any aspect of the individual financings.

Paris Club: A forum at which a country's debt owed to or guaranteed/insured by governments is restructured. A Paris Club arrangement usually requires the debtor government to seek comparable relief from nongovernmental creditors.

Performance Bond: Guarantee issued by a financial institution on behalf of a supplier to assure the buyer that the supplier will perform according to the supply contract. In some countries, insurance or guarantee coverage is available to protect the supplier or the bank/insurance company issuing the bond from the unjustified or capricious calling of the performance bond.

Political Risk: Insurance or guarantee cover that protects the exporter or financing bank from nonpayment by the buyer or borrower because of political events in the buyer's country or a third country through which either goods or payment must pass. The specific political events generally include lack of foreign exchange; default of sovereign entity; general moratorium on external debt; cancellation or nonrenewable of export or import licenses or import restrictions; delay in transfer of payments; and war, civil war, and certain other events that prevent the exporter from performing under the supply contract or the buyer from making payment.

Post-Shipped Period: Period of time extending from shipment date to the final payment by the foreign buyer.

Preliminary Commitment: An offer of financing subject to the final award of the export contract and on the ECA's final review.

Premium Rate: Cost of export credit insurance per unit, usually calculated on the gross invoice value for short-term sales or on the financed portion for medium- and long-term sales.

Pre-Shipped Period: The period from the date of contract signing to the date of shipment.

Protracted Default Risk: A commercial risk typically defined by export credit agencies as payment not received six months or longer past maturity.

Recourse: The right of a bank or export credit agency to demand payment from the maker of a draft or endorser of a note it has purchased, if the primary obligor fails to pay. Banks often finance exporters with recourse for transactions or portions of transactions that are not insured or guaranteed.

Reinsurance: One export credit agency (the lead ECA) provides the entire financing while other ECAs provide reinsurance proportionally based on their nations' share of the export (e.g., in the event of a claim, the lead ECA would pay the entire claim and be reimbursed by the other ECAs proportionally according to their exporters' share).

Repayment Term: Schedule of payments to the exporter for goods purchased by a foreign buyer. The length of repayment terms generally reflects the type of product exported, the size of the transaction, the type of buyer, etc.

Rescheduling: Occurs when a debtor (public or private borrower) is unable to meet the original schedule of repayment called for in its loan agreement. Rather than repudiate or default, the debtor renegotiates the loan agreement, restructuring the payment schedule to provide additional terms to meet its obligations.

Short Term: Repayment terms generally of up to 180 days, or exceptionally up to 365 days. Berne Union guidelines for short-term credit insurance refer to repayment terms of up to two years depending on the product and the size of transaction.

Sovereign Buyer: A buyer that is owned by a national government and has the full faith and credit backing of that government when entering into sales or credit agreements.

Special Buyer Credit Limits: Maximum amount of credit set by the export credit agency that will be covered on a specified buyer when an exporter's shipments exceed the discretionary credit limit.

Supplier Credit: Financial arrangement in which the supplier (exporter) extends credit to the buyer to finance the buyer's purchases. Normally the buyer pays a portion of the contract value in cash and issues a promissory note or accepts a draft to evidence the obligation to pay the remainder to the exporter.

Tenor: Total repayment period. Also referred to as term.

Third Country Cost: Costs of procurement necessary for a project incurred in a country other than that in which either the project or the prime contractor is located. Some export credit agencies will cover such costs up to an amount equal to the cash payment.

Tied Aid Program: A government-to-government concessional financing of public sector capital projects in developing countries. Tied aid is provided by the aid agencies of the rich-country governments, sometimes in conjunction with their national export credit agencies. Tied aid differs from typical export credit terms offered by ECAs in that it usually involves total maturities longer than 20 years, interest rates equal to one-half to two-thirds of market rates in the currency of denomination, or large grants.

Waiting Period: The period following occurrence of a loss during which exporters or banks must wait before filing a claim with an export credit insurance agency.

Whole Turnover Policy: Insurance or guarantee cover for all or a negotiated portion of the export transactions of an exporter or bank, generally at a lower premium than for specific transactions due to the speed of risks. Also called a global policy.

Customary and Maximum Repayment Benefits

Products or Contract Value	Repayment Terms
Small & Medium Unit Value Items	
< $75,000	2 Years Customary
$75,001–$150,000	3 Years Customary
$150,001–$300,000	4 Years Customary
$300,001–$10,000,000	5 Years Customary
Breeding & Dairy Cattle	
< $150,000	2 Years Customary
> $150,000	3 Years Customary
Large Fleets of Vehicles	5 Years Customary
Propeller-Driven Airplanes & Helicopters	5 Years Maximum
Turbo-Driven Airplanes,	
< 30 Passengers	7 Years Maximum
Self-Propelled Ships	8 Years Maximum
	(12 Years Max from 1996)
Capital Goods to Category I Countries	5 Years Max W/O OECD notification
> $10,000,000	8.5 Years with OECD notification
Complete Projects, Category I Countries	8.5 Years with OECD notification
Capital Goods to Category II Countries	
> $10,000,000	10 Years Maximum
Complete Projects, Category II Countries	10 Years Maximum
Complete Power Plants	10 Years Customary
	12 Years Max with OECD notification
Large Passenger Aircraft	12 Years Customary/Maximum
Nuclear Power Plants	15 Years Maximum

Source: *Financing and Insuring Exports: A User's Guide to Ex-Im Bank Programs*
Export-Import Bank of the United States
Business Development Group
811 Vermont Avenue, N.W.
Washington, D.C. 20571
Tel: (202) 565-3946
Fax: (202) 565-3880

OECD Country Term Categories

NEW CATEGORY I COUNTRIES

Rule 1: Maximum 5-year repayment term, without OECD notification.
Rule 2: With OECD prior notification, maximum 8.5 years repayment term.
Rule 3: Direct loan financing of local costs is prohibited.

Andorra, Antigua (2), Argentina (3), Aruba, Australia, Austria, Bahamas (3), Barbados (3), Belgium, Bermuda, Brunei, Canada, Cyprus (3), Denmark, Faeroes, Finland, France, French Guiana, French Polynesia, Germany, Gibraltar, Greece, Greenland, Guadeloupe, Hong Kong, Iceland, Ireland, Israel, Italy, Japan, Kuwait, Libya, Liechtenstein, Luxembourg, Macao (2), Malta (3), Martinique, Monaco, Montserrat (2), Netherlands, Netherlands Antilles (3), New Caledonia, New Zealand, Norway, Oman (3), Portugal (3), Qatar, Reunion, San Marino, Saudi Arabia, Singapore (3), Slovenia (3), South Korea (2), Spain, Sweden, Switzerland, Seychelles (2), Taiwan (2), United Arab Emirates, United Kingdom, United States, Vatican City.

1. The OECD Secretariat will update this list annually. It includes all countries "too rich" to qualify for World Bank loans. The current cut-off point is $4,715 per capita GNP in 1992 U.S. dollars. With dollar inflation, the cut-off point will rise each year. The dollar GNPs are by the World Bank Atlas Method.
2. For these countries, 10-year terms are permitted for a transition period. New PCs/LIs with 10-year terms may be issued through August 31, 1996. All PCs/LIs with 10-year terms must expire by February 28, 1997.
3. For these countries, direct loan financing of local costs is permitted for a transition period. New PCs/LIs with loan financing of local costs may be issued through April 30, 1995. All PCs/LIs with loan financing of local costs must expire by September 30, 1995.

NEW CATEGORY II COUNTRIES

Rule 1: Maximum 10-year repayment term, without OECD notification.

All countries not included in Category I above.

FORMER CATEGORY III COUNTRIES

Still eligible for matrix (SDR-based) rate until August 31, 1995.

Angola, Bangladesh, Benin, Bolivia, Burkina, Burma, (Myanmar), Burundi, Cambodia, Cameroon, Central African Republic, Chad, China, Comoros, Congo, Egypt, El Salvador, Equatorial Guinea, Ethiopia, Gambia, Ghana, Grenada, Guinea, Guinea-Bissau, Guyana, Haiti, Honduras, India, Indonesia, Kenya, Laos, Lesotho, Liberia, Madagascar, Malawi, Mali, Mauritania, Mozambique, Nepal, Nicaragua, Niger, Pakistan, Philippines, Rwanda, St. Vincent, Sao Tome and Principe, Senegal, Sierra Leone, Solomon Islands, Somalia, Sri Lanka, Sudan, Tanzania, Thailand, Togo, Tonga, Uganda, Vanuatu, Vietnam, Yemen, Zaire, Zambia, Zimbabwe.

NOTE: Not all countries listed are eligible for Ex-Im Bank financing.

Source: *Financing and Insuring Exports: A User's Guide to Ex-Im Bank Programs*
Export-Import Bank of the United States
Business Development Group
811 Vermont Avenue, N.W.
Washington, D.C. 20571
Tel: (202) 565-3946
Fax: (202) 565-3880

Sample LI and Term Sheet From Ex-Im Bank

January 21, 200A

Mr. Ted Williams
American Drill Company
100 Celtics Drive
St. Louis, MO 12345
Fax No. (314) 555-1313/Telephone No. (314) 555-1212

Re: Letter of Interest No. LI070000XX - Estasia

Dear Mr. Williams:

We are pleased to provide you with Ex-Im Bank's Letter of Interest for Farmland Corporation in Estasia. Our review of the participant and product information in your application indicates that Ex-Im Bank support may be available for this transaction. This Letter of Interest is not, however, a financing commitment. The indicative terms referenced in this Letter of Interest are valid until July 14, 200A.

The Term Sheet attached to this Letter of Interest sets forth Ex-Im Bank's indicative terms of support based upon the transaction information we have received to date. If, however, the U.S. exporter is facing foreign competition which is supported by a foreign export credit agency offering more favorable financing terms, Ex-Im Bank may consider matching those terms.

Please note that Ex-Im Bank support generally is provided only where there is a demonstrated need, either to meet competition from a foreign export credit agency supporting a foreign exporter or to overcome a lack of financing from private sources for the U.S. export.

The limited nature of our review of a request for a Letter of Interest does not include evaluation of all the issues that may arise in Ex-Im Bank's consideration of financial support. The attached Program Guidelines set forth Ex-Im Bank's general policies and requirements which you should consider as you structure this transaction. Please specifically refer to section XXXX of the Program Guidelines. Ex-Im Bank will complete a thorough review of policy and creditworthiness issues at the time of Final Commitment application.

If you would like Ex-Im Bank to consider issuing a Final Commitment, the borrower (in the case of either a direct loan or a guarantee) or the lender (in the case of a guarantee) must submit a complete Final Commitment application, together with a copy of the export contract between the U.S. exporter and the foreign buyer. Only those eligible items shipped no earlier than the date of this Letter of Interest (and a maximum of 24 months before Ex-Im Bank receives a complete Final Commitment application) may be considered for Ex-Im Bank support. (Please note that the shipments more than 12 months prior to a Final Commitment Application may affect repayment terms.) In addition, all long-term cases can obtain local cost support when the costs are connected to the U.S. exporter's responsibilities in carrying out his contract.

If you have any questions about this Letter of Interest, please contact the Ex-Im Bank International Business Development Officer, at telephone (202) 565-3XXX.

Sincerely,
Jeffrey L. Miller
Group Vice President
Structured & Trade Finance Group

Enclosures

TERM SHEET FOR LETTER OF INTEREST NO. LI070000XX

Exporter	American Drill Company, St. Louis, MO
Supplier	American Drill Company, St. Louis, MO
Buyer	Farmland Corporation, Bruin, Estasia
End-user	Farmland Corporation, Bruin, Estasia
Borrower	Farmland Corporation, Bruin, Estasia
Guarantor (1.01)*	See Program Guidelines

Goods and Services (Items): Five model #DR7246 Drilling Bits, and Spare Parts

U.S. Content	$ 5,100,000
Eligible Foreign Content	$ 400,000
Contract Price	$ 5,500,000
Less: Cash Payment (Minimum - 15% of Contract Price)	$ 825,000
Amount of Contract Price Financed (Financed Portion 85%)	$ 4,675,000

Ex-Im Bank Category of Risk	Sovereign	( )
	Political Risk Only	( )
	Public Non-Sovereign	( )
	Private	(X)
Program Options Available	Direct Loan	(X)
	Guaranteed Loan	(X)
	Medium-Term Insurance	(X)

Maximum Repayment Term (1.05*) 10 semiannual payments from the Starting Point.

Interest Rates (1.04*)

Direct Loan — The Ex-Im Bank Lending Rate as defined in section 1.04 of the Program Guidelines. The Ex-Im Bank Lending Rate applicable to the minimum repayment term indicated above is 5.31% per annum from January 15, 200A-February 14, 200A

Guaranteed — Loan To be determined by Guaranteed Lender

Commitment Fee (1.02*)

Direct Loan — 1/2 of 1% per annum

Guaranteed Loan — 1/8 of 1% per annum

Exposure Fee (1.03*) — Refer to attached Exposure Fee Advice for information concerning Ex-Im Bank's determination of Exposure Fees. Ex-Im Bank will specify the fee at the time of issuance of a Preliminary or Final Commitment.

LI Expiry Date (1.13*) — July 14, 200A

*Refer to indicated section of attached Program Guidelines for additional information.

Sample EFIC Letter
of Indication
Application Form

LETTER OF INTEREST

APPLICATION

OMB No. 3048-0005
Expires 10/31/2004

Please type. Processing of applications may be delayed if the requested information is not provided.

1. **Applicant.** The applicant may be any responsible individual, financial institution or non-financial enterprise. • Check if applicant has been assisted by a city or state export agency and provide the name of the agency:

Applicant name:	Duns #:
Contact person:	Phone #:
Position title:	Fax #:
Street Address:	City:
State/Province:	Postal Code:	Country:
Taxpayer ID #:	

2. **Exporter.** The "exporter" is the company which contracts with the buyer for the sale of the U.S. goods and services. • Check if the exporter is also the applicant. If not, complete the information below.

Exporter name:	Duns #:
Street address:	Phone #:
City:	State:	Postal code:
Taxpayer ID #:	

3. **Supplier.** The "supplier" is the U.S. company which manufactures the goods and/or performs the services to be exported. • Check if the supplier is also the exporter. • Check if the supplier is not determined. If neither applies, attach the same information for the primary supplier as requested above for the exporter. Information on additional suppliers is not required for an LI.

4. **Borrower.** The "borrower" is the company which agrees to repay the Ex-Im Bank direct or guaranteed loan. Complete the information below. Check the box for "public sector" if the borrower is at least 50% directly or indirectly owned by a government. Check the box for "private sector" if the borrower is less than 50% owned by a government.

Contact person:	Fax #:
Borrower name:	Duns #:
Street address:	City:	• • public sector	• • private sector
State/Province:	Postal Code:	Country:

5. **Buyer and End-user.** The "buyer" is the company which contracts with the exporter for the purchase of the U.S. goods and services. The "end-user" is the foreign company which utilizes the U.S. goods and services in its business. • Check if the borrower, buyer, and end-user are not the same entity. If box is checked, attach the same information for the buyer and the end-user as requested above for the borrower.

6. **Export Items.** The "export items" are the goods and services to be exported from the U.S.

   6a. **Large Aircraft.** • Check if the export items include aircraft which, in a passenger configuration, contain more than 70 seats. If box is checked, complete *Attachment A.*

   6b. **Military.** • Check if the buyer is associated in *any* way with the military, if *any* export items are to be used by the military, or if *any* export items are defense articles or have a military application.

   6c. **Limited Recourse Project Finance.** • Check if you want a Letter of Interest issued by the Project Finance Division. If box is checked, complete *Attachment D.*

   6d. **Description of Export Items.** Briefly describe the principal goods and services, including the *type, quantity, model number and capacity (if applicable), and SIC Code.* For an aircraft transaction, include a description of the engines.

OMB No. 3048-0005
Expires: 10/31/2004

LETTER OF INTEREST

APPLICATION

6e. **Utilization of Export Items.** Briefly describe the principal business activity of the *end-user*. If the export items are to be used in a project, also provide the name, location, purpose, and scope of the project.

7. **Financing Type Requested.** Check applicable box(es). You may request both a direct loan and a guarantee. If both financing options are acceptable to Ex-Im Bank, they will be indicated in the LI as options. Refer to *Attachment A* if the transaction involves the export of new large aircraft.

- Direct Loans
- Comprehensive Guarantee
- Political Risk Guarantee

8. **Contract Price.** The "contract price" is the *amount to be shown in the supplier's invoice related to goods to be exported from the U.S. and services to be performed by U.S. companies*. If there is more than one supplier, the contract price is the sum of the suppliers' invoice amounts. The "eligible foreign content" is the portion of the contract price representing components to be purchased by the sup-plier outside the U.S. and *incorporated in the U.S. into the items to be exported*. Costs to be incurred in the end-user's country are not considered eligible foreign content. Note that the eligible foreign content, if any, is part of the contract price.

8a. **Contract Price: $ _____** (including eligible foreign content)

8b. **Eligible Foreign Content: $ _____**

9. **Foreign Competition.** • Check if, to the best of your knowledge, there is at least one entity offering non-U.S. goods and/or services in *direct* competition for this specific export sale.

10. **Other U.S. Government Agencies.** • Check if an application for support of this export contract or related project has been filed with the Agency for International Development, Maritime Administration, Overseas Private Investment Corporation or Trade Development Agency.

11. **Environmental Effects.** If 85% of the contract price exceeds $10,000,000, complete *Attachment B*. Attachment B is not required for aircraft transactions.

12. **Tied Aid Capital Projects Fund.** If you want Ex-Im Bank to preclude or counter a tied aid offer, complete *Attachment C*.

13. **Certifications.** The undersigned certifies that the facts stated and the representations made in this application and any attachments to this application are true, to the best of the applicant's knowledge and belief after due diligence, and that the applicant has not omitted any material facts.

The undersigned further certifies that it is not currently, nor has it been within the preceding three years: 1) debarred, suspended or declared ineligible from participating in any Federal program; 2) formally proposed for debarment, with a final determination still pending; 3) voluntarily excluded from participation in a Federal transaction; or 4) indicted, convicted or had a civil judgment rendered against it for any of the offenses listed in the Regulations Governing Debarment and Suspension (Governmentwide Nonprocurement Debarment and Suspension Regulations: Common Rule), 53 fed. Reg. 19204 (1988).

Applicant (company) name: _____

Name and title of authorized officer: _____

Signature of authorized officer: _____ Date: _____

Payment, payable to the Export-Import Bank of the U.S., must accompany application; please indicate: • Visa • Mastercard • Check

Account #: _____ Expiration Date: _____

Signature: _____

Ex-Im Bank would be pleased to assist you in applying for financial support. If you have any questions, please contact the Business Development Division (Telephone: 202-565-3900 or Fax: 202-565-3931). For information concerning financing of large aircraft and ancillary equipment, please contact the Aircraft Finance Division (Telephone: 202-565-3550 or Fax: 202-565-3558).

Taxpayer Identifying Numbers: Ex-Im Bank intends to use the taxpayer identifying numbers furnished on this application for purposes of collecting and reporting on any claims arising out of such persons' or business entities' relationships with the U.S. government.

EIB Form 96-9
Revised 04/99

2

OMB No. 3048-0005
Expires: 10/31/2004

LETTER OF INTEREST

APPLICATION

Public Burden Statement: Public burden reporting for this collection of information is estimated to average 20 minutes per response, including time required for searching existing data sources, gathering the necessary data, providing the information required, and reviewing the final collection. Send comments on the accuracy of this esti-mate of the burden and recommendations for reducing it to: Office of Management and Budget, Paperwork Reduction Project (#3048-0004), Washington, D.C. 20503.

EIB Form 96-9
Revised 04/99

3

ECGD's Impact Screening and Analysis Procedures

PO Box 2200 2 Exchange Tower Harbour Exchange Square London E14 9GS

AN INTRODUCTION TO ECGD's IMPACT SCREENING AND ANALYSIS PROCEDURES

It is UK Government policy to promote Sustainable Development. ECGD, therefore, must consider, in its risk assessment, environmental, social and human rights issues which could impact materially on the construction, operation or economic viability of the project, the local and global environment and the relevant communities. We will consider support only if, in our judgement and after taking account of all mitigating measures, the positive effects of the project outweigh any adverse impacts.

Provision of information

Since each case is unique, its circumstances will determine what information is available to our customers. Our request for information is based on 3 principles:

1. We will analyse all requests for support.
2. We expect investors, project leaders and suppliers of components which form a major part of a project to provide us with full information about the impacts of the business/project/goods.
3. We expect applicants who are suppliers of goods/services which may form only a minor part of a project to provide full information about the impacts of these goods/services and to assist us in obtaining information about the impacts of the project.

Where necessary, the relevant Underwriter and/or ECGD's Business Principles Unit will provide guidance on what further information is needed in order to enable ECGD to take a decision on project impacts.

We recognise that, in some circumstances, not all the information requested will be available at the time of the submission of the application/proposal form. The existence of relevant company policies, ISO14001/EMAS certification and a record of good performance will be helpful if this is the case.

Standards

- As a minimum, ECGD expects all projects/goods/services to comply with host/destination country legislation, regulations and standards.
- Suppliers of goods and services forming only a minor part of a project will normally be expected to comply with UK legislation, regulations or standards. Any departures from this will need to be justified to the satisfaction of ECGD.
- Projects/goods/services that comply with an international standard (e.g. World Bank, IFC or relevant regional Development Bank) will not normally be investigated further for environmental impacts (except, possibly, for verification of compliance).
- Host/destination country or project standards which are below international standards may be unacceptable and would need to be justified. ECGD will use international standards as benchmarks against which to make this judgement. We will look to the customer/exporter to provide this justification wherever possible.

Should you have any further questions on this subject, please contact the relevant Underwriter or the Business Principles Unit (David Allwood 020 7512 followed by extension 7323 or Martin McKee x7072).

Commercial in Confidence

IMPACT QUESTIONNAIRE FOR CUSTOMERS
(Form IQ1a)

Questions 1 to 7 of this questionnaire should be answered for all applications for support, irrespective of value, with the exception of defence equipment and aerospace business (which are subject to separate considerations). It is essential that investors, project leaders and suppliers of components which form a major part of a project respond to all the remaining questions. Other applicants should answer as many of these as they are able. If applicants consider that to provide a full response to any of questions 8 to 13 would be unduly onerous then they should indicate this in the space provided for the response to that question and provide a brief explanation of why this is the case.

Questions must be answered fully and truthfully to the best of your knowledge and belief. If the space provided is insufficient, please continue your answers on your headed notepaper and attach it to the form. (If completing the questionnaire in the electronic form, please start text responses in the grey boxes provided.)

Provision of all relevant information will facilitate ECGD's response by minimising the need to find the information from other sources. Please note, however, that ECGD may need further information beyond that provided in the questionnaire.

Customers will be required to submit these forms (together with, where appropriate, any necessary supplementary information) to underwriters prior to ECGD being asked to underwrite a deal or provide any commitment of cover. You will, however, normally be able to obtain a non-committal indication of potential ECGD support before providing us with a completed Impact Questionnaire (IQ).

For certain types of business (e.g. Limited Recourse Project Finance, Power Projects, Mining Projects) where there are likely to be major impacts, it would be useful for ECGD to be provided with outline project impact information as soon as ECGD support is being considered.

Please read the Introduction and Guidance Notes before starting to complete the questionnaire.

Detailed notes regarding specific questions (marked 📖) are provided in Annex 1 of the questionnaire. Further assistance may be obtained by contacting the relevant Underwriter or the Business Principles Unit at ECGD.

Subject to our obligations to Parliament as a Government Department all information provided in this questionnaire will be treated as Commercial in Confidence until you tell us otherwise. Please tell us when you can release us from this commitment.

Exporter's/Investor's Name:
Buyer's/Enterprise Name:
Project Country/ies:

Commercial in Confidence

CASE OUTLINE AND GENERAL INFORMATION

1 Please give a brief description of the goods/services/project that you are supplying/investing in. *(including contractual obligations, the stage reached in bidding/development, the extent to which you are able to influence the design or specification of the goods/project and whether the goods/services/project relate to an extension or modification of an existing plant/project).*
Goods:

Project:

2 Are any other Export Credit Agencies (ECAs) or International Finance Institutions (IFIs) involved in the project?
☐ Yes ☐ No ☐ Don't know

If yes, please state names of IFIs or ECAs involved.

3 (a) If you have corporate Environment, Occupational Health & Safety, Social Issues or Human Rights policies and/or your company subscribes to ISO 14001/EMAS accreditation, please attach relevant details (if not previously provided).

☐ Copy of policies/certificates previously provided to ECGD

☐ Copy of policies/certificates attached

☐ No policies/accreditation in place thus none attached

(b) Please attach details of any documented Environment, Occupational Health & Safety or Social Issues policy statements issued by the project developer or owner.

☐ Copy of policies attached ☐ None issued ☐ Don't know

(c) Is the project owner/developer ISO 14001/EMAS accredited?

☐ Copy of certificate attached ☐ No ☐ Don't know

4 (a) Will the goods/services that you are supplying/investing in or has the project/business been designed to meet recognised environmental standards? *(Please indicate, where appropriate, the relevant standards for both the goods and the associated project.)*

Goods:
☐ Host Country ☐ UK /EU ☐ World Bank ☐ IFC ☐ Other ☐ None
Project:
☐ Host Country ☐ UK /EU ☐ World Bank ☐ IFC ☐ Other ☐ None
If None, please explain

(b) If the project/business has been designed to meet any other environmental performance standards please identify and provide a copy of these.

Environmental standard:

☐ Copy attached

Commercial in Confidence

5   (a) Has an Environmental Impact Assessment (EIA) or Social Impact Assessment (SIA) been prepared or is one planned?   Please attach details of any social or environmental management and monitoring plan that has been developed for the project. *(Annex 2 contains the contents list of a typical EIA.)*

EIA: ☐ Yes   ☐ No   ☐ Planned   ☐ Don't know
SIA: ☐ Yes   ☐ No   ☐ Planned   ☐ Don't know

If Yes, please attach. If an EIA or SIA is planned, please forward a copy of the Terms of Reference and timescales for completion.

Management & monitoring plan:
☐ Copy attached   ☐ None available thus not attached   ☐ Don't know

(b) Where the goods or project impact on the local population and an EIA or SIA has not been prepared, have they (or their authorised representatives) been consulted?

☐ Yes   ☐ No   ☐ Don't know

If Yes, please give details, including any mitigation or compensation measures

OCCUPATIONAL HEALTH AND SAFETY

6   Please indicate whether the goods/services/project that you are supplying/investing in will be compliant with UK or Destination/Host Country Health and Safety standards and supply details of any Health and Safety guidance that you supply to the users/operators of your goods/ projects.

Standards:
☐ UK   ☐ Destination/host country   ☐ Other   ☐ None

If Other or None please give details.

Guidance:
☐ Attached   ☐ None provided thus not attached

ENVIRONMENTAL IMPACTS

7   Will the goods/services/project have any actual or potential environmental impacts in any of the following areas? *(Please mark relevant boxes.)*

(The Guidance notes in Annex 1 contain specific guidance for the responses to each of these areas.)

☐ Water pollution or extraction   ☐ Damage to wildlife or habitats
☐ Local air quality   ☐ Climate change (Kyoto Protocol)
☐ Acid deposition   ☐ Ozone depletion (Montreal Protocol)
☐ Use of hazardous substances   ☐ Production of damaging or toxic waste
☐ Noise pollution
☐ Degradation of land (e.g. soil contamination, erosion or salinisation)
☐ Other adverse environmental impacts, please specify:

☐ Beneficial environmental impacts, please specify:

If there are actual or potential environmental impacts, please give details (including any mitigating factors, consultants' reports, choice of technology, etc.).

Commercial in Confidence

8   (a) Please give the exact geographical location of the project:

     (b) As or for what is the project site currently used?

     ☐ Urban   ☐ Industrial   ☐ Greenfield   ☐ Other – please specify

     (c) Please indicate if the goods/services/project will be located in or could have an environmental impact upon any of the following: *(please mark box(es))*

     ☐ Semi-arid areas and desert margins
     ☐ Properties on World Heritage List
        (for list see website http://www.unesco.org/whc/heritage.htm)
     ☐ Tropical or sub-tropical forests (especially primary forests)
     ☐ Rivers, lakes, coastline, coral reefs and wetlands, including mangroves
     ☐ National Parks, nationally designated nature reserves and all other conservation areas, and the margins of these
     ☐ Habitat of endangered species of flora or fauna or areas of high concentrations of biological diversity
     ☐ Habitats providing important resources for vulnerable groups (e.g. indigenous or tribal groups)
     ☐ Areas largely untouched by humans (wildlands)
     ☐ Areas of high concentration of population or industrial activity where further development could create significant environmental problems
     ☐ Other areas of local interest or sensitive locations – please provide details

     Please note that for projects located in any of the above, ECGD is likely to require an Environmental Impact Assessment (EIA). (Annex 2 contains the contents list of a typical EIA.)

9   In which of the following sectors is the project for which you are supplying goods/services/investment? *(please mark box)*

     Natural Resources
     ☐ Mining and mineral extraction   ☐ Forestry
     ☐ Irrigation   ☐ Large scale water reservoir
     ☐ Oil and gas field development   ☐ Aquaculture

     Infrastructure, Utilities and Public Works
     ☐ Dams and hydropower   ☐ Pipelines or electricity transmission
     ☐ Nuclear power plant   ☐ Thermal or geo-thermal power plant
     ☐ Tourism   ☐ Water abstraction
     ☐ Transport infrastructure construction (road, rail, port, harbour, airport, bridges, tunnels etc. or part thereof)
     ☐ Coastal structure or flood protection construction
     ☐ Solid waste or waste water treatment infrastructure or equipment

     Industry
     ☐ Pulp and paper processing   ☐ Tanning
     ☐ Waste incineration   ☐ Agroindustry   ☐ Agrochemicals
     ☐ Mineral processing   ☐ Genetically modified organisms (GMOs)
     ☐ Chemical / Pharmaceuticals manufacture or storage
     ☐ Metal production or processing (including smelting, electroplating etc.)
     ☐ *Other (please specify)*

     Please note that for large or greenfield projects in any of the sectors listed above, ECGD is likely to require an Environmental Impact Assessment (EIA). ECGD also reserves the right to request an EIA in other sectors where there are potential environmental sensitivities. (Annex 2 contains the contents list of a typical EIA.)

Commercial in Confidence

SOCIAL AND HUMAN RIGHTS IMPACTS

10   Will the goods or project cause, require, bring about or stimulate any of the
following?
*(The Guidance notes in Annex 1 contain specific guidance for the responses in each of
these areas.)*

☐ Resettlement of the local population
☐ Compulsory acquisition of land
☐ Displacement of, or damage to, existing industry or agriculture
☐ Job losses among the local population
☐ Child labour
☐ Bonded or forced labour
☐ Large-scale influx of workers
☐ Damage to sites of cultural, historic or scientific interest
☐ Impact on minority or vulnerable communities

Please provide details of any of these that apply.

*Please note that for projects involving any of the above ECGD is likely to require a
Social Impact Assessment.*

☐ Other social drawbacks, losses, or disadvantages, please specify:

☐ Social benefits, please specify:

11   Do the security arrangements for the contract/project make use of armed
personnel (either from private security firms or state security organisations)?

☐ Yes   ☐ No   ☐ Don't know

If you answered Yes to this question, please provide details.

12   Will the benefits of the goods/project (including employment opportunities for local
people) be open to all, regardless of race, religion, gender, social grouping, etc.?

☐ Yes   ☐ No   ☐ Don't know

If No, please provide details and justification of selection process.

13   Please give details of any other information that you think may be relevant to ECGD's
assessment of the impact of this project, including any positive impacts not previously
identified.

Commercial in Confidence

DECLARATION

We declare that:

1. if there are any material changes in the information provided in response to this Impact Questionnaire prior to ECGD approving support we will advise ECGD immediately;

2. if this Impact Questionnaire has been transmitted by electronic means, we have not amended any of the declarations or the questions contained in the Impact Questionnaire (form IQ1) provided to us by ECGD;

3. the facts stated and the representations made in this form and in any related discussions or correspondence are, to the best of our knowledge and belief, true and that we have neither misrepresented nor omitted any fact nor failed to provide any information known to us which is material to ECGD's assessment of the impact of the contract or the project to which it relates.

Signed on behalf of (Company Name)   :

Signature   :

Name (block capitals)   :

Capacity of signatory   :

(Signatory must be an authorised officer on behalf of the Company)

Date   :

ANNEX 1 – CUSTOMERS' GUIDANCE NOTES

These notes provide detailed guidance to customers as they complete ECGD's Impact Questionnaire (IQ). They are intended to help you identify the quantity and quality of information required when answering some of the less straightforward questions which are marked with the ⌨ symbol underneath the question number.

If further assistance is required, it may be obtained by contacting the relevant Underwriter or the Business Principles Unit at ECGD.

QUESTION 1

Please give a brief description of the goods/services/project that you are supplying/investing in (including contractual obligations, the stage reached in bidding/development, the extent to which you are able to influence the design or specification of the goods/project and whether the goods/services/project relate to an extension or modification of an existing plant/project).

GUIDANCE NOTES

Please describe the reason/market need for the project.

Please include quantitative information (productive capacity, main raw materials and energy consumptions, number of operators/employees required etc.).

For extension of existing plants, please state both the existing size or capacity of the plant/project and the increase in size or capacity.

QUESTION 2

Are any other Export Credit Agencies (ECAs) or International Finance Institutions (IFIs) involved in the project?
If yes, please state names of IFIs or ECAs involved.

GUIDANCE NOTE

Your answer will assist us in reducing the duplication of requests for information and in establishing common project standards e.g. the use of the World Bank standards. For example, ECGD may be able to make use of assessments/investigations undertaken by or for International Finance Institutions (IFC, EBRD etc.) or other ECAs and may wish to co-ordinate its activities with them in order to streamline the process of investigation and analysis. Provision of contact details for the relevant people involved would facilitate this.

QUESTION 3

(a) If you have corporate Environment, Occupational Health & Safety, Social Issues or Human Rights policies and/or your company subscribes to ISO 14001/EMAS accreditation, please attach relevant details (if not previously provided).

GUIDANCE NOTE

ECGD encourages its customers to demonstrate their commitment to Sustainable Development through the development and publication of relevant policies and the implementation of appropriate environmental management systems (EMS) which should be verified/accredited where possible. Since EMS certificates are awarded for individual sites, please provide copies of the certificate(s) for the site(s) connected with each specific request for support.

Your Human Rights policies might contain, for example, your policy on equal opportunities.

QUESTION 4

ANNEX 1 – CUSTOMERS' GUIDANCE NOTES

been designed to meet recognised environmental standards?

(b) If the project/business has been designed to meet any other environmental performance standards please identify and provide a copy of these.

GUIDANCE NOTES

ECGD is interested in the impacts of both the goods/services being supplied and also any associated project of which the goods/services form a part.

ECGD 'benchmarks' projects against a range of internationally recognised standards (UK, EU, World Bank, IFC, and relevant regional Development Banks). You should assume that ECGD has copies of all the major international standards. If Host country standards or some other standard is being used then please provide a copy of these.

We accept that products which are identical to those sold in the UK comply with EU standards. Host country or project standards which are below international standards may be unacceptable and would need to be justified. ECGD will use international standards as benchmarks against which to make this judgement.

If there are no applicable or appropriate environmental standards please provide an explanation of why this is the case.

QUESTION 6

Please indicate whether the goods/services/project that you are supplying/investing in will be compliant with UK or Destination/Host Country Health and Safety standards and supply details of any Health and Safety guidance that you supply to the users/operators of your goods/ projects.

GUIDANCE NOTE

ECGD needs to satisfy itself that due regard is being paid to Health & Safety issues. If the guidance that you normally supply is extensive then please provide a contents list only in the first instance.

QUESTION 7

Will the goods/services/project have any actual or potential environmental impacts in any of the following areas?

GUIDANCE NOTES

Please identify all areas of impact and provide sufficient information for ECGD to determine whether or not impacts resulting from normal operations or the reasonably predictable consequences of misuse or breakdown of equipment are significant. Please also include information on any mitigating factors and consultants reports. Many projects will have impacts in several of the areas listed. Early identification of these and provision of relevant information will facilitate our analysis of your application. The following questions may assist in determining the appropriate answer (impact/no impact) and the type and detail of information required.

Water pollution or extraction

Is the consumption of water or disposal of liquid effluent likely to impact on other users of this supply? How much water will be required and where will it come from? How much effluent will be generated? What are the contaminants of the effluent and their concentrations?

Damage to wildlife or habitats

ANNEX 1 – CUSTOMERS' GUIDANCE NOTES

Is a change of land use necessary eg. agricultural to industrial? Does the project involve the clearance of land? What is the present use of the land? Are any compensating features planned eg. provision of greenbelt areas?

Local air quality

Do the goods or project produce dust or fumes? What are the sources and levels of emissions? What mitigation systems are installed? How efficient is any filtration equipment?

Climate Change (Kyoto Protocol)

For projects involving generation of power from fossil fuels, ECGD may wish to report CO_2 emissions per unit of power generation. For these projects, what is the expected net annual production of carbon dioxide? (If required, ECGD can provide a simple methodology for calculating annual CO_2 emissions.)

What quantities of other greenhouse gases will be produced? (Other greenhouse gases are: methane, nitrous oxide, sulphahexafluoride, hydrofluorocarbons & perfluorocarbons.) These last 2 are also ozone depleters.)

Acid Deposition

What fuel is proposed to be used and what is its sulphur content? Has low sulphur or biofuel been considered? Is flue gas desulphurisation equipment proposed? If so, please provide details of the specifications.

Ozone depletion (Montreal Protocol)

Are CFCs or HCFCs used in refrigeration or air-conditioning systems? Have alternatives been considered? Are any other ozone depleters used? Details of the Montreal Protocol including a list of ozone depleters can be found on the UNEP website at: http://www.unep.ch/ozone/mont_t.htm

Use of hazardous substances

What hazardous substances are used in the goods and project, eg. are polychlorinated biphenyls (PCBs) present in transformers, capacitors or gas pipelines? What processes or procedural systems are there to prevent or deal with the escape of any such hazardous substances?

Production of damaging or toxic waste

What quantities of solid waste are produced? What damaging or toxic substances are contained in the waste and in what quantities are they present? Is waste production minimised? What arrangements have been made for the safe storage and/or disposal of wastes?

Noise pollution

Are the noise levels at 1 metre from the equipment above 85dB(a)?

Will operations cease at night or will there be 24 hour operation? For industrial and commercial areas the noise level at the site boundary should not exceed 70 dB(a). For residential areas the noise level at the site boundary should not exceed 55 dB(a) during daytime and 45 dB(a) at night.

Degradation of land (e.g. soil contamination, erosion or salinisation)

What steps will be taken to ensure that land degradation is avoided eg. bunding of tanks/other measures to prevent spillage? What plans are there for site restoration after the project has closed?

Other adverse environmental impacts, please specify

Provide details of any other adverse environmental impacts that you are aware of.

ANNEX 1 – CUSTOMERS' GUIDANCE NOTES

Other beneficial environmental impacts, please specify

Please ensure that all environmental benefits are clearly identified and quantified where possible. Benefits could include reduction in pollution, technology transfer, skills transfer and training and opportunities for local entrepreneurs.

If there are actual or potential environmental impacts, please give details (including any mitigating factors, consultants' reports, choice of technology, etc.).

Please provide details of any reports including the Terms of Reference, producer of the report and the summary of the report (or full report if it is short).

QUESTION 10

Will the goods or project cause, require, bring about or stimulate any of the following?

GUIDANCE NOTES

Please provide sufficient information for ECGD to determine whether or not the impacts that you are aware of, after enquiry appropriate to your role in the project, are significant. The following questions may assist in determining the appropriate answer (yes/no) and the type and detail of information required.

Resettlement of the local population

Are people being moved from or excluded from the site of the project, particularly on an involuntary basis? How many are involved? How long have they lived or worked on the site? What is the source of this data and how reliable is it?

Compulsory acquisition of land

Is land being acquired by or on behalf of the project company through compulsory purchase systems? How and by whom are the assets and resource base being valued? Are current inhabitants/users being offered alternative land or cash or both? Are equivalent or better services and infrastructure being provided?

Displacement of or damage to existing industry or agriculture

Are alternative jobs (with appropriate training) being offered? Is the whole community being consulted?

Job losses among the local population

Are job losses expected to arise as a result of the project? What opportunities for re-employment or re-training are being provided?

Child labour

Are any children under 14 employed? What mechanisms are being put in place to monitor this? Do any children accompany their parent(s) onto the business premises?

Bonded or forced labour

Is any of the work extracted for no payment and/or under threat of force or penalty e.g. does the employer hold workers' identity documents? Is work extracted as payment for debt?

Large-scale influx of workers

Will the business (or sub-contractors) import a non-local work-force requiring accommodation and access to facilities for a period of more than 3 months eg. during a construction phase? How many will be employed and for how long? Have opportunities been offered to local workers?

Damage to sites of cultural, historic or scientific interest

Does the project affect a religious or ancestral site, or natural resources ascribed by local people with cultural or sacred significance? Is the site near to a recognised World Heritage site? Is the site near to a recognised site of special scientific interest?

ANNEX 1 – CUSTOMERS' GUIDANCE NOTES

Impact on minority or vulnerable communities

Are any of the above impacts likely to have a disproportionate effect on national, ethnic or religious minority communities or other vulnerable groups in the country concerned?

Please provide details of any of these that apply.

Other social drawbacks, losses or disadvantages

Social benefits

ECGD is keen to recognise social benefits arising from the project.

QUESTION 11

Do the security arrangements for the contract/project make use of armed personnel (either from private security firms or state security organisations)?

GUIDANCE NOTES

Please indicate, as far you are aware, the extent of armed security that the contract or project will use (e.g. number of armed personnel). If possible, include details of rules or procedures in place governing conduct of personnel and sub-contractors, including on the use of force.

Projects making use of extensive security arrangements may need to take account of the impact of those arrangements in a Social Impact Assessment (SIA).

QUESTION 12

Will the benefits of the goods/project (including employment opportunities for local people) be open to all, regardless of race, religion, gender, social grouping, etc.?

GUIDANCE NOTES

Please indicate whether you are aware of, and, if possible, give reasons for, any discriminatory practices relating to the opportunities to derive benefits from the exported goods or the various phases of the project (construction, operation, product use, and decommissioning). We do not expect positive discrimination to ensure equality in the distribution of benefits but we encourage equality of opportunity to share in the benefits.

ANNEX 2 – CONTENTS LIST FOR EIA

CONTENTS OF AN ENVIRONMENTAL IMPACT ASSESSMENT
WORLD BANK (OPERATIONAL DIRECTIVE 4.01 OF WORLD BANK)

ECGD requires that Environmental Impact Assessments (EIAs) of projects conform to a recognised format and coverage. This is the content page list used by the World Bank. EIAs which conform to other internationally recognised standards of good practice would also be acceptable.

1   Description of project

  -    location, type, purpose & scope of project, size, onsite and offsite components, technologies to be employed, construction scheduling

  -    information on the applicant and the role of the host country government

2   Description of existing environment

  -    project area and size, location and physical ecological and socio-economic/cultural conditions

  -    results of site audit, if conducted, and results of participatory input from affected population, if conducted

3   Potential environmental impacts of a proposed project

  -    analysis of beneficial and adverse impacts of the project, and their significance, potential mitigation for adverse impacts and identification of impacts for which no mitigation is available

4   Host country regulatory requirements and permits

  -    host country regulatory framework, including ECA and applicable host country regional and local requirements

5   Description of project monitoring and environmental management plan

  -    discussion of the scope and effectiveness of existing environmental monitoring or proposed environmental management programs and recommendations for any additional monitoring if needed or appropriate

6   Discussion of identified environmental issues and potential mitigation measures applicable to project specifics such as

  -    air quality and the maintenance of ambient air quality

  -    water use and quality including protection of surface and groundwater resources

  -    wastewater management such as handling, processing, storage and disposal of dangerous or toxic materials

  -    effect of natural hazards including measures to mitigate environmental risks due to seismicity, landslides, flooding, etc

  -    ecological considerations such as protection of biodiversity and ecosystems and conservation of natural resources in conjunction with sensitive sites such as those containing endangered species

  -    maintaining the socio-economic and cultural context through development of resettlement plans, measures to preserve historical sites and artefacts etc

In addition, the following aspects should be addressed

  Public participation within the host country in the preparation of the EIA

  Procedure for comparing the environmental effects of alternatives to the project

Export Credit Agencies

OECD COUNTRIES

COUNTRIES	Name of ECA	Internet address	PE*	S-T Post E**	M to L-T PE***	PF****
1 Australia	Export Finance and Insurance Company (EFIC)	www.efic.gov.au		X	X	
2 Austria	Oesterreichische Kontrollbank Aktiengesellschaft (OeKB)	www.OeKB.co.at		X	X	X
3 Belgium	Office National du Ducroire/National Delcrederendienst (ONDD)	www.ducroire.be or www.delcredere.be		X	X	X
4 Canada	Export Development Canada (EDC)	www.edc.ca		X	X	X
5 Czech Republic	Exportni garancni a pjist ovaci spolecnost, a.s. (EGAP)	www.egap.cz	X	X	X	
6 Czech Republic	Czech Export Bank	www.ceb.cz			X	
7 Denmark	Eksport Kredit Fonden (EKF)	www.ekf.dk		X	X	X
8 Finland	Finnvera plc	www.finnvera.fi			X	X
9 France	Compagnie Francaise d. Assurance pour le Commerce Exterieur (Coface)	www.coface.com or www.cofacerating.com			X	X
10 Germany	Kreditanstlt für Wiederaufbau (KfW)	www.kfw.de		X	X	X
11 Germany	Hermes Kreditversicherungs-Aktiengesellschaft AG (Hermes)	www.hermes-kredit.com		X	X	X
12 Greece	Export Credit Insurance Organization (ECIO)	www.oaep.gr		X		X
13 Hungary	Hungarian Export Credit Insurance Ltd. (MEHIB)	www.mehib.hu/english/	X	X	X	
14 Italy	Instituto per i Servizi Assicurativi del Commercio Estero (SACE)	www.isace.it		X	X	X
15 Japan	Japan Bank For International Cooperation (JBIC)	www.jbic.go.jp/english/	X	X	X	X
16 Korea	Korea Export Insurance Corporation	www.keic.or.kr	X	X	X	X
17 Korea	Korea Eximbank		X	X	X	X
18 Netherlands	Nederlandsche Credietverzekering Maatschppij N.V. (NCM)	www.ncmgroup.com	X	X		X

* Pre-Export
** Short-Term Post Export
*** Medium- to Long-Term Post Export
**** Project Finance

OECD COUNTRIES

COUNTRIES	Name of ECA	Internet address	PE*	S-T Post E**	M to L-T PE***	PF****
19 Norway	The Norwegian Guarantee Institute for Export Credits (GIEK)	www.giek.no	X	X	X	X
20 Poland	Export Credit Insurance Corporation KUKE	www.kuke.com.pl		X	X	X
21 Portugal	Companhia de Seguro de Creditos, SA (COSEC)	www.cosec.pt	X	X	X	X
22 Portugal	Conselho de Garantias Financeiras (CGF)					
23 Spain	Compania Espanola de Seguros de Credito a la Exportacion, S.A. (CESCE) or Spanish Export Credit Insurance Company	www.cesce.com		X	X	X
24 Sweden	Exportkreditnämnden (EKN)	www.ekn.se		X	X	X
25 Sweden	The Swedish Export Credit Corporation (SEK)	www.sek.sk		X	X	X
26 Sweden	The Swedish International Development Co-Operation (Sida)	www.sida.se				X
27 Switzerland	Swiss Export Risk Guarantee Agency (ERG)	www.swiss-erg.com	X	X	X	X
28 Switzerland	Investment Risk Guarantee (IRG)	www.swiss-irg.com		X	X	X
29 Switzerland	State Secretariat of Economic Affairs (SECO)			X	X	X
30 Turkey	Export Credit Bank of Turkey (Turk Eximbank)	www.eximbank.gov.tr	X	X	X	X
31 United Kingdom	Export Credits Guarantee Department (ECGD)	www.ecgd.gov.uk		X	X	X
32 United States	U.S. Export Import Bank	www.exim.gov	X	X	X	X

* Pre-Export   *** Medium- to Long-Term Post Export

** Short-Term Post Export   **** Project Finance

NON-OECD COUNTRIES

COUNTRIES	Name of ECA	Internet address	PROGRAMS			
			PE*	S-T Post E**	M to L-T PE***	PF****
1 Argentina	Banco de Inversion y Comercio Exterior (BICE) or Foreign Commerce and Investment Bank	www.bice.com.ar	X	X	X	X
2 Brazil	Banco Nacional de Desenvolvimento Economico e Social (BNDES) or Brazilian Development Bank Export Import Division	www.bndes.gov.br/english/	X	X	X	X
3 Colombia	Banco de Comercio Exterior de Colombia (BANCOLDEX)	www.bancoldex.gov.co	X	X	X	X
4 Colombia	SEGUREXPO	www.segurexpo.com	X	X		
5 Croatia	HBOR	www.hbor.hr	X	X	X	X
6 Cyprus	Export Credit Insurance Service (ECIS)					
7 Ecuador	Corporacion Financiera Nacional (CFN) or National Finance Corporation	www.cfn.fin.ec	X	X		X
8 Hong Kong	Hong Kong Export Credit Insurance Corporation (HKECIC)	www.hkecic.com	X	X	X	
9 India	Export-Import Bank of India (Ex-Im India)	www.eximbankindia.com	X	X	X	X
10 India	Export Credit Guarantee Corporation (ECGC)	www.ecgindia.com	X	X	X	
11 Indonesia	Asuransi Ekspor Indonesia (ASEI)	www.asei.co.id	X	X		
12 Ireland	Export Credit Division		X	X	X	
13 Israel	The Israel Foreign Trade Risks Insurance Corporation (IFTRIC)	www.iftric.co.il	X	X	X	X
14 Jamaica	National Export-Import Bank of Jamaica Limited (EXIM Bank)	www.eximbankja.com	X	X	X	X

*   Pre-Export   ***   Medium- to Long-Term Post Export
**   Short-Term Post Export   ****   Project Finance

NON-OECD COUNTRIES

COUNTRIES	Name of ECA	Internet address	PE*	PROGRAMS S-T Post E**	M to L-T PE***	PF****
15 Luxembourg	Societe Nationale de Credit et d'Investissement (SNCI)	www.snci.lu	X	X	X	X
16 Malaysia	Malaysia Export Credit Insurance Berhad (MECIB)	www.mecib.com	X	X	X	X
17 Mexico	Banco de Comercio Exterior, S.N.C. or Mexican Bank for Foreign Trade	www.bancomext.gob.mx	X	X	X	X
18 New Zealand	Gerling NCM EXGO	www.exgo.co.nz	X	X		
19 Oman	ECGA	www.ecgaoman.com	X	X		
20 Romania	Eximbank of Romania	www.eximbank.ro	X	X	X	X
21 Russia	RosEximBank (website in Russian only)	www.rosexim.com		X		
22 Singapore	Export Insurance Corporation of Singapore Ltd. (ECICS)	www.ecics.com.sg	X	X	X	
23 Slovak	Export-Import Bank of Slovakia	www.eximbanka.sk		X	X	
24 Slovenia	Slovene Export Corporation (SEC)	www.sid.si	X	X	X	X
25 Sri Lanka	Sri Lanka Export Credit Insurance Corporation (SLECIC)	www.tradenetsl.lk/slecic/#WAS		X		
26 Taiwan	Taipei Export-Import Bank of China (Eximbank)	www.eximbank.com.tw		X	X	
27 Thailand	Export-Import Bank of Thailand	www.exim.go.th	X	X	X	X
28 Trinidad	Trinidad and Tobago Export Credit Insurance Co. (EXCICO)		X	X		
29 Uzbekistan	Uzbekinvest National Export-Import Insurance Company (UNIC)	www.unic.gov.uz/index-e.html	X			
30 Zimbabwe	Credit Insurance Zimbabwe	www.firstre.com/other/InsuranceDirectory/zimbabwe/credit.html				

* Pre-Export	*** Medium- to Long-Term Post Export		
** Short-Term Post Export	**** Project Finance		

REGIONAL AGENCIES THAT PROVIDE EXPORT FINANCING PROGRAMS

Name of ECA	Internet address	PROGRAMS			
		PE*	S-T Post E**	M to L-T PE***	PF****
1 AFREXIM	www.afreximbank.com	X	X	X	X
2 ATFP	www.atfp.org.ae	X	X	X	
3 BLADEX	www.blx.com/eng.html		X		
4 CABEI	www.bcie.org		X		X
5 CAF (Corporacion Andina de Fomento)	www.caf.com		X	X	X
6 EBRD (European Bank for Reconstruction and Development)	www.ebrd.com	X		X	X
7 ICIEC (Islamic Corporation for Insurance of Investments and Export Credits)	www.iciec.org		X	X	
8 IADB	www.iadb.org	X	X	X	X
9 IAIGC	www.iaigc.org				X
10 ISDB	www.isdb.org	X	X	X	X
11 OECS	www.oecs.org	X			X
12 PTA BANK	www.ptabank.co.ke		X		X

*	Pre-Export	***	Medium- to Long-Term Post Export
**	Short-Term Post Export	****	Project Finance

INDEX

A

ABB Export Bank, 8
Accounts receivable insurance,
Canada, EDC, 14
AFREXIM Bank. See African
Export-Import Bank
Africa
African Export-Import Bank
(AFREXIM Bank), 133-136,
225-227
Eastern and Southern African
Trade and Development
Bank (PTA Bank), 227-229
African Export-Import Bank
(AFREXIM Bank), 133-136,
225-227
Agroprocessor loan, 174-175
Aid finance
Finland, Finnvera plc, 27-28
Netherlands, NCM, 68
Norway, GEIK, 73
Switzerland, SECO, 96-97
United States, Ex-Im Bank,
131-132
Airbus Industrie, 31
Aluminum Smelting Company
(ALSCON), 135
Andean Development
Corporation, 163
Angloco Ltd., 106
Arab Trade Financing Program
(ATFP), 229-230
Argentina, Foreign Commerce
and Investment Bank (BICE),
136-138
ASEI. See Indonesia Export
Credit Agency
ATFP. See Arab Trade Financing
Program

Australia, Export Finance and
Insurance Company (EFIC),
1-5
Austria, Oesterreichische
Kontrollbank
Aktiengesellschaft (OeKB),
6-10

B

Banco Industrial de Venezuela,
163
BANCOLDEX. See Bank of
Foreign Commerce of
Colombia
Banco Mercantil, 163
BANCOMEXT. See Mexican
Bank for Foreign Trade
Bank guarantees
Africa, AFREXIM Bank, 226
Austria, OeKB, 7-8
Europe, EBRD, 239-240
Greece, ECIO, 39-40
Israel, IFTRIC, 170-171
Italy, SACE, 46
Korea, Ex-Im Bank, 59
Korea, KEIC, 57-58
Malaysia, MECIB, 180
Netherlands, NCM, 67
New Zealand, EXGO, 188
Portugal, COSEC and CGF, 84
Romania, Eximbank, 194
Singapore, ECICS, 198
Slovenia, SEC, 205-206
Spain, CESCE, 88
Sri Lanka, SLECIC, 208-209
Switzerland, ERG, 98
Banking services
Corporacion Andina de
Fomento, 235
Colombia, BANCOLDEX, 145